Produce Pete's "Farmacopeia"

Produce Pete's "Farmacopeia"

Pete Napolitano

HEARST BOOKS

NEW YORK

Library of Congress Cataloging-in-Publication Data

Napolitano, Pete.
    Produce Pete's farmacopeia : from apples to zucchini, and everything in between / by Pete Napolitano.
        p.   cm.
    Includes index.
    ISBN 0-688-12847-5
    1. Cookery.   2. Fruit.   3. Vegetables.   I. Title.
TX714.N366   1994
641.6'4—dc20   94-16421
                                                                CIP

Printed in the United States of America

First Edition

1 2 3 4 5 6 7 8 9 10

BOOK DESIGN BY RICHARD ORIOLO

To the two most important people in my life: First, my wife, Betty, whose love and understanding for over thirty years makes my life worthwhile. And my mom, who is no longer with me but whose voice I hear every day as she speaks to me through the wind.

Acknowledgments

I'd like to thank The Weekend *Today* Show staff and crew: Magee, Bill, Bobby, Cindy, IraJoe, Kim, Mike, Mary, Lynn, Sharon, Warren, Ken, and Bruno. I'm also grateful to Matt Lauer, Rene Hambley, Laura Geller, Jim Sebastian, Fred Ciardi, Jill Blackstone, Carl Menk, Rosemary Henri (my mentor), Kathy Banks (who "became" me during the writing of this book), and Megan Newman, my editor at William Morrow.

And finally, with grateful appreciation to all the crew at Napolitano's Produce, our loyal customers for over forty-five years, and the following:

L & P Corp.
 Pat, Louie, Marc, Jimmy, MRP,
  Michael, JoJo, Andy, and the crew
S. Katzman Produce
 Steve, Mario, Lonnie, MRK, and the
 crew
Shapiro & Cohen
 Dennis, George, Joey, and the crew
Finest Fruits, Inc.
 Cooper, the Mushroom King
Krisp Pak Sales Corp.
M & R Tomato Distributors, Inc.
Square Produce Co.
D'Arrigo Bros. Co.
 "Andy Boy"
Rubin Bros., Inc.
J & J Produce

Mike Siegel, Inc.
Wishnatzki & Nathel
Junior's Produce
 Junior, Louie, and the crew
Ven-Co Produce, Inc.
 Louis, Jimmy, Paulie, and the crew
Robert Freeman Produce
Porricelli Bros.
Fierman Produce Exchange
J. Renella Produce, Inc.
D'Agostino
 John Vasadoli
A. J. Trucco
The Alden Group
 Laura Baddish
Underwood Ranches
Exotic Produce EH, Inc.

California Food

Lib's Restaurant
  Rich and Judy

Patsy's Restaurant, New York

Banana Dist. of N.Y., Inc.

Post & Taback, Inc.

RLB Food Distributors
  Jeff Shilling
  Peter Damiano

Comfort Hall Farms
  John Sharp

T. M. Kovacevich, Inc.

Smith Farms

Groff Farms

Arturo's Restaurant

Blood's Orchards

Perrones Farm

Phillips Mushroom Farm

Caigene Fresh, Inc.

California Tree Fruit Agreement

California Avocado Commission

Calavo Foods, Inc.

Frieda's, Inc.

Produce for Better Health Foundation (5-a-Day—For Better Health)

Pacific Bartlett Growers, Inc.
  Arthur O'Leary

Blue Anchor, Inc., fresh fruit growers
  Thanks, Karen

Produce Marketing Association

United States Department of Agriculture

Chilean Winter Fruit Association

Caryl Saunders Associates

California Kiwi Fruit

New York Hall of Science

Konica U.S.A., Inc.

The Agricultural Export Co. of Israel
  Toni Farella

Washington State Fruit Commission

Sunkist Growers, Inc.

Hawaiian Papaya Commission

California Strawberry Advisory Board

Idaho Potato Commission

Del Monte Brands

California Table Grape Commission

California Artichoke Advisory Board

Florida Department of Citrus

National Onion Association

The Packer, Shawnee Mission, Kansas

New York State Apple Commission

And thanks to following people for their generous contributions of their recipes: Lee Bruno, Bob and Loel Welch, Tess Garbarino, Adele Bull, Louise Napolitano (my mom), Peter Napolitano (my dad), Dolores Napolitano, Betty Napolitano, Andy Persichetti, Wally Smith, Julia Donaldson, Jimmy Quick, John Sharp, Marie Diana, Lu Anne Napolitano, Ken Otto, Virginia P., Catherine Faison, Peter D., and Eva Rosenblatt.

Winter

Spring

Summer

Fall

Introduction

Napolitano's Produce has been on the same corner in Bergenfield, New Jersey, for thirty-five years now. Back in 1959, when my father first opened up there, my mother prepared a lot of the family's meals on a stove at the back of the store. She did it because she couldn't leave her customers to go home and fix dinner—even though home was an apartment upstairs. She'd cook *gumbroit*, she'd cook pasta fusul, she'd cook peppers and eggs and other simple but fabulous dishes. And whenever people came in and smelled what Momma was cooking, they bought more vegetables. They'd drift to the back and hang around her stove, asking questions about whatever she was stirring up. Then they'd buy eggplants, shallots, peppers, escarole, and all sorts of things, take them home, and cook them the way my mother told them to. And they started bringing in and exchanging their own family recipes. My mother moved a lot of produce that way!

This book is dedicated to her memory—and to everyone who enjoys good food, enjoys feeding their families and friends, but doesn't have a lot of time to do it.

My family has been in the produce business for three generations now—with a fourth generation coming up. My father's father came to this country from Italy around the turn of the century. My father was eight when my grandfather died. He was the youngest of twenty—count 'em—twenty children. What other business can you go into when you have twenty kids, except something to do with food?

Introduction

My father grew up working in the store, and when he had kids, we worked, too. Through most of the fifties, he sold produce from the back of a truck. Growing up in Tenafly, New Jersey, and going to grade school with doctors' and lawyers' kids, I can still remember how I wanted to crawl under a rock when my father came to pick me up at school in his beat-up truck with bunches of bananas hanging off the back! My brother and I started helping him sell produce really young.

In the forty years I've worked with produce, a lot of things have become second nature to me: what time of year navel oranges are at their sweetest and juiciest. When a spot of mold on the skin may mean a ripe, sweet melon inside. When "new" potatoes aren't new at all. And, thanks to my mother, I absorbed a lot of things about preparing fresh vegetables and fruits—the *simple* rules for cooking that let you really enjoy the wonderful flavors of good-quality fresh produce, including all those ordinary vegetables most Americans take for granted.

My mother was Irish, and she learned a lot of her cooking from my grandmother. She used to make a tomato sauce in a frying pan—she'd cut up peppers, fresh tomatoes, and onions and make a marinara in ten minutes. Fresh marinara sauce is very popular now; it's on the menu at good restaurants; it's at the grocer's packaged in plastic. My mother made it out of necessity. It was fresh, it was fast, it was inexpensive, and it was exactly the kind of food most nutritionists now recommend.

Just as my mother learned from my grandmother, my wife, Betty—a skillful cook in her own right—learned a lot from my mother. What's life all about but learning good things and passing them on from one generation to the next? Betty works like my mother did, and like 55 percent of all the women in America. She gets home at five o'clock, and she can whip up a good meal in fifteen minutes. Good meals that can be quickly prepared are a real necessity for most of us, and I'm especially pleased to be able to include recipes from the cooks in my family, and not just for preparing exotic or unfamiliar vegetables, but for home-style "fast foods" and dishes you can make when you think there's not really anything in the house to eat.

If you think about it, all our lives are wrapped up in food. Thanksgiving, Christmas, seders, birthdays, weddings, anniversaries—even wakes—all of them are commemorated when people sit down at a table and share a meal. The smell of a fresh apple pie baking, or of basil and garlic and olive oil warming in a pan, can bring on a flood of feelings and memories. Food and memory, memory and food.

Introduction

When I was a little boy, my family lived next to a cemetery in Tenafly. We had a big, old house—I mean this house was ancient. Out back was an equally ancient garage that was half falling down. My brother David and I made ourselves a little clubhouse back there. We fixed it up with some old lumber and a few nails, the usual stuff kids manage to lay their hands on. The one big disadvantage of our special place, as far as we were concerned, was that it was where my mother kept the pickle barrel. Every year she pickled a big batch of cheese peppers in a gigantic old whiskey barrel right there in our clubhouse. She filled that barrel brimming to the top with fresh white vinegar. Then she'd take bushels of cheese peppers and just dump them in—without even cleaning them. Next she put about a case of unpeeled garlic into a net bag, then she took a hammer and pounded away at it until the heads were broken up and very well bruised. In they went, with the peppers and vinegar. We couldn't believe how much stuff she put in there! Next she tossed in salt and pickling spices. Finally she added a little water, gave the whole thing a few stirs, then picked up her hammer and her spice cans and left our clubhouse in peace again.

She'd do this in September, and my brother and I always dreaded it. We hated the way it smelled up our clubhouse. In September and October you'd get a few warm days, and you'd see flies and other bugs flying around that pickle barrel, and my brother and I would get completely disgusted with the whole thing. We used to say to each other, "We're not gonna eat those. Mommy made those. We're *never* gonna eat those."

Now there was no heat back there, of course, and as the winter came on and we got our first hard freeze, the vinegar water started freezing over. By the middle of the winter there would be a thick layer of ice at the top of the barrel. It was so solid that you had to take an ice pick to it to get into the peppers. My mother would go out there in the cold, chop the ice away, scoop down to get those peppers, and bring them in to the table. I have to say that when she brought those peppers in, we forgot all about the flies. Those peppers were *terrific*. To this day I can't remember tasting another pepper as good as those were.

In the summer, during corn season, our day would sometimes start at two or three o'clock in the morning, when we got a delivery of fresh sweet corn. Farmers would get up in the middle of the night to pick it, because the sugar in sweet corn—at least in the older varieties—starts to turn to starch within a day. Farmers would load their trucks in the middle of the night and start deliveries well before dawn. My mother used

Introduction

to wake us at three or four A.M. to come down and help unload those trucks. I hated having to get up in the middle of the night, but Mom made sure we got our reward. She'd put a pot of water on that stove in the back of the store, and once it was boiling she'd take a bunch of those ears, husk them, and drop them into the pot. That's another taste I'll never forget: sweet corn taken straight off a farmer's truck and cooked by my mother in the middle of the night.

Now that I'm an adult, when we send the truck up to Wally's for sweet corn and it comes back loaded with fresh, green ears, this comes pretty close to those times of my childhood.

As the years have passed, we've built up quite a nice retail business. It is more than a family business—it is a neighborhood affair. We've made friends with the farmers who supplied us. We've become friends with customers who have stayed with us for forty years.

Good times, hard times, struggling to make a dollar. No matter how hard times got, my father and mother fed our family, and fed us well. The success we eventually achieved came from hard work. My father always used to say, ''You only get out what you put into it, kid.'' We worked hard, but my childhood was never boring. I learned a little bit about so many things—jack-of-all-trades, master of none. But I learned a little about a lot, and I try to pass it on.

In 1969, when my father retired, I bought the business from him, reorganized it as Napolitano's Produce, Incorporated, and started to change things around a little bit. Times were changing, the economy was changing. By the middle seventies, women were starting to go back to work. Things started to rise in price, and more and more families needed two incomes to live. I thought I had put in long hours as a young man, but in the seventies I started going into the market at one o'clock in the morning and not coming home until six o'clock at night. As the years went on and my family started to grow up, I started to fall into my father's mold. By the mid-eighties I really didn't want to be in the produce business anymore. I had been in it my whole life, and although I'd made the choice as a young man to go into it full-time, it didn't seem like a choice. I felt like I was stuck.

But sometimes good things happen to you. Around April 1989, when we were just opening the store for the season, I got a phone call from a local television station, WWOR, Channel 9. We had just had the Chilean grape scare, when cyanide was found in some grapes imported from Chile. WWOR wanted me to come on *People Are Talking* to discuss what was going on with the grapes. We were really busy at the time, so I said no, thank you very much, but I really didn't want to go on the show. I was also thinking I could never get up in front of a television camera—I'd be too nervous. The woman said, "What happens if we send a limo for you?" I said no, really, thanks very much, but I really didn't want to do it. So I gave her the names of three other produce people I thought might be interested.

But sometimes good things happen, sometimes you do the right thing. WWOR called me back and said look, these other people aren't interested, would you please come, we need someone in the business to talk about this problem. My wife, Betty, then tells me, "You're crazy. Why don't you go? It might be good for business. Besides, it's only a one-shot thing. And everyone should have their one minute of fame."

So I gave in. And when I got down to the station, I met the person who changed my professional life from that day forward. Her name was Rosemary Henri. She was the producer of *People Are Talking*. I wanted to know what to do, and she told me to talk about grapes. Well, that just made me nervous. What was I going to say? As far as I was concerned, the whole thing was a fluke. But Rosemary said, "Look, you know your business. Just go out and talk about the grapes." And the piece of advice I'll always remember: "Just look into the camera, just as if you were looking in the eyes of someone sitting across the table from you. Just as if you were ringing the register and talking to someone."

And that's what I did. I talked about the grape scare with Richard Bey, one of the co-hosts, and I gave him a little information. I told him I really didn't think the grapes were doused with cyanide in Chile, but that it was some kind of sabotage committed here. Cyanide is actually an acid and grapes have a very thin skin. If they'd been coated with cyanide in Chile, by the time the grapes got here they would have looked like little raisins. Now I'm no scientist; that just seemed to me to be common sense.

Richard said, "So, Pete, you're not afraid?" And I said, "No, I'm not afraid. This is just my opinion—I'm no expert—but I'm not afraid." Then I plucked a grape out of a bunch and popped it into my mouth.

Well, everybody was very stunned, they thought all Chilean grapes were loaded with cyanide and I was going to drop dead right on the stage.

That came as a surprise to *me*—and it was surprising that people were interested

Introduction

not only in the grapes but in a lot of other things having to do with produce. After the spot, Rosemary came up to me and said, "Have you ever done this before?" And I said no. And she said, "I saw something there—a little *rough*—but I saw something. Would you like to come back once in a while?" I thought it was a lot of fun and I said sure.

When I got home I said to Betty, you know they're real nice, they tried to make me feel right at home, in fact they even asked me back again, which of course they never will, but it was nice.

My next surprise came about three or four weeks later, when they called and asked me to come in and talk about some other little thing to do with produce. Then they asked me again and again. Then one day I got another call from Rosemary, and she said, "Pete I'd like you to come in. We've got some things we'd like to discuss." When I went in, she told me that WWOR wanted me to be a regular on the show and to come in once a week to talk a little about produce. Well, I almost hit the floor—I was flabbergasted. You know, when you see yourself on TV for the first or second time, chances are you'll think you really look like a fool. I thought so! But the main thing was, I was me. I was Pete Napolitano, a regular guy, the same guy who puts your peaches into the bag and rings them up down at Napolitano's. People seemed to relate to that.

It was Rosemary Henri who gave me the tag "Pete, your produce pal," and I began doing regular segments on *People Are Talking* once a week for whatever time was allotted to me—whether five minutes or fifteen. As the show went on, we started to get mail. We'd get one hundred letters, two hundred letters a week. People were interested in what was going on.

You get an allotted time in television, and when you're on camera a technician will hold up cue cards that tell you how long you have: three minutes, two minutes, one minute, and then "BREAK." When they tell you to break, you break! One day I was doing a segment and they'd held up the cards—three minutes, two minutes, one minute, then all of a sudden they gave me a hand signal: "STRETCH! STRETCH!" Well, I had wound up and I didn't really have any more to say about the fruit of the day, so I thought fast and said, "Well, why don't we have someone from the studio audience come down and try this?" I don't remember what it was, maybe a fig or something, but a couple of people came down and tasted and enjoyed it. That's how we ended the segment, and the folks on the set liked it a lot.

I thought about it when I got home, and concluded that while talking about produce is fine, people really want to do know what to *do* with the stuff. Betty is an excellent cook, so I decided why not have her cook up a recipe for each segment? So Betty started doing recipes for the show. Then we started getting four hundred, six hundred, eight hundred letters a week or more, asking for those recipes.

One of the biggest compliments I ever got was from a guy who wrote to say he'd been stationed with the Navy in the Caribbean for three or four years and never touched a mango. Then he saw my spot on the *Today* show, and he decided to give them another try. Now he eats three or four a week.

Five servings of fruits and vegetables a day is one of the most important things you can do for your health. According to the U.S. Department of Health and Human Services and the National Cancer Institute, 35 percent of the deaths in this country may be related to what we eat—a diet high on fats and low in fiber. Fruits and vegetables reduce your risks because they're low in fat and are a rich source of vitamin A, vitamin C, and other essential nutrients, and are high in fiber. Five servings a day will lower your risk of cancer and heart disease.

There are hundreds of varieties of produce on the market, and more new things coming in every year as horticulturalists develop new strains and suppliers develop better ways of shipping in imports. Every day is a new day in the produce field. Try some new things every once in a while. Ask your produce man to stock things you're interested in. And try some of the great old-fashioned vegetables and fruits like winter squash or rhubarb or quince if you've been passing them by. They'll add great variety and a great nutritional boost to your diet.

As I've always said, if you eat right, you'll live right—and you'll have a good time along the way. Enjoy!

Introduction

Apple

I love apple season. There are few things better than a good apple eaten out of hand. Whether the flesh is mild and sweet or tart and winey, when you bite into it, a fresh-picked apple will make a crisp cracking sound and you'll get a spurt of juice.

There's a season for everything, and the main season for American apples starts the last half of October. I've probably said this a thousand times, but our problem in the United States is that we try to buy produce out of season. Many varieties will keep well late into winter, but by summer most apples have been stored for seven or eight months. No wonder they are soft, mealy, and without juice. When peaches and melons come in, stay away from apples. Come back when there's a snap in the air, and you'll remember what makes apples so good.

Apples are one of the most esteemed fruits in the Northern Hemisphere, in part because they're so versatile. They're delicious raw, baked, dried, or made into applesauce. They make great pies, apple butter, apple jelly, chutney, cider, and cider vinegar, and they're a welcome addition to dozens of other dishes. A member of the rose family, apples have been known since ancient times and were cultivated by the Egyptians, Greeks, and Romans. Many places grow wonderful apples now, but overall, the United States produces the finest apple crops in the world. The Northwest, the East Coast, and parts of the Midwest—regions where the seasons change—grow the best apples. They're not a fruit for hot climates.

Only a few of the thousands of varieties of apples grown today are mass marketed, but there are many more out there than Red Delicious, Golden Delicious, and Macs. There are very old and very new varieties you may never have heard of. If you're north of the Mason-Dixon line, you're going to find the best apples at local farm markets and stands, where they're fresh-picked, and you're likely to find great varieties you'd never see at the supermarket.

Season The vast majority of apples are picked from September through November and either sold immediately or put into cold storage, where some keep well and some don't. The peak of the season for domestic varieties—when most stored apples still retain their snap—is generally over by December. A few will last through the early spring, but by March it's hard even to find a good Winesap.

Selecting In most cases look for very firm, bright-colored fruit with no bruises and with the stem still on—a good indication that you've got an apple that's not overripe. The apple should feel heavy in the hand for its size and have a good shine on it. A dull look usually means the fruit has been in storage too long, although some excellent varieties like Winesaps and eastern Golden Delicious have relatively rough skin with little or no sheen. As always, use your nose. An apple that smells great is going to taste great.

Varieties For the sake of comparison, I've listed the four most familiar apples first: Red and Golden Delicious, McIntosh, and Rome Beauty. Following these are some less familiar varieties you should know about.

Red Delicious First developed in Iowa at the end of the nineteenth century, Red Delicious apples are our most familiar and popular apples. It's not hard to see why: they have great color, a sweet taste, and they're very crisp. A thick-skinned apple that ranges in size from very small to very large, Red Delicious is one variety you'll always find in supermarkets. The bright color and distinctive shape—rounded at the top, with points around the bottom—make it an easy sell.

On the East Coast, Red Delicious are grown as far north as Maine and as far south as Virginia and even the Carolinas. But the northern states—regions where the nights are cool during the growing season—produce the best apples. Red Delicious

from the Northeast are a little less shiny, a little smaller, and not as red as those grown in the Northwest, but they're hard, they're juicy, and they're usually a lot sweeter than the western apples.

When you're selecting Red Delicious, look for hard, unbruised, shiny fruit that's heavy in the hand. Except for those grown locally, a dull skin means the apple is getting old and has a little heat in it.

Red delicious from the Northwest are available year round, but by late spring, after they've been stored, they're going to be soft, mealy, and without juice. You'll get good Red Delicious from October through early May. Wherever they're from, these apples are better for eating than for cooking or baking.

Golden Delicious Despite their name and similar shape, Golden Delicious apples are an entirely different variety from Red Delicious. They tend to be a little smaller, have a much more tender skin, and are a little better for cooking than the red, although they're still best eaten out of hand. They also appear earlier in the season, stay in the stores longer, and keep a little longer than the red.

On the East Coast, local Golden Delicious apples start out a little greener than those from the Northwest, but by November they are a deep gold color with russet specks. Late in the season, after the frost, they're a real treat. Look for local Golden Delicious apples at produce and farm stands—you're not likely to find them at the supermarket. And don't be afraid to buy them after a frost; they're actually a lot sweeter and much crisper then. And you haven't lived if you've never had a pie made from local Golden Delicious apples. Locals are harder and crisper than the northwestern Goldens; they store better, and after they've turned deep gold, they develop an incredible fragrance. We keep a bin of local Golden Delicious outside the store even into Christmas. Leaving them outside to get a touch of frost—*not* a hard freeze—turns them sweet as sugar. Don't be afraid of a little scarring or flecks of brown, and when you find a bin of them with that deep yellow, freckled skin, don't pass them up. They're unbelievably good.

McIntosh McIntosh is America's most famous apple. New York State produces the largest number of Macs in the United States. One of the earliest apples of the season, McIntoshes start to appear in the middle of September if the temperature drops below

Apple

60°F. But wait until the end of September or early October to buy and eat Macs; then you'll get an apple that has matured on the tree and has a wonderful flavor—any earlier and it will taste green.

Early Macs are excellent eaten out of hand and very good for pies; they're slightly tart and crisp. As the season goes on, they get redder and sweeter. By late winter Macs are mostly red; they're sweet, but the crunch and juice have left them. A fresh McIntosh is very juicy and has a tender flesh. The best Macs are produced in the Midwest and Northeast. They're not very good bakers because they turn to mush in the oven, but mix them with other apples in pie, make applesauce from them, or eat them raw.

When choosing a Mac, don't worry if its color is more green than red, so long as it has a little red blush on it. As with any apple, make sure the stem is still attached—a reliable indication that it's not overripe. Macs keep very well—up to three or four weeks—in a cool place (like a root cellar or a porch that is protected from freezing). If your only option is to keep them in a heated house, refrigerate them.

Rome Beauty A late fall apple, the Rome Beauty is medium to large, oval shaped, and usually has a flat bottom, which makes it especially suitable for baking. Romes hold their shape and texture in cooking and are good for pies when they're mixed with other varieties. They're one of the best, if not the best, for baking because they have a thick skin that helps the apple keep its shape. I don't recommend a Rome for eating out of hand; even at the beginning of the season, it tends to be dry.

The trick to baking Rome apples is to turn off the heat when they're about done but leave them in the oven another ten minutes so that the apples keep from falling apart.

Old and New Varieties Worth Looking For

Cortland A Cortland's skin is dark red over green and flecked all over with rust; it has a very white, juicy flesh and a medium-tart to sweet flavor. A lot of people think Cortlands make the best apple pies. Their flavor sweetens when they're cooked. Cortlands are a lot harder than Macs, although their thin skin bruises easily. Primarily grown in Maine, New York, Massachusetts, and other parts of New England, Cortlands are found at farm stands and produce markets but rarely in the supermarket. They're especially great in salads because they are less apt to discolor after being cut.

Apple

Empire A cross between the Red Delicious and the McIntosh, the Empire is one of the best apples I've ever eaten; it is firm and crisp like a Delicious, but juicy like a Mac.

This hybrid keeps a lot better and comes out of storage better than McIntoshes. When choosing Empires, make sure the apples are nice and shiny, heavy in the hand, free of bruises, and still have their stems. Empires are perfect for pies and baking. But the best way to eat them is to just take a bite.

Greening Greenings ripen early, usually right at end of summer, during the last week or two of August. Many people feel that small, tart Greenings are the best pie apple in the world. People used them years ago when there were fewer hybrids available and the methods of cold storage hadn't been perfected; because of their tough, thick skin, they kept better than other varieties. Today most greenings are bought by canners, so you don't see them very frequently in the markets. Those that do make it to market don't have much flavor, and even for pie making they're best when mixed with other varieties.

Lady Apple Lady Apples are the oldest variety known, first cultivated by the Romans. The French loved them and thought they were a royal apple; early American colonists thought of them as a symbol of wealth. Lady Apples are not available everywhere, but where they are, they make their appearance just before Thanksgiving and stay until Christmas. Very small, with bright red and yellow coloring, they are a cheerful holiday fruit that's fun to eat (two bites is all it takes). Don't peel Lady Apples because the peel adds to the winey, semisweet taste of the flesh. You can cook them with lamb, pork, or ham, use them as a garnish, or add them to roasted vegetables such as potatoes. My mother used to drop them into our Christmas stockings and use them as ornaments on the tree. They also look especially pretty on a wreath. Left out, they dry nicely; refrigerated, they last up to four weeks.

Macoun A cross between the McIntosh and the Jersey Black (an old apple variety), Macouns first appeared in the 1920s. They range from very small to medium in size and have a flecked, maroon-red skin. The flesh is crisp, very white, and very juicy, making Macouns one of the most popular if not *the* most popular apple in the Northeast. They don't hold up in storage very well, so they should be eaten in season only—and

Apple

the season is very short. You should start looking for Macouns at the beginning of October, and sometime between the end of October and mid-November they will pass their prime in storage and will start breaking down. Look for firm, bright apples free of bruises. Their small size makes them great for lunch boxes and snacks. The supply is short and the demand is high, so the price is high, but they're worth it. When you see fresh Macouns, grab them.

Winesap One of the oldest American varieties, the Winesap is a terrific all-round eating apple. It is hard and juicy, with a very crisp texture and a tart, winey taste. I think of Winesaps as real country apples with a rusty-red, speckled skin and pure white flesh. Usually picked after the first frost, they are still fresh from November through mid-December, and they also come out of storage better than any other apple: nice and hard and very, very juicy. That's unusual for an apple: cold storage makes most of them steadily lose their juice, but a Winesap will sometimes last until April in cold storage and still retain its snap.

Winesaps are excellent for cider or juice and are also great in pies. They're not found in many supermarkets, so look for them at local farm and produce markets. The skin of a Winesap is going to be a little rough, usually with some green on it, but don't worry about that.

Hard-to-Find Varieties

Jonathan A Jonathan is a very round, deep yellow apple with bright red stripes and creamy white, semisweet flesh. Although not very hard it is good for just about anything—cooking or eating out of hand. In days gone by, Jonathans were one of our most popular varieties, but they're hard to find now except in the Midwest. They don't store well, which is strange because they have a tough skin.

Opalescent When I hear the word Opalescent, I think of my childhood. When my mom and dad first opened their farm stand, Opalescent was one of the most popular sellers. In old family photos you'll see bushel baskets full of them at the stand. Now, unless you're talking to an old-timer, most people have never heard of Opalescents. They are large apples, mostly green, with a red blush and large white specks. They're very hard, tart, and juicy, they don't bruise easily, they store very well, and they're one of the few early apples that are hard and juicy when fully ripe. Opalescents are great

for baking and their aroma is wonderful; I can still remember the scent wafting through the house when Mom was baking them. Opalescents come out in early September; if you find them in your area, buy them—then send me a postcard and let me know where you found them. They're a real treat.

Other Older Varieties

Baldwin, Northern Spy, Winter Banana, York, and other older varieties of apples have all but disappeared except from farm stands in the North. If you do find these varieties in your area, look for firm, medium-sized, bright fruit that are free of bruises. Avoid large, dark apples, which are likely to be soft, dry, and mealy.

New Zealand Apples

If you're craving apples in summer, look for the New Zealand varieties. Early New Zealand settlers brought apple seeds with them, and they've been cultivating, improving, and developing new varieties ever since. They're responsible for four excellent apples: the Gala, the Royal Gala, the Braeburn, and the Granny Smith. New Zealand introduced the Granny Smith apple to North America about thirty years ago. In recent years Washington State and British Columbia have begun cultivating the Gala, which is becoming more popular here too.

Apple Cider

Fresh apple cider is really no more than liquefied apples, made by crushing apples—peels, cores, and all—then straining the juice from the pulp. Years ago farmers and producers used a hand-cranked press, almost like a vise, to pulverize the apples. Fresh unpasteurized apple juice with no preservatives has to be refrigerated immediately and will keep no more than two or three days before it starts turning to vinegar. Pasteurized apple juice, with preservatives added, will keep two or three weeks in the refrigerator.

At Napolitano's, as the holidays approach and the weather starts getting colder, we heat apple cider with cinnamon sticks and serve it to our customers. The aroma alone almost makes it worth doing, but it's a festive, no-caffeine, nonalcoholic, relatively low-calorie drink that warms you up and tastes great.

New Zealand apples are shipped fresh from harvesting, while many U.S. apples are put in cold storage, then shipped. The Galas and Braeburns are packaged with great care, so they're usually in prime condition at the market, with smooth, unblemished skin and firm flesh. Like all apples, the New Zealands keep well for several weeks in a paper or plastic bag in your refrigerator. Even though they're not waxed, you should wash them before eating. They're outstanding eaten fresh and are equally good cooked.

Gala and Royal Gala The Gala and the more fragrant Royal Gala varieties are the result of crossing a superb British apple called Cox's Orange Pippin with Red and Golden Delicious apples. They both have a thin, creamy yellow skin. The Gala is striped with pink, while the Royal Gala has a crimson red blush. They both have relatively tender flesh and a mild taste, but they're crisp, sweet, and juicy. Imported Gala and Royal Gala apples are available April through June. Galas from Washington and British Columbia are available from September to December.

Braeburn Available here only since the mid-1980s, the Braeburn is the newest variety developed in New Zealand. It is medium to large in size and has a greenish gold skin striped with red. Very firm, juicy, and sweet, the Braeburn is a terrific apple and

holds up well. It is in season from May through August, when domestic apples are out of the picture.

Granny Smith The Granny Smith is a hard, crunchy, green-skinned apple with a tart taste. A hybrid of the Green Pippin originally grown in England, it has a high juice content and keeps very well. Granny Smiths originated in Australia and are imported mostly from Australia and New Zealand, although we get a few from South Africa, and producers are starting to grow them in Chile and Argentina, which also have opposite growing seasons from ours. France and the U.S. (California and Washington State) are starting to grow them as well, but I think the imports are still tops in taste. Granny Smiths are shipped around the world and start arriving in the U.S. around the middle of April. The season lasts into July and sometimes even through August. Like the other New Zealand apples, they're excellent when you want a good apple out of season.

The Granny Smith is a medium to large apple with a very juicy, white, tart, super-hard flesh. As the season progresses, Granny Smiths get sweeter. I suggest peeling them because the green skin tends to be tough and is coated with oil for shipping. Although they're not particularly good for baking, Granny Smiths are great for pies. They're more expensive than domestic apples, so you should expect near perfection in them. Avoid bruised apples, and never buy a yellow Granny Smith, which will be juice-less and tasteless.

About Alar

Americans buy with their eyes, and alar is used to make red apples turn really red and shiny and to be uniform in size and shape. Growers have been using alar for one hundred years as a growth retardant and insect repellent. It also produces perfect-looking fruit.

If you assembled two different panels of doctors and agriculturalists, one would say alar is harmful, and the the other would say it is absolutely safe. You're not going to get agreement on this, and so it's a choice you as a consumer have to make. I've been eating apples all my life—they're practically my favorite fruit—and I don't worry about alar.

Apple

Betty's Apple Crumb Pie
6 to 8 servings

6 large apples

3 tablespoons sugar

3 teaspoons ground cinnamon

2 teaspoons instant tapioca

1 baked 9-inch pie shell

2 tablespoons unsalted butter

CRUMB TOPPING

1½ cups flour

1 teaspoon ground cinnamon

¾ cup brown sugar

¾ cup (1½ sticks) butter

Preheat the oven to 375°F.

Peel, core, and slice the apples and place in a large bowl. Add the sugar, cinnamon, and tapioca and stir together until the apples are well coated. Spoon the apple mixture into the pie shell. Dot with butter or margarine and set aside.

For the crumb topping, place the flour, cinnamon, and sugar in a large bowl and cut in the butter with a pastry blender or two knives until the mixture has the texture of coarse cornmeal. Sprinkle the crumb mixture on top of the apples. Bake the pie for 40 to 45 minutes.

Apple

Lib's Apple Crisp   6 servings

> **2 cups peeled and sliced Granny Smith apples**
>
> **2 cups peeled and sliced Rome Beauty apples**
>
> **2 cups flour**
>
> **2 cups sugar**
>
> **2 eggs, beaten**
>
> **ground cinnamon to taste**
>
> **½ cup (1 stick) unsalted butter, melted**

Preheat the oven to 350°F.

Arrange the apples in a baking dish. In a small bowl, mix the flour, sugar, and beaten eggs to crumb consistency with a fork (do not use an electric beater). Sprinkle the crumb mixture over the apples.

In a separate bowl, stir the cinnamon into the melted butter and pour over the apple-crumb mixture. Bake for 30 to 45 minutes, or until the apples are soft and lightly browned. Serve warm with ice cream or whipped cream.

Apple or Asian Pear

Known variously as apple pears, Asian pears, Oriental pears, sand pears, or shalea (which means "sand pears" in Chinese), these fruits have a thin, smooth skin and a crispy crunch like that of a hard apple. They are very, very juicy, with a strong pear taste and granular texture. Apple pears originated in northern Asia and were cultivated long before Bartlett, Bosc, or other North American varieties. Similar in flavor to a Bartlett or Comice pear, but with a heavier perfume and the characteristic crunchy texture, the apple pear has a strong flavor at room temperature that becomes more delicate after slight chilling.

Apple or Asian Pear

Apple pears are *not* a cross between a pear and an apple (a hybrid that has never been successfully achieved, by the way). Although grown mainly in Asia and exported to the U.S., they are now cultivated commercially in California and Washington. New Zealand, where the pears are called nashi, also exports the fruit to the United States, as does Brazil. Asian apple pears are still held in the highest esteem, however, and a variety known as Twentieth Century from China has commanded as much as three dollars apiece in our markets.

There are approximately one thousand varieties of apple pears, but only a few are grown commercially. The two main varieties we see here are Twentieth Century and Hosui. They range in size from quite small (smaller than a tennis ball) to a pound or pound and a half. The Twentieth Century has a very pale, almost white, glossy skin, and looks something like a large, round apple. The Hosui, my favorite, has a golden brown, russet skin, almost like that of a Bosc, which is a pretty contrast to the white flesh. It's even sweeter and juicier than the Twentieth Century.

Season Because they're grown in many parts of the world, apple pears are available virtually year round. New Zealand apple pears are available from January to April; those from Taiwan from June to mid-October. American and Japanese varieties are available from August to December.

Selecting Unlike pears, which must be picked before they're ripe, apple pears are ripened on the tree before they're harvested and usually can be eaten immediately. They have a thin skin and show scars but these blemishes are only skin deep and don't affect the taste or quality of the flesh. Apple pears are pollinated and picked by hand and individually wrapped for shipping. Ordinarily those imported from China and Japan are wrapped in a kind of netting, while those from California are packed in plastic cells.

Storing Leave apple pears at room temperature if you're going to eat them within a week. If properly refrigerated, they will keep well for weeks—the russet Hosui, which has the longest shelf life, for up to two months. Wrap them individually in paper towels or tissue paper so they don't touch each other, then refrigerate in a plastic bag or in the crisper.

Apple or Asian Pear

Apple pears are usually washed and enjoyed in their natural state. Because of their very high water content, apple pears don't freeze well and tend to fall apart when cooked, but they can be baked or poached like pears. They make a good garnish for hot or cold meats and are excellent in fruit salads (the crisp texture and flavor complement other fruits), and they go well with cottage cheese or yogurt dressing. Apple pears also make an excellent juice when pureed or put through an extractor.

Apricot

When apricots arrive in the store, I know that summer has finally arrived and all the other hot-weather fruits are not far behind. A good apricot is small, round, delicate, and glows with golden color. About the size of a plum and similar in appearance to a very small peach, a ripe apricot is sweet, fragrant, richly colored, and extremely fragile. It is also one of the richest sources of beta carotene (vitamin A). Apricots are delicious and low in calories eaten out of hand; they're also great poached with a little sugar, turned into jam or fillings for layer cakes, made into tarts, dried, or glacéed.

Although apricots from China were introduced to Europe by Alexander the Great, they apparently disappeared at some point during the Roman Empire. Some say that the Moors reintroduced them when they conquered Spain, but apricots definitely reappeared during the Crusades. And it's certain that Franciscan friars brought them to California, which still grows the bulk of the crop in the United States. Although we get a few out of Idaho, I think those from California are the best. They're surpassed in flavor only by apricots from Morocco, where weather and soil conditions produce wonderful apricots. The trouble is, they're so fragile they must be picked hard and shipped under refrigeration and often don't ripen properly. Too many times in and out of the refrigerator, and an apricot becomes dry and woody. If you see great-looking apricots from Morocco, try them, but your safest bet is the California apricot, mainly because it travels a shorter distance.

California apricots are at their peak from May through August. Later in the fall, apricots from Idaho appear. Winter fruit from Chile, Australia, and New Zealand are not worth buying, simply because they've been picked too green (which means they will be very hard, very woody). Australian apricots are fine in Australia, but not here.

Season

Selecting Since apricots will ripen off the tree, in many instances your best bet is to buy firm fruit and take it home to ripen. Firm apricots should be gold, with no traces of green. A good ripe one will be a rich allover gold, often with a red blush, and the flesh will be soft. Avoid wrinkled apricots, which are old.

Because they are so tender, ripe apricots will often show small bruises or soft spots. Don't let that worry you, as it is usually a sign that the fruit is ripe and sweet (but don't select fruit that is bruised all over—something that can happen in a self-service market where dozens of people may have squeezed the life out of the fruit). Although Napolitano's is self-service, we try to keep the apricots near the check-out counter so that we can help our customers with them. Do yourself and your neighbors a favor, and handle apricots and other fragile fruit very carefully.

Storing Leave hard apricots on the counter in a warm place for as long as five or six days to ripen, until very gold in color and soft to the touch. A ripe apricot may be refrigerated, but not for more than a day or two. Like peaches, apricots dry out fairly quickly in the refrigerator.

Preparing A fresh ripe apricot is a sublime treat. But this fragrant fruit is also delicious gently poached, or try the Apricot Mousse featured here.

Apricot Mousse   6 servings

1¾ cups water

1 package (6 ounces) lemon-flavored gelatin

8 ripe apricots

2 tablespoons brandy or apricot brandy

1 cup fresh whipped cream

In a large saucepan, bring the water to a boil. Remove from the heat, add the gelatin, and stir until dissolved. Set aside and allow to cool.

Apricot

Rinse the apricots well, halve, and remove the pits. Puree in a blender or food processor until smooth. Add the pureed apricots and brandy to the cooled gelatin mixture and refrigerate until slightly thickened (about 1 hour). Beat the apricot mixture slightly, then fold in the whipped cream. Transfer the mousse to a mold or serving dish and chill until firm.

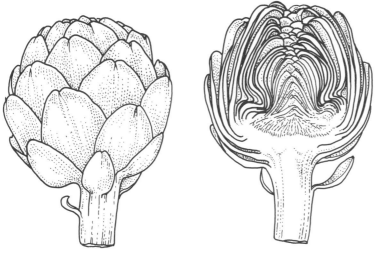

Artichoke

Artichokes are actually the giant, unopened buds of a flowering plant—an edible relative of the thistle. They've been a favorite in Spain, Italy, and other Mediterranean countries for hundreds of years, but many people here still think of them as fairly exotic.

Although they take a little time to eat—there's no way you can wolf down an artichoke—they're actually fun to dismantle, and the tender flesh at the base of the leaves and especially at the heart has a distinctive sweet, nutty taste that's absolutely delicious. Artichokes can be prepared in dozens of ways, and I like all of them.

The largest crop of artichokes is still produced in Mediterranean countries, but California is the biggest supplier in the U.S. Castroville, located near San Francisco,

Artichoke

How to Eat an Artichoke Start with your fingers. A whole cooked artichoke should be eaten by removing one leaf at a time and pulling it between your teeth to remove the soft, tender flesh at the base. Discard what's left. A lot of people like to dip the leaf in a bit of melted butter or hollandaise first, but they're delicious plain or with a less fattening sauce. When all the fleshy leaves have been removed, use a small knife or even a spoon to scrape away and discard the hairy "choke" that covers the base. The last part is the best: the heart, which is the tenderest, sweetest part of an artichoke.

calls itself the Artichoke Capital of the World, and the whole economy of the place revolves around the vegetable—there's even a statue of an artichoke in the middle of town. With its cool, humid, foggy weather, the area is perfect for growing good artichokes.

There are three basic types of artichoke, plus a new "thornless" variety that's beginning to appear on the market. The *globe* type is the most common, with a large, fairly round shape and smallish barbs on the tips of the leaves. The *oval* artichoke is very thorny, with a longer, more pointed leaf. The taste of both is identical, and they can be cooked in the same way, but I find that globe artichokes are usually more tender.

The third type is the small, loose *baby artichoke,* which is often marinated whole in vinegar and oil after it has been washed and dethorned. Most baby artichokes don't have many thorns in the first place, and they can be eaten whole, without removing the "choke."

Thornless artichokes are also available. I find them to be excellent if they're from California but unreliable if they've been imported from Mexico or Chile. The imports are difficult to cook properly because it's hard to get the timing right—some cook fast and tender; others take an hour and either stay raw or suddenly turn to mush. The imports are usually a paler green than the California crop, but if you're in doubt, ask your produce manager.

Artichoke 16

The peak of the season is in March, April, and May, when California producers ship nearly half the annual crop, but artichokes often show up in the fall. The worst time for artichokes is in the dead of summer (July and August), when growing conditions are too hot and dry for good artichokes. However, they are available year round.

Selecting

Look for fat, firm-looking buds with dense, tightly packed leaves of a uniform dusty green. Lots of black spots, tired color, or opened leaves indicate an older artichoke that will have a woody taste. An artichoke with one or two black spots, on the other hand, isn't always a bad risk. Don't worry if the artichoke is discolored on the stem end—you're going to cut that part off. When selecting an artichoke, gently pull back the central leaves, taking care not to prick yourself on the thorns, and look into the heart. If there is no black showing inside, the artichoke is good. At home you can be more aggressive—turn the artichoke upside down and give it a good whack or two on the counter to make the leaves open out more easily.

Artichokes that have developed purpling on the leaves have been exposed to too much hot sun and will be much less tender. An artichoke that shows some bronzing and peeling has had a touch of frost, which won't hurt the flavor and may in fact improve it. If you're unsure about what kind of discoloration is okay and what kind is not, a good rule of thumb is not to buy discolored artichokes in the summer.

Storing

Artichokes are quite perishable. Use them as soon as possible. Refrigerate for one week only, if necessary.

Preparing

There are a thousand ways to cook artichokes, but one thing to avoid is to cook them in an aluminum pot since they will turn a gray-green color. To prepare them for the pot, rinse the artichokes in cold water, handling them carefully so that you don't prick yourself on the pointed barbs at the end of each leaf. The barbs are softer and easier to handle after the artichoke is cooked, but many people prefer to remove them beforehand by snipping off the tips of the leaves with kitchen shears or scissors. Remove the thorns from baby artichokes that you intend to eat whole.

Artichoke

Betty's Stuffed Artichokes   4 servings

4 medium-sized artichokes

2 cups bread crumbs

¼ cup Parmesan cheese

1 tablespoon garlic powder

½ teaspoon salt

½ teaspoon freshly ground black pepper

½ cup (1 stick) butter, melted

¼ cup olive oil

Rinse the artichokes well, remove the small outer leaves, cut off the stems, and slice about 1 inch off the tops.

In a large bowl, combine the bread crumbs, Parmesan cheese, garlic powder, salt, and pepper. Add the melted butter and oil and mix well.

Turn the artichokes upside down and press firmly to spread the leaves. Turn right side up and stuff the bread crumb mixture into the center and surrounding layers of leaves. Carefully stand the stuffed artichokes in a large pot with about 1½ inches of water in the bottom. Cover and steam over high heat about 10 minutes. Reduce the heat to medium and steam for 20 to 30 minutes, or until the artichokes are tender, checking the water level occasionally and adding more boiling water as needed.

Artichoke

Arugula

I think arugula (ah-*roo*-goo-lah) is my favorite salad green. While this Italian favorite hasn't been discovered in all parts of the country yet, its popularity is growing. In New York City's Little Italy, you'll see people growing arugula in tiny backyard plots and even in pots on windowsills. Few self-respecting Italian cooks will go without it for long.

Also known as rocket or rocket salad in Great Britain and the United States, *rucola* in Italy, and *roquette* in France, arugula originated in the Mediterranean and was introduced to North America by Italian immigrants. It's another ancient cultivar—the Romans thought eating it would bring them good luck. It is now cultivated worldwide and is in such demand from restaurants that we grow it in the Napolitano greenhouses during the winter.

Arugula has fine, smooth, dark green leaves that are notched toward the bottom of the stem. A member of the mustard family and closely related to radishes, it has a sharp, spicy flavor that is somewhat similar to watercress; if it has no bite, it isn't fresh. The peppery taste actually gets hotter in the field as the weather gets hotter.

Season

Available year round.

Selecting

Always buy arugula with the roots still attached. It will lose its zip and flavor fast enough with them on—and even faster with them off. Look for bright, tender, fresh-looking leaves with no signs of yellowing or dark spots. They should not be at all limp.

Storing

Because the flavor and texture fade very fast, use arugula as soon as possible after purchasing. If you have to keep it a day or two, *don't* wash it or remove the roots—just sprinkle with a little water, wrap in paper towels or a clean cloth towel, put in a plastic bag, and refrigerate. Remove the roots and wash only when you're ready to use it. Arugula tends to be very sandy, so wash it well, as you would spinach.

Preparing

Arugula makes a terrific salad all by itself, dressed with a little vinegar, olive oil, garlic, salt, and pepper. It also adds a wonderful tart, peppery taste mixed into a salad of milder lettuces and greens. I think it's great on sandwiches, especially tomato sandwiches.

Arugula is delicious added raw to pasta with a little garlic and oil—the hot pasta steams it just enough. Or you can sauté some minced garlic in olive oil, then toss in a bunch of arugula, sauté briefly, and pour over cooked pasta. The oil will pick up the flavor of the arugula. Be careful not to overcook arugula or it will lose its characteristic peppery flavor.

Arugula can also be frozen or dried and used as an herb. When it's dried, it loses some of its bite, but not all of it, as it tends to do when it's overcooked.

Arugula Salad   4 servings

2 bunches arugula, washed and trimmed

½ head radicchio, washed and sliced

1 Belgian endive, washed and sliced

1 small onion, sliced

¼ cup olive oil

¼ cup balsamic vinegar

salt and freshly ground black pepper to taste

Tear the arugula into bite-sized pieces and combine in a large salad bowl with the radicchio, endive, and onion. In a small bowl, combine the oil, vinegar, salt, and pepper. Pour over salad and toss well.

Variations

Arugula and Radicchio Clean one bunch of arugula, a small head of radicchio, and a few chicory leaves. Tear them into a salad bowl and toss with a dressing of olive oil, balsamic vinegar, a little minced garlic, salt, and freshly ground pepper to taste.

Arugula Italian Style Clean one bunch of arugula and about half a head of Boston lettuce. Tear into a salad bowl and add sliced tomatoes, sweet onion rings, and coarsely chopped scallions with some of the green tops. Toss with a dressing of olive oil, the juice of a lemon, a clove of minced garlic, a bit of oregano, salt, and freshly ground pepper to taste.

Arugula

Asparagus

Once thought of as a harbinger of spring, asparagus is now available nearly year round. This vegetable delicacy has a flavor like no other. Asparagus is actually the sweet, tender, early shoot of a plant in the lily family. In the industry it's referred to as grass.

Edible asparagus grows best in temperate climates, where the ground freezes in winter but the growing season is warm. It can range in size from very thin—called pencil grass—to jumbo grass, which can be as big around as a nickel. A lot of people think that thin stalks are younger, but that's not the case at all. It's true that a mature asparagus spear is tough and woody, but old asparagus can come in any size.

Asparagus basically comes in three colors: green, white, and purple. Most common is the long green asparagus. White asparagus is simply green asparagus that has been covered with soil to blanch out the color. The flavor is about the same, but the texture may be more tender. Purple asparagus is purple at the tip and at leaf points and tends to have a pale stalk.

Because it is very difficult to grow and harvest, asparagus costs more per pound than most other vegetables, but to most of us the taste is worth the expense. Asparagus is also extremely perishable and is usually shipped in wooden boxes with water pads on the bottom to keep the fresh-cut stems moist.

Season

Imported asparagus is available year round at high prices. Asparagus is less expensive during the North American harvest, which is from April to June.

Selecting

Look for tight, dry tips, which should be fresh green or purplish—never yellowed or going to seed. The tops should never be wet. *Smell* the asparagus—it should have no odor. A bad-smelling spear is a bad asparagus.

The base of the asparagus is usually white, woody, and tough, and the more white on the stalk, the more you're going to have to throw away. With white varieties of asparagus, which are generally available only in fancy fruit markets, gauging toughness by the amount of white doesn't quite work. However, the tough part of the stem will look slightly dry and woody.

Generally, there is very little difference in taste and texture between long, short, thick, or thin asparagus. The important determining factor is *freshness*. But do pick asparagus of a uniform size so that it will cook evenly.

Storing Asparagus is best if you buy it the day you plan to use it. Refrigerate it as soon as you get it home. If necessary, you can keep it as long as three or four days under refrigeration.

Preparing Gently wash the asparagus and snap off the tough bottom ends (snap them in two with your hands instead of cutting them, and they'll break just above the tough part). Steam them or braise in a small amount of water, but *don't* overcook. Overcooking will turn asparagus into a tasteless mush. Each spear needs to be soft all over, but the tips tend to cook faster than the stem ends. Try standing them up in a narrow pot and steaming them in about an inch of water. My Irish grandmother used to cook asparagus in a coffeepot: she'd tie them in a bunch with string, stand them in an inch or two of water, and cook about five minutes, or until tender but still crisp. You can also sauté asparagus for three or four minutes with butter, adding a spoonful of water as necessary to prevent burning.

What is true for most fresh vegetables is especially true for fresh asparagus: the less you do to it, the better it tastes. Asparagus is a treat lightly cooked and dressed with no more than a little butter and salt. For variety it can be added to soups, used raw in salads, or blanched and served cold in a vinaigrette. It's also a terrific addition to pasta dishes.

Asparagus

Baked Crusty-Crumb Asparagus

4 to 6 servings

18 to 24 spears asparagus

6 tablespoons butter

1 small yellow onion, chopped

3 cloves garlic, chopped

2 tablespoons chopped Italian parsley

2 tablespoons chopped fresh tarragon

2 cups bread crumbs

Preheat the oven to 350°F.

Blanch the asparagus in a skillet of boiling water and place in a buttered shallow baking pan.

In a skillet, melt the butter and sauté the onion, garlic, parsley, and tarragon. Add the bread crumbs and mix well. Spoon the bread crumb mixture over the asparagus and cover the pan with foil. Bake for 10 to 15 minutes. Remove the foil and bake at 400°F for an additional 5 minutes.

Asparagus

Avocado

If I were stranded on a desert island and could have only one food, it would be the avocado. The rich, buttery-smooth flesh of an avocado is on a lot of people's lists as a delicious but fattening treat. It's true that avocados have a high oil content, but they are also packed with vitamins A, C, and E—the primary vitamins in the antioxidant group that protect the cells in human tissue. A high protein content makes avocados a good meat substitute, and unlike animal fat, the fat is *not* saturated. The big surprise in avocados is how high they are in dietary fiber—they have one of the highest fiber contents of any fruit or vegetable.

Avocados grow abundantly in warm climates. Europeans discovered them when Cortez arrived on these shores in the sixteenth century, but avocados had been eaten for centuries by native Americans. Excavators have unearthed avocado pits in Peru that date to before A.D. 900.

Everyone knows that Mexican and southwestern cuisines include a lot of avocados, but the fruit—especially the Hass variety—has become extremely popular in the Far East. The French also love avocados, consuming an average of four pounds a year per person, while the average American consumes two pounds—that is, outside the state of California, where the average consumption is six pounds a year. In the U.S. the biggest consumption of avocados nationwide is on Superbowl Sunday.

When ripe, an avocado has pale yellow to gold flesh and a delicate, sweet, nutty flavor. Above the equator the fruit blooms between February and May, but it is harvested year round. Unlike most fruits, an avocado doesn't have to be picked at a certain peak time; it can remain on the tree quite a while. Like pears, avocados ripen only after they are picked, and the firm fruits ship well. Once a relatively expensive delicacy, avocados have steadily decreased in price as the fruit has become more widely available, and now they're quite reasonable.

Varieties

California avocados are generally Guatemalan varieties, and in my opinion they are the best. They include the famous Hass, the Fuerte, and the Reed, which are relatively small compared to Florida avocados and have a thick, pebbly skin. Sometimes called alligator pears because of their rough skin, these have a higher oil content than the larger Florida varieties and a richer, creamier taste.

The Hass is small to medium in size and oval in shape, with a very pebbled skin that goes from dark green to purplish black, a high oil content, and a buttery taste. The Hass strain was discovered by a postman named Randolph Hass, who patented it in 1935. It was resisted at first by consumers, but because of its distinctively nutty, rich taste, it's now the most popular variety in the U.S. and accounts for 80 percent of the California crop.

The Fuerte strain was developed by Henry Dalton a few miles east of Los Angeles, near what is now Azusa, in 1848. Trees set out near Santa Barbara in 1871 have thrived for more than a century. These are medium-sized, pear-shaped fruits with a skin that's somewhat pebbled but smoother than the Hass. The skin starts out green and fairly shiny, then becomes duller with darker spots as the avocado ripens. The Fuerte doesn't peel as easily as the Hass, and it needs to be thoroughly ripe when it's eaten. Because it stores so well, it's available eight months of the year.

The Reed is roundish and large. It looks more like a Florida avocado, although it has slight pebbling on the skin.

Florida avocados are generally Mexican varieties. Smooth-skinned and very clean looking, they can grow to be very large. They contain less oil and more water than the rough-skinned California varieties, and although they're generally much less expensive and have a good flavor, they're not as sweet and nutty-tasting. Florida varieties include Booth, Lula, and Taylor.

Mexican avocados that are imported are, in my opinion, better than the Mexican varieties grown in Florida. High in quality *and* the least expensive, Mexican avocados include the Bacon and Zutano, which are available twice a year—in early spring and again in early fall. Both are well suited to guacamole and salads.

Because each variety has a different season, avocados are available year round. **Season**

California Varieties	Florida and Mexican Varieties
Hass:	**Booth, Lula, Taylor:**
Available year round	End of June through February
April to November—height	**Zutano:**
Fuerte:	October through May
November to July	**Bacon:**
Reed:	November through July
March to September	

Selecting Choose unbruised, unscarred fruit with no wrinkles, and *don't* squeeze the fruit or you'll bruise it. Look at the stem end: if the avocado is ripe, the stem will pull right out. The best strategy is to buy avocados when they're still a bit green and firm and ripen them at home.

Storing Leave firm avocados out on the counter for a few days to ripen. Early in the season avocados will take six to nine days to ripen. Late in the season they'll take only one to five days. That's because fruit left longer on the tree has matured to the point that it will ripen quickly after picking. To hasten the ripening process, put avocados in a paper bag or a drawer. Some people think they ripen best wrapped in foil.

Don't refrigerate avocados. They can turn to mush in as little as a day under refrigeration. Avocado flesh exposed to the air will darken very quickly. Some people think that leaving the pit in prevents discoloring, but the primary factor is keeping air away from the flesh—so wrap a cut avocado in plastic, refrigerate, and use it as soon as possible. Peeled and sliced avocados should be sprinkled with lemon or lime juice to retard discoloration; the citric acid also brings out the flavor.

To peel, cut the avocado lengthwise around the pit, then rotate the two halves in opposite directions. Gently put the tip of a spoon under the pit; if it comes out easily, the avocado is ripe. You can scoop the flesh out of the shell with a spoon, but in many cases the avocado will peel like a banana—just turn it over on the cut side and pull off the skin with your fingers.

Avocados are great with a sprinkle of lemon or lime juice and salt. Mashed avocado is, of course, the primary ingredient in guacamole, but the fruit is also delicious sliced and served with slices of ripe red tomato, or cut into slivers and added to tossed green salads. For a pretty salad plate, cut avocados in half lengthwise, leaving skins on, and remove the pits. Arrange on a bed of lettuce and fill the centers with crab, tuna, or chicken salad. Garnish with additional raw fresh vegetables and serve with bread if desired. An avocado pureed with a little lemon juice, salt, other seasonings, and perhaps a dab of olive oil makes a great creamy salad dressing for lettuce or other greens.

Avocados are also good on sandwiches. Any combination of avocado, bacon, lettuce, tomato, turkey, and chicken makes a great sandwich.

Italian-Style Avocados   4 servings

2 large avocados

4 green leaf or Boston lettuce leaves

2 tomatoes, sliced

4 scallions, chopped

1 cucumber, sliced

1 small onion, chopped

3 cloves garlic, chopped

3 tablespoons chopped fresh parsley or dried parsley

3 tablespoons chopped fresh basil or dried basil

¾ cup olive oil

½ teaspoon salt

½ teaspoon freshly ground black pepper

Peel the avocados, cut in half lengthwise, and take out the pits. On a large platter, arrange the lettuce leaves, tomatoes, scallions, and cucumber slices. Place the avocado halves on top. In an electric blender, combine the onion, garlic, parsley, basil, olive oil, salt, and pepper and blend until smooth. Pour over the avocados. Serve with your favorite Italian bread or rolls.

Avocado

Grow Your Own Avocado Plant

The pit of an avocado will grow into a hardy houseplant. First wash and dry it, then insert three toothpicks around the perimeter, about halfway down from the pointed end. Fill a narrow-necked jar with tepid water, then balance the pit—broad end down—over the top so that the base of the pit is below the water line. Make sure the base (the root end) is submerged at all times and change the water frequently. If you have a small narrow-necked vase or a hyacinth glass—used for forcing hyacinth bulbs—you won't need the toothpicks.

Keep the seed out of direct sunlight until the bottom splits and roots emerge, which will take anywhere from two to six weeks. Then plant in a pot filled with ordinary potting soil. As soon as you see a little more growth, put the plant in a sunny window. Avocados will grow in moderate light, but the more light, the better. You can put the plants out on the patio in the spring if you take care to harden them off by exposing them gradually to more and more light. If temperatures in your area never drop below freezing, you can plant your avocado directly in the ground. Water frequently and liberally.

Avocado

Banana

The most familiar of the tropical fruits, bananas are in abundant supply at moderate prices twelve months of the year. The top exporters of bananas are the Central American countries of Costa Rica, Honduras, Ecuador, and Panama, but bananas are grown in tropical areas all over the world.

Bananas grow in clusters called "hands" that usually include twelve to fourteen bananas; these in turn grow on huge stalks of seven to twelve hands on a plant that's actually an enormous, treelike herb. Because they ripen best off the tree and are fragile and easily bruised when ripe, bananas are shipped green and usually arrive at the market with a fair amount of green still showing.

There are special varieties of banana that include red-skinned and miniature versions, but the main difference you'll find in them is their high price, not their flavor or texture.

Season

Bananas are available year round.

Selecting

For the best eating, choose firm, unscarred bananas that are greenish to greenish yellow and ripen them at home. A golden yellow banana is ripe and fragile, and the flesh may be bruised even though you can't see bruises on the skin. Don't buy bananas if they're *grass* green; they may deteriorate without ever ripening, especially if they've been exposed to cold temperatures. And don't be afraid of bananas with brown specks on the peel; these are loaded with sugar and taste great.

Storing   For use in the fruit bowl, try buying bananas at various stages of ripeness, from fairly green to greenish yellow. That way you'll be able to keep up with the fruit. Once fully ripe, bananas deteriorate fairly rapidly; if necessary, refrigerate fully ripe fruit. Refrigeration will turn the skin an unappetizing black, but it won't really harm the fruit inside.

Preparing   Other than simply peeled and eaten or sliced on cereal, peeled bananas are great pierced with a stick, dipped in chocolate, and frozen. Also try them sliced and sautéed briefly in butter and brown sugar (and a little rum if you wish), then served over ice cream. Overripe bananas are perfect for baking in banana-nut bread, banana cake, or muffins—even when the skins are nearly all black.

Banana Crisp   6 servings

6 medium-sized bananas, peeled
¼ teaspoon salt
¾ cup vanilla wafer crumbs
¼ cup unsalted butter, melted
⅓ cup packed brown sugar
1 teaspoon ground cinnamon
whipped cream or Cool Whip

Preheat the oven to 350°F.

Slice the bananas into ½-inch rounds. Grease a large casserole and arrange the banana slices on the bottom. Sprinkle with salt.

In a bowl, combine the vanilla wafer crumbs with the melted butter. Add the brown sugar and cinnamon and mix well. Sprinkle over the bananas. Bake for approximately 20 minutes, or until browned. Serve warm or cold and top with whipped cream or Cool Whip.

Banana

• *The New England Journal of Medicine* has revealed that one extra serving of potassium per day as found in bananas can cut the risk of death from stroke by 40 percent.

• Bananas are low in sodium and high in potassium and they help maintain healthy cardiovascular muscle tissue, thus aiding in the prevention of heart disease.

• Doctors of patients treated for hypertension now recommend a supplement of bananas.

• Bananas are highly recommended for use in ulcer-control diets.

• Bananas are usually the first solid food fed to infants since the fruit is easily digestible, mild flavored, and smooth textured.

• Bananas are used to supplement the diets of the elderly since they contain fibers helpful in alleviating digestion problems.

Bean, String or Snap

String beans are so named because years ago they had a "string"—a tough fiber that ran from one tip to the other. While the string has been bred out of most varieties you'll see on the market, the name has stuck. Although there are several varieties, they're generally divided into two categories—bush beans, which have a rounded pod, and pole beans, which are usually large and relatively flat. One of the best of the flat pole beans is the Kentucky Wonder—a bright green, fairly broad bean that reaches six to eight inches in length. When fresh, young, and velvety, Kentucky Wonders have a sweet taste and an excellent, crisp texture.

One virtue of pole beans is that they're usually picked by hand. There is a definite difference between hand-picked and machine-picked beans. Machine-picked beans are usually a less tender variety—they have to be tough to survive machine picking. Machines also pick everything off in the row, while farm workers are a bit more selective. Although hand-picked beans are more expensive than the others, they may be a better buy in the long run because there's less waste.

Season Fresh green beans are available year round, but they are best in early winter, early summer, and early fall. That's when you'll get the early part of the crop. Beans picked early in the season are smaller, sweeter, and more velvety. You don't want a long, thick, or bumpy pod that shows the outline of the beans inside. These are too mature, and will be tough and tasteless.

The best beans are local ones that can be shipped to your market within one or two days of harvest, rather than crops that may have been a week in transit.

Selecting Look for small to medium-sized pods that are velvety-looking and bright green, with no signs of wilting or wrinkling. Fresh green beans should be tender enough to eat raw. The USDA classifies string beans as snap beans, and that's exactly what the bean should do when you bend one—snap. If it's rubbery and bends, it will taste rubbery too.

Storing Do not wash string beans until you're ready to use them. Refrigerate in a paper bag or unsealed plastic bag, and they'll keep well for a day or two, although it's best to use them as soon as possible. If you've had them longer and they're starting to wilt, you may be able to revive them in ice-cold water. Otherwise, add them to soups or stews.

Preparing Tender young green beans can be added raw to crudité plates. To cook, simply steam or cook in a small amount of water in a covered pan for five to eight minutes, adding a dab of butter, salt, and pepper if desired. Don't overcook! String beans also freeze well if blanched for two minutes before freezing.

Bean, String or Snap

Mama Louise's Potato and String Bean Salad

6 to 8 servings

2 pounds potatoes, peeled and cubed

1 pound string beans

½ cup corn or other light oil

¼ cup wine vinegar

pinch of garlic powder

½ teaspoon salt

½ teaspoon freshly ground black pepper

In a large saucepan of water, boil the potatoes until fork-tender. Drain and set aside to cool. In a medium-sized saucepan, steam the string beans until barely tender. Drain and run quickly under cold water to set their color. Set aside to cool.

In a large bowl, combine potatoes, beans, oil, vinegar, garlic powder, salt, and pepper. Mix well. Add more oil and vinegar if needed. Serve chilled or at room temperature.

Beet

A lot of people don't realize it, but beets and their greens are actually two vegetables: the tender tops have a sweet, buttery flavor like spinach, and they're one of the highest sources of potassium and iron you can find. The brilliant red beet roots have about the highest sugar content of any vegetable.

Fresh beets were much more popular in Grandma's day than they are now. People have gotten used to buying them in jars or cans, but fresh beets have a much more delicate flavor than processed beets, and they're not hard to prepare.

Season Beets are available year round, but they're at their peak between April and August. The best beets can be found at farm stands and markets that sell local produce.

Beet

Selecting The red beet root should be hard, with a fresh-looking tail at the root end. There should be no cuts in the flesh, and the color should be a good, deep red. The top leaves should be crisp and fresh-looking. Always try to buy beets with the tops on.

Storing Beets without the tops get soft faster than those with them on. If you aren't going to prepare the beets right away, store them in the refrigerator with their tops *on*.

Preparing The roots are dirty, so they should be washed thoroughly, but avoid using a brush because beets have a very thin skin. Always cook beets whole, and leave a bit of the stem on—this helps keep the root from bleeding. Peel and slice only *after* cooking. Once beets have been cooked, they can be run under cold water and the skins will remove easily. Cooked beets can be served with butter or a little lemon juice and are good pickled and served cold.

To prepare the tops, wash carefully, as you would spinach, to remove any traces of sand. Remove the coarse part of the red stem, steam briefly with some ground pepper and herbs as desired; then add a bit of butter and salt and enjoy as you would fresh spinach. Fresh, raw beet tops can also be added to tossed salads.

If you have a juicer or extracter, give beet juice a try. It is excellent combined with carrot juice, plus a little apple juice for extra sweetness.

Beet

Belgian Endive

Also called whiteleaf or witloof chicory, Belgian endive is a salad "green" that's grown indoors away from the light. The nearly white, broad leaves of Belgian endive form a close head that's shaped something like a squat ear of corn—broader at the base, with a tapered top. The tender leaves add a distinctive bittersweet flavor when sliced and eaten raw in salads, but Belgian endive is also tender and delicate when lightly braised and served as a side vegetable.

Belgian endive is produced by forcing chicory roots, much as you'd force a narcissus bulb in the winter. The first crop was actually an accident. A Belgian farmer left a load of chicory roots in the darkness of his barn, planning to feed them to his pigs. When he next checked on them, the roots had started to sprout small, crisp, green-white leaves. He tasted them, found them delicious, and a multimillion dollar industry was born. The only seed is actually chicory seed. The chicory is grown, then the roots are harvested, covered, and replanted. Once the "palms" form, they have to be shipped immediately because they are so perishable. The plant is totally manipulated by humans, and the timing is critical. That's why Belgian endive is so expensive. With increased means of production, however, we should see the price of Belgian endive drop considerably in the near future.

Nearly all that is sold here is imported from Belgium. Before World War II, U.S. farmers attempted to produce Belgian endive in Michigan, but the results were disappointing. Today only a few crops are produced—some in various parts of Long Island—but the bulk of the crop is imported.

Season

Belgian endive is available year round, but it's best during cool spring weather—between March and June.

Selecting

Look for endive that's more white than any other color; any green on the leaves will be very bitter-tasting. In contrast to most plants, green on the tips of Belgian endive indicates the plants are old, not young. Short, fat heads are better than long, thin ones. The plant should be crisp-looking, with no brown spots or wilted edges.

Belgian Endive

Endive Salad

2 small endives

1 head red leaf lettuce

1 small head radicchio

1 small can mandarin oranges, drained

salt and pepper to taste

¼ cup balsamic vinegar

¼ cup olive oil

pinch of oregano

Wash the endive, red leaf lettuce, and radicchio, and drain well in a colander. Dry greens thoroughly, then tear into bite-sized pieces and place in a large bowl. Top with mandarin oranges, sprinkle with salt and pepper, and toss with balsamic vinegar, olive oil, and oregano.

Belgian Endive

Berry
Blackberry

Some of the best memories of my childhood are of picking blackberries from a wild patch near a neighbor's yard in Tenafly, New Jersey—a patch now long gone. A bramble and a member of the rose family, blackberries will grow like weeds in the right climate, and in more rural areas they can still sometimes be seen growing by the side of the road. What we get on the market are cultivated varieties. Although they're grown in almost every state, the biggest crops come from the Pacific Northwest, Michigan, and New Jersey. The greater part of the crop is sold to processors for jams and jellies, but you'll find fresh blackberries at roadside stands, farm markets, and good produce stores during the summer, usually in half-pint boxes.

Season

Blackberries are available from May until September, with the peak usually in June and July. Winter berries are imported from Chile.

Selecting

A blackberry on the vine ripens from green to purple to black; a ripe one is just about jet black and will almost fall off the vine with a gentle touch. If you pick them yourself, look for the blackest berries you can find. If you have to tug at them to get them off the vine, they aren't really ripe.

Blackberries are usually marketed by the half pint. The container is usually cardboard, so check the bottom for stains. If it's badly stained, pass it by. Avoid berries that are very soft or wet, show signs of mildew, or seem to be stuck together in the container.

Storing

Since they're not hollow, blackberries will keep a little longer than raspberries, but you want to use them within two days of purchase or picking. Don't keep 'em—eat 'em!

Like all berries, blackberries should be refrigerated *unwashed*. Spread them out on a tray or in a shallow basket so that they're not packed on top of each other.

Preparing

Rinse the berries quickly in cold water right before you're ready to serve. *Never wash any berry until you're ready to eat it*. Blackberries are delicious eaten as is, with cream and sugar, or added to other sliced fresh fruits such as peaches. They make intensely flavored pies and jams.

Blueberry

In produce markets blueberries come in two varieties: wild and cultivated. The wild ones are quite small and tart, while the cultivated varieties are bigger, sweeter, and I think have a lot of flavor. Blueberries grow in clusters at the top of the bush; new cultivars grow high off the ground and can be picked by machine. That means that while they're in season, they're in bountiful supply.

Most fruits and vegetables originated in Asia or Europe, but blueberries are strictly a North American food. Although they're grown worldwide, North America still produces 95 percent of the world's crop. They have a very short season—only cherries and apricots are shorter—yet we still produce more than 200 million pounds. Blueberries are available between June and September from the Carolinas, Michigan, and New England, as well as from the garden state of New Jersey. Without a doubt the biggest, best, and sweetest berries come from Hammonton and Vineland, New Jersey.

Season The first blueberries of the season—from Florida—show up on the market at the beginning of May, but I don't think they are as good as those from states a little farther north. Good berries from the Carolinas start appearing in late May. Late in June a huge New Jersey crop comes in; then in July berries from Oregon, Washington, Michigan, and Massachusetts come on the market; in August crops from Maine arrive, and in late August, berries from British Columbia. Although it's always best to buy local produce, blueberries stand up to shipping much better than other berries, basically because they're small and round and pack compactly.

Selecting To get the best value for your money, try to buy local berries. Buy them at the top of their yield in your own community, and eat your fill while they're in season. Look for firm, plump, dry, deep blue berries of a uniform size. A dusty bloom on the outside is an excellent sign of freshness. Seven or eight days after harvest, that bloom will disappear, but it's not something that will wash off in cold water. The dusty blue sheen on the berry is nature's way of protecting it from the sun, and it's your way of knowing

Berry 38

the berry is fresh, so make sure the berries look dry and have that dusty blue look. A paler, reddish purple color is usually an indication the berry isn't ripe. Also check to be sure the box isn't wet underneath—which is an indication of overripe, ruined fruit.

Fresh blueberries will keep unrefrigerated for two days and for up to ten days in your refrigerator. If you're not going to eat them plain or bake them into pies, muffins, or pancakes, you can freeze them just as they come from the market: wrap the whole package and stick it in the freezer. As they defrost, blueberries lose their firm consistency, but they stay sweet. You can use them semifrozen in fresh fruit salads, or bake with them.

Blueberry Torte   6 to 8 servings

½ cup (1 stick) unsalted butter

1 teaspoon vanilla extract

½ cup plus 2 tablespoons sugar

3 egg yolks

½ cup cornstarch

1 cup flour

1¼ teaspoons baking powder

2 cups fresh blueberries

1 tablespoon ground cinnamon

Preheat the oven to 350°F.

Using an electric mixer, combine the butter, vanilla, ½ cup sugar, egg yolks, cornstarch, flour, and baking powder. When well blended, press the mixture into the bottom and sides of a greased 8-inch square or 9-inch round baking pan.

In a large bowl, mix the blueberries with the remaining 2 tablespoons sugar and the cinnamon until the fruit is well coated. Pour into the prepared pan and bake for 1 hour. Serve hot or cold.

Blueberry Tea Cakes   Makes about 24 small cakes

CRUMB TOPPING

½ cup sugar

¼ cup flour

½ teaspoon ground cinnamon

¼ cup unsalted butter or margarine, melted

BATTER

2 cups sifted flour

2 teaspoons baking powder

½ teaspoon salt

¼ cup butter

¾ cup sugar

1 egg

½ cup milk

2 cups blueberries

Preheat the oven to 375°F. Grease muffin cups or line with paper liners.

To make the topping, combine the sugar, flour, and cinnamon in a small bowl. Drizzle the melted butter over the mixture and combine with a fork or your fingers until it forms crumbs. Set aside.

To make the batter, sift together the flour, baking powder, and salt, and set aside.

In a large mixing bowl, cream together the butter and sugar and beat until fluffy. Beat in the egg, then add the milk gradually, beating after each addition. Add the batter mixture a small quantity at a time, beating after each addition. Beat until smooth.

Fold the blueberries into the batter, stirring gently by hand until they are evenly distributed. Spoon the mixture into muffin tins and sprinkle each cake with a little crumb topping. Bake 40 to 45 minutes, or until golden brown.

Berry

Boysenberry

Boysenberries are an experimental cross developed by a man named Boysen, who crossed the blackberry with a raspberry and got a slightly larger and sweeter berry that, except for its lighter color, looks like a blackberry. Boysenberries are more fragile than blackberries and have slightly softer seeds. They are ripe when they turn deep purple; if they're too pale, they'll be bitter. Boysenberries are one of the more popular hybrids of the blackberry; other hybrids include the loganberry and youngberry.

Season

Boysenberries are in season in late summer and fall.

Selecting

Select as you would blackberries, except look for a dark purple rather than black color. Boysenberries are available at roadside stands, farm markets, and most fruit stands.

Storing

Store as you would blackberries.

Preparing

Rinse briefly in cold water just before serving. Boysenberries are excellent with cream, in cereal, with whipped cream, and on ice cream. They make a terrific sorbet or ice cream—boysenberry ice cream is one of my favorites. They also make a delicious cobbler or deep-dish pie.

Raspberry

Raspberries are an extraordinarily flavorful fruit with a tart-sweet, almost floral taste that can't be duplicated. A bramble fruit and cousin to the blackberry, raspberries once flourished wild in North America; now almost all are cultivated and available only in limited supplies. Unlike blackberries, which are relatively firm, raspberries are hollow and are therefore extremely fragile. The plants themselves have a low yield, and the berries frequently break when they're picked, further reducing the quantity that can be shipped fresh. Because of all these factors, in the winter raspberries can be as high as six or seven dollars a half-pint—and that's wholesale! At the height of the season, however, you can enjoy them at more reasonable prices, especially if they are local.

Ninety-nine percent of commercially cultivated raspberries are red, but there are

Berry

also black and golden varieties. Black raspberries can be quite good, but golden raspberries are not as sweet or flavorful as the red. For my money, rose-red raspberries can't be beat. Although they're never inexpensive, try to enjoy them when they're in season. There is no finer berry.

Season Raspberries are most abundant during June, July, and August. Local raspberries are available for about three to four weeks during the summer; the exact month will depend upon your region. (Most cultivars do not thrive in the South.) Some farmers will grow two crops, with the first ripening in late June and early July, and the second in September or early October.

Raspberries from California are available from summer through early fall; in the late fall raspberries arrive from the Pacific Northwest, and in the winter, from Chile.

Selecting Look for local raspberries at roadside stands or farm markets. If you find a farm that offers pick-your-own berries, don't pass them up. Like a ripe blackberry, a ripe raspberry will practically fall off the vine into your hand.

At the market select dry, firm fruits with excellent form and hollow centers. Avoid soft, wet, or mildewed berries, berries that seem to be stuck together, and fruit in badly stained containers.

Storing Always refrigerate, and use the same day of purchase if at all possible.

Preparing Rinse briefly in cold water just before serving. Raspberries are delicious fresh and whole as is or with a little cream. Fresh raspberries are also wonderful pureed, slightly sweetened, and used as a sauce for ice cream, custards, or other fruits. Freeze the puree for an elegant sorbet.

Salad with Greens, Reds, and Whites   4 servings

1 bunch watercress, washed

2 heads Bibb or Boston lettuce, washed

1 pound mushrooms, sliced

1 bunch white radishes, sliced

½ cup Raspberry Vinaigrette

1 cup raspberries

Place the greens, mushrooms, and radishes in a large bowl. Drizzle with vinaigrette and toss. Sprinkle the berries over the salad.

Raspberry Vinaigrette   4 servings

¼ cup raspberry vinegar

½ teaspoon salt

½ teaspoon raspberry mustard

½ teaspoon freshly ground black pepper

1 cup olive oil

In a mixing bowl, combine the vinegar, salt, mustard, and pepper. Drizzle in the olive oil and mix with a whisk until all the ingredients are blended.

Berry

Raspberry Torte 4 to 6 servings

1 cup graham cracker crumbs

¾ cup sugar

¼ cup unsalted butter, softened

8 ounces cream cheese

2 eggs

2 cups Raspberry Filling

whipped cream (optional)

Preheat the oven to 350°F. Grease an 8-inch square or 9-inch round baking pan.

In a small mixing bowl, combine the graham cracker crumbs, half of the sugar, and the butter until blended. Press into the bottom of the pan.

In a large mixing bowl, beat the cream cheese, gradually adding the remaining sugar, until smooth. Add the eggs and blend thoroughly. Pour into the prepared pan and bake for 30 minutes. Let cool, then add the filling. Chill and serve with whipped cream if desired.

Raspberry Filling 4 to 6 servings

½ cup sugar

2 tablespoons cornstarch or arrowroot

pinch ground nutmeg

¼ cup water

1 tablespoon unsalted butter

1½ cups raspberries

In a small saucepan over moderate heat, combine the sugar, cornstarch, and nutmeg. Gradually add the water and stir. Add the butter and raspberries and bring to a boil, stirring gently. Boil for 2 minutes, or until thickened.

Berry

Butter Cookies with Raspberry Preserves

Makes 4 dozen

½ **pound unsalted butter**

½ **cup confectioners' sugar**

½ **teaspoon salt**

1 teaspoon vanilla extract

2 cups flour

raspberry preserves

Preheat the oven to 400°F.

In a mixing bowl, cream the butter, sugar, salt, and vanilla. Add the flour and mix well. Using your hands, roll the dough into small balls and place on ungreased baking sheets. In the center of each cookie, press lightly with your thumb and fill the centers with raspberry preserves. Bake for 10 minutes, or until lightly golden.

Strawberry

If there's any such thing as an all-American fruit, it's strawberries. They're our most popular dessert fruit. In most places local strawberries have a very short season. You can, of course, buy them year round, but like a lot of good things, the best strawberries are still the ones you get locally during those few brief weeks that they're in season.

The first refrigerated shipment of strawberries in this country was made in 1843, when 40,000 quarts were shipped out of Cincinnati. That's a lot of strawberries. But in 1992, California shipped more than 5,160,000 quarts *every day*. More than 300,000 acres of strawberries are now cultivated worldwide—half of them in the United States. California is the biggest producer, and I think it grows the best commercially produced strawberries. We also get strawberries from Florida, New Zealand, Argentina, and Chile. Mexico and Guatemala also grow them, but I don't think they have much flavor.

Berry

Varieties Although there are different strawberry strains, there are three basic types: wild strawberries (often called *fraises des bois*), commercially grown hybrids, and local strawberries. I put locals into a separate category because, compared to strawberries grown and shipped from California and Florida, local strawberries—picked ripe by hand and sold close to home—taste totally different.

For hundreds of years wild strawberries were the only ones available. They're most frequently found in alfalfa and clover fields, where they seem to grow best. Very tiny, with a tart, delicate flavor, wild strawberries show up in late June in most places.

Although wild strawberries are native to the Americas, most commercially grown berries are produced from hybrids first developed in France, where wild strawberries imported from Virginia were planted next to yellow Chilean strawberries. These varieties cross-pollinated to produce a sweet red berry several times larger than its wild cousin.

A local strawberry is simply any strawberry grown and sold not far from where you are. They're ripened right on the plant and picked by hand. Vine-ripened berries are darker and sweeter than shipped berries, but they're very, very fragile. Local strawberries are picked early every morning, when the dew is still on them. The whole season lasts only about three weeks—usually from mid-June to early July. But too much rain in June can ruin the entire crop. One year there were heavy rains in our part of New Jersey during strawberry season, and we had strawberries for only two days! So when those first ripe local berries appear at your market, grab 'em.

Commercial cultivars are bred to be firmer and heartier than most varieties so that they'll stand up to shipping. And, of course, they're shipped under refrigeration, which is an absolute necessity. Strawberries are an exception to my no-refrigeration rule. They *must* be refrigerated.

Right now the top-of-the-line commercially grown strawberry is the Driscoll Stem. It's the great big one with the stem cut long. It looks spectacular and is good for desserts like chocolate fondue. But I still look for small berries: I think they have the best flavor.

Berry

When you're selecting strawberries, look for bright, deep red, glossy berries with fresh **Selecting** green caps, leaves, and stems. They should also be dry. Look at the bottom of the box: there should be no red stains or seepage showing. And, of course, stay away from berries that have turned dull and bluish. They're goners.

Storing

Rule 1:	**Rule 2:**	**Rule 3:**
Refrigerate.	Refrigerate.	Refrigerate.

Strawberries, like most other berries, won't ripen any further once they're pulled from the vine. Nothing you can do at home will make a green berry ripen. And once the berry cap is pulled, it will deteriorate very quickly. You can hold ripe strawberries in the refrigerator a day or two and still have pretty good berries, but the best thing to do is to eat strawberries the same day you buy them.

Preparing

Just as important: store the strawberries untouched. Never, ever wash or remove the strawberry cap until you're ready to eat the berry. Then just wash the berries with a gentle spray of cool water and remove the caps *after* the berries have drained.

The no-touch rule also holds if you're planning to freeze the berries. Just pop them into a plastic bag and put them into the freezer unwashed and uncapped. Rinse briefly and remove the caps only when you're ready to serve.

Season

Wild strawberries: early June, where available

Local strawberries: in most areas, mid-June and early July

California strawberries: January through November, with peak in March through May

Florida strawberries: December through May, with peak in March and April

Imports: from New Zealand and Chile, November through April; from Mexico and Guatemala, early spring

Berry

Strawberry Muffins   Makes 12 muffins

1½ cups coarsely chopped strawberries

¾ cup sugar

1¾ cups flour

½ teaspoon baking soda

¼ teaspoon ground nutmeg

¼ teaspoon salt

2 eggs, beaten

¼ cup unsalted butter, melted

1 teaspoon vanilla extract

Preheat the oven to 425°F. Grease muffin cups or line with paper liners.

In a small bowl, combine the strawberries and ½ cup of the sugar. Set aside for 1 hour. Drain, reserving the liquid in a separate bowl.

In a medium-sized bowl, combine the flour, baking soda, nutmeg, and salt. In a separate bowl, mix the eggs, butter, vanilla, remaining ¼ cup sugar, and strawberry liquid. Stir until well combined. Fold in the dry ingredients until just moistened, taking care not to overmix. Fold in the strawberries.

Spoon into muffin cups and bake for approximately 20 minutes, or until a toothpick inserted in the center of one comes out clean. Serve warm.

Chocolate-Covered Strawberries   6 to 8 servings

5 ounces milk chocolate

4 ounces semisweet chocolate chips

3 pints large, fresh strawberries with stems

Place both kinds of chocolate in a small saucepan and stir over very low heat until melted. Dip in the strawberries one at a time until coated with chocolate, being careful not to cover the stem. Place the strawberries on a greased baking sheet or tray and immediately place in the refrigerator. Chill until the chocolate hardens. These can be prepared a day in advance.

Strawberry Pie   6 to 8 servings

3 pints strawberries, washed and hulled

1 cup sugar

3 tablespoons cornstarch

½ cup water

1 baked 9-inch pie shell

whipped cream (optional)

Crush enough of the strawberries to make 1 cup. In a saucepan, combine the crushed berries, sugar, cornstarch, and water. Cook over moderate heat, stirring constantly, until the mixture thickens. Remove from the heat and set aside to cool.

Slice the remaining strawberries and place them in the pie shell. Pour the cooked mixture over the top and refrigerate for 3 hours, or until the pie is set. Serve with whipped cream if desired.

49   Berry

Strawberry Angel Pie

6 to 8 servings

CRUST

4 egg whites

¼ teaspoon cream of tartar

1 cup sugar

FILLING

4 egg yolks

½ cup sugar

1 teaspoon lemon juice

1½ cups fresh strawberries, crushed and drained, reserving liquid

1 teaspoon unflavored gelatin

¼ cup cold water

1 cup heavy cream

Preheat the oven to 250°F.

Prepare the crust. In a large bowl, beat the egg whites until frothy. Add the cream of tartar and continue beating until the egg whites are stiff. Add the sugar and beat in. Spread the egg whites evenly over a 9-inch pie plate. Bake for 20 minutes, then increase the oven temperature to 300°F and bake an additional 40 minutes.

In the meantime, prepare the filling. In a medium-sized saucepan, combine the egg yolks, sugar, and lemon juice. Add the reserved strawberry liquid and cook over moderate heat until the mixture thickens. Remove from the heat.

In a small bowl, sprinkle the gelatin over the cold water and let sit for 3 to 4 minutes, until the gelatin softens. Add to the filling mixture along with the crushed strawberries and set aside to cool.

Beat the heavy cream until stiff and spread a thin layer onto the cooled pie shell. Cover with the strawberry filling and top with the remaining whipped cream. Chill well before serving.

Berry

Broccoli

Kids who call broccoli "trees" are imitating the Romans, who called it *bracchium*, meaning "strong branch or arm." Their nickname for it was "the five green fingers of Jupiter," and they ate a lot of it. Broccoli is one of the cruciferous vegetables—in the cabbage family—that is packed with beta carotene, the precursor to vitamin A that researchers believe has anticarcinogenic properties.

Thomas Jefferson first brought broccoli seeds from Italy to Monticello. Although broccoli flourished there, Jefferson wasn't fond of it—probably because it was cooked to death. Broccoli didn't really catch on in the U.S. until the twentieth century; as Italian immigration increased, Italian farmers started growing it in California. They knew how to cook it, and by the mid-1920s broccoli was becoming more popular. Although broccoli is grown almost everywhere, the bulk of the crop is still grown in California.

Season

A cool-weather crop planted in the spring and fall, broccoli is available year round, but the peak of the season is March through November. It's usually very consistently priced, but when the price jumps up 30 to 40 percent, you know it's out of season and in short supply.

Selecting

Look for a firm, clean stalk with tight, bluish-green florets. Check the stalks to make sure they're not too thick and hard—they will be a bit woody. Most important, the florets should be tightly closed and the broccoli should have little or no fragrance. Broccoli is eaten at an immature stage; left to grow in the field, the buds will open into yellow flowers. Buds that are starting to open and look yellowish will be mushy and have a strong cabbage taste. Use your nose when you're selecting broccoli: if a head has an odor, it's not good.

Storing

Broccoli will keep up to seven days if refrigerated and kept moist. You can break apart the stalks and put them in ice water or spread crushed ice on top. Or wrap broccoli in a plastic bag with a damp paper towel and place in the crisper.

Preparing The less you do to broccoli, the more it will do for you. Broccoli will lose up to 30 percent of its vitamins and minerals when it's cooked, so for nutritional reasons as well as good flavor, never overcook it. Broccoli is also very good raw on a platter of crudités, added to other vegetables in a salad, or served with dips.

At certain times of the year, broccoli may harbor a bug or worm or both. When cleaning, soak the head in salted water about fifteen minutes, and the critters will float to the top.

Broccoli can be prepared in countless ways. Sauté it with a little garlic and onion. Add it to pasta, or serve it blanched and cooled in a vinaigrette. It's excellent simply steamed for a few minutes and served with a dab of butter or squeeze of lemon—or both. To steam, put it in about half an inch of salted water, stem ends down. Don't let the buds touch the water—they'll cook very quickly and will get mushy and disintegrate. Cover and cook over low to medium heat for no more than four to five minutes— just until it's fork tender. Check the pot once or twice to make sure there is adequate liquid in the bottom to keep from burning, and add a few tablespoons of water as needed. Properly cooked, broccoli has a delicate flavor and arrives at the table tender-crisp and bright green. If you're going to add lemon or vinegar, do it at the last minute because they tend to drab the color.

At my house, we also eat broccoli in a stir-fry, with snow peas and pork. And in the wintertime I love Betty's Cream of Broccoli Soup. It's rich, but is it good!

Broccoli

Cream of Broccoli Soup   4 servings

¼ cup unsalted butter

¼ cup chopped onions

2 tablespoons flour

2 10¾-ounce cans chicken broth

½ cup heavy cream

1 cup half & half

¼ teaspoon salt

½ teaspoon ground black pepper

1 head broccoli, trimmed and chopped

In a large soup pot, melt the butter over moderate heat. Add the onions and sauté until translucent. Sprinkle in the flour and stir until the mixture has thickened. Add the chicken broth, heavy cream, half & half, salt, pepper, and broccoli. Gently stir together. Cover and bring to a boil, stirring occasionally. Turn heat to low and simmer for an additional 15 minutes. Serve.

Broccoli

Andy's Raw Broccoli Salad
6 to 8 servings

SALAD

2 heads broccoli, cut into small pieces

½ cup golden raisins

⅓ cup hulled sunflower seeds

½ small red onion, diced

½ pound bacon, cooked and crumbled

DRESSING

1 cup mayonnaise

2 tablespoons red wine vinegar

¼ cup sugar

In a large bowl, mix together all the salad ingredients. In a small bowl, whisk together the dressing ingredients, then stir into the salad until well mixed. Chill and serve.

Broccoli à la Dolores

6 servings

2 heads broccoli

1 pound Velveeta cheese

½ cup milk

2 tablespoons chopped onion

2 tablespoons diced red bell pepper

1½ cups Ritz cracker crumbs

3 tablespoons butter or margarine

Preheat the oven to 375°F.

In a large saucepan, steam the broccoli until fork-tender. In a small saucepan, melt the cheese on low heat, then add the milk, onion, and bell pepper. Stir until well blended.

Layer the ingredients in a large casserole, beginning with the melted cheese, then adding the broccoli and sprinkling with the cracker crumbs. Dot the crumb layer with butter and repeat. Sprinkle the final layer with additional cracker crumbs. Cover and bake for 20 minutes, then uncover the casserole and bake an additional 5 minutes, until the crumb topping is lightly browned.

Broccoli

Patsy's Pasta Primavera   4 servings

1 pound ziti

3 teaspoons salt

2 tablespoons olive oil

1 teaspoon chopped garlic

¼ cup broccoli florets

¼ cup chopped carrots

¼ cup chopped mushrooms

¼ cup water

¼ cup chopped tomatoes

¼ cup chopped zucchini

splash white wine

2 sprigs fresh basil

pinch freshly ground black pepper

In a large pot, bring 3 quarts of water to a boil. Add the ziti and 2½ teaspoons of the salt. Cook until al dente.

In the meantime, heat the olive oil in a large skillet, add the garlic, and sauté until golden. Add the broccoli, carrots, mushrooms, and water. Cover and simmer for about 3 minutes, then add the tomatoes, zucchini, white wine, basil, pepper, and remaining salt.

When the ziti is cooked and drained, transfer it to a serving dish and stir in a little of the sauce. Spoon the remaining sauce over the top and serve.

Broccoli   56

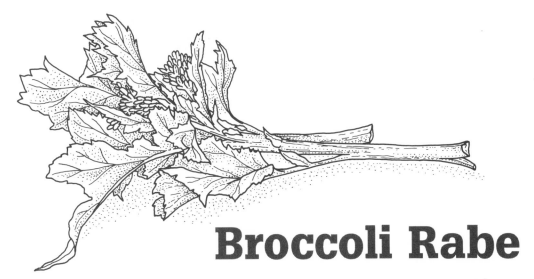

Broccoli Rabe

Broccoli rabe is a nonheading variety of broccoli that's also known as *broccoletti di rape*, *brocoletto*, rapini, *choy sum*, or Chinese flowering cabbage. It has long, thin, leafy stalks topped with small florets that look like tiny broccoli florets. The florets or flowers are quite delicate; the leaves slightly bitter.

Once highly prized by the Romans and cultivated all over the southern Mediterranean, broccoli rabe didn't appear in more northern areas of Europe until the sixteenth century, and didn't appear in North America until the 1920s, when Italian farmers brought it to the United States. For years broccoli rabe was favored mainly in the Italian and Asian communities here. In the old days broccoli rabe was a staple and sold for twenty-five cents a pound, maybe ten cents a pound. In my father's family broccoli rabe was used to flavor all kinds of filling dishes when meat was just too expensive. They'd have it with pasta, with potatoes—they'd even make broccoli rabe sandwiches! They had it so much that my father once swore he'd never eat it again. Now it's a yuppie food that shows up in trendy restaurants and fetches $1.98 a pound at the market.

Even though it's a little pricey now, broccoli rabe is still a great vegetable. It packs a wallop and has a bitter zest that gives a real lift to bland foods.

Season

Broccoli rabe is most plentiful between late fall and early spring. It is grown in various places all over the continent, including Quebec, California, Arizona, and other states, so it's usually available year round, except for a couple of months in midsummer—usually June and July.

Selecting At the market you'll usually find broccoli rabe displayed in a refrigerator case sprinkled with ice because it wilts very easily. Choose firm, green, small stems with compact heads. Like broccoli, the flower buds that make up the florets should be tightly closed and dark green, not open or yellow. The Andy Boy label is the top of the line when it comes to broccoli rabe and should be bought whenever possible.

Storing Store broccoli rabe in your refrigerator crisper unwashed, either wrapped in a wet towel or in a plastic bag. It will keep two or three days. For longer storage, blanch and freeze.

Preparing To prepare, rinse thoroughly in cold water, shake off, and cut off the bottoms of the stalks (they're too tough to eat). Broccoli rabe is much better cooked than raw. Raw, it's very bitter but has no other flavor. Even a light steaming brings out its distinctive taste. As a side vegetable, broccoli rabe yields only about one serving per pound because it cooks way down. You can cook it like broccoli, but whether you braise, sauté, boil, or steam it, you only need to cook it for eight to ten minutes. Most Italians like broccoli rabe al dente—cooked about six minutes. You can steam it in water or chicken broth, or sauté it with oil and garlic. Some people like it as a cold salad: steamed, then cooled and dressed with oil, hot peppers, garlic, and other seasonings. For terrific potatoes, add steamed broccoli rabe to boiled potatoes and dress with olive oil and garlic. Broccoli rabe also makes a great sauce for pasta when steamed and combined with olive oil, garlic, and hot sausages.

Broccoli Rabe

Betty's Sausage and Broccoli Rabe

6 to 8 servings

2 pounds cooked hot or sweet Italian sausage

2 pounds broccoli rabe, rinsed well

3 cloves garlic

¼ cup olive oil

1 teaspoon ground red (cayenne) pepper

salt and freshly ground black pepper to taste

1½ pounds hot cooked pasta

In a large skillet, brown the sausage, then slice into ½-inch rounds; set aside. Trim off the lower 2 inches of the broccoli rabe stems. In a large pan, brown the garlic in the olive oil, add the broccoli rabe, cover, and simmer over medium heat for about 12 minutes. Add the sausage, ground red pepper, salt, and pepper and simmer until the broccoli rabe is tender, about 5 minutes. Toss with the cooked pasta.

Brussels Sprout

You could say I owe my television career to Brussels sprouts. When I was doing a local TV program, I was called by NBC to interview for a show called *House Party*. There were several people up for the spot. I'm Italian and feel more comfortable talking with my hands, so I decided to take along something to demonstrate. I brought a stalk of Brussels sprouts, got up in front of the producers, and said, ''Honey, I shrunk the cabbage.'' I got a little laugh—and the *House Party* job.

A lot of people think of Brussels sprouts as cute little cabbages but prefer not to eat them, usually because they've only had them mushy and overcooked. Brussels sprouts should be steamed or simmered very briefly, just until they're beyond the raw stage. That way they'll stay nice and green on the outside, they'll have a beautiful white color inside, and they'll be delicious. Trust me!

Brussels Sprout

Brussels sprouts are the newest member of the cabbage family—a mere two hundred years old—compared to head cabbage, which has been cultivated for thousands of years. They grow clustered on a thick stalk, although they are most often sold loose or packaged in pint cartons. In the fall you may see them fresh on the stem, especially at local farm stores. Buy them that way when you can. They're fresh, and they'll stay fresh a lot longer than cut sprouts. If you have room, you can put the whole stalk in the refrigerator, and the Brussels sprouts will keep a long time without wilting or yellowing.

Season Brussels sprouts are available most of the year, but they thrive in cold, damp weather and are best in the late fall and early spring. Brussels sprouts from California—the biggest producer—are available from October through March. High-quality sprouts are also grown on Long Island and in upper New York State; these are most likely to be on the market in the fall.

Selecting Look for fresh green sprouts that are free of wilt, yellowing, or spots. Buy them on the stalk when you can.

Storing Cut Brussels sprouts will last up to a week in the refrigerator, even longer if they're still on the stem.

Preparing To cook, rinse the sprouts and remove any wilted or yellow leaves. Score the stem ends with a knife. Bring a large pot of salted water to a boil over high heat, then add the sprouts and cook just until tender—about seven to ten minutes. To steam, place in a steamer basket over, but not touching, boiling water, cover, and steam just until the sprouts are tender but still firm—al dente, as the Italians say—which will take about ten to fifteen minutes. Do not overcook! You should be able to pierce each sprout easily with a cooking fork. The very tiny sprouts are very sweet and good raw. Try adding them to a platter of crudités or to a green salad—they're delicious.

Brussels Sprout

Cabbage

One of the least expensive and most available of all vegetables, cabbage is a food staple in Europe and northern Africa and has been around for more than four thousand years. Long associated with boarding-house cooking and lingering smells, cabbage has been reinstated as one of the members of the important crucifer family—vegetables that contain important anticancer nutrients.

The problem with cabbage is the usual one: most people overcook it. When it's cooked quickly and evenly, cabbage has a mild, sweet flavor and a pleasing texture; eaten raw, it has a spicier flavor and crunchy texture.

The difference between green and white cabbage is that the green comes straight in from the field, while the white has been blanched. In upper New York State, for example, growers cut the heads and then bury them in trenches to blanch the leaves and protect the heads from freezing. This method gives us cabbage all winter long. Many people think that cabbage with a touch of frost on it is sweeter too.

Savoy cabbage has puckered, wrinkly leaves and forms a looser head. Red cabbage is a different variety altogether. Both are good simmered in vinegar and allowed to cool overnight, then served as a side dish with veal or pork.

 Cabbage

Season Available year round at reasonable prices.

Selecting Select hard, round heads with crisp outer leaves that are free of rust or yellowing. Red cabbage and Savoy cabbage should be crisp and brightly colored. None of them should show black edges or other signs of rot.

Storing Refrigerate in a plastic bag or in the crisper drawer. Cabbage will keep well for weeks. If the outer leaves turn yellow or dry out, just peel them off. The cabbage underneath will still be good.

Preparing Pull off and rinse the green outer leaves for stuffing. The head may be cut into wedges for steaming, sliced thin for sautéing, shredded raw and mixed with salad greens, or made into coleslaw. For a tasty winter salad, shred cabbage together with apples and carrots, then add raisins and nuts and toss with a dressing. Cabbage is excellent added to stir-fries, pickled, made into sauerkraut, or cooked and served with corned beef, smoked pork, or German sausage.

Cardoon

An old Italian favorite, cardoon is also known as *cardoni* or *cardone*. It looks like pale, overgrown celery, with long, flexible stalks lined with jagged leaves. The outer stalks are very fibrous and covered with prickly thorns; the inner stalks are pale, tender, and succulent.

Cardoon is never eaten raw, but it's delicious cooked—when breaded and fried, it tastes almost like veal cutlet. The flavor is like a cross between artichoke and celery. Cardoon is a traditional dish among Italians around Thanksgiving and Christmas, but the vegetable is often hard to find because most people don't know what to do with it.

A relative of the globe artichoke, cardoon is a member of the composite family, a name that derives from the Latin for thistle and includes lettuce, dandelion, endive, and Jerusalem artichoke. It originated in the Mediterranean area and was widespread through southern Europe by the Middle Ages. Well liked by the Romans, cardoon was consumed in large quantities by pregnant women, who believed it would give them male children. Cardoon is now grown mainly in Italy, France, Spain, Argentina, and

Australia. Early colonists and Italian settlers in North America first cultivated cardoon on the East Coast and later in California, which is about the only place in the U.S. that grows it commercially. But you can still find cardoon growing wild on the roadsides in New Jersey and other eastern states.

Available September to March, mostly in Italian specialty markets.

Season

Cardoon comes in gigantic stalks that range from six to ten pounds. Look for firm, very crisp cardoon with a touch of dew on it—almost as if you were choosing celery. The large top leaves are always cut off when it's harvested, and discoloration at the cut edge is normal.

Selecting

Since the stalks are so large, you may not want to use more than half at a time. Cut the cardoon crosswise and use the top half first—the base will keep longer. Wrap it in a damp paper towel, place in a paper or plastic bag, refrigerate in the crisper, and it will hold a week or two but no longer. Never let it dry out—dried-out cardoon is inedible.

Storing

Cardoon is usually precooked before use in recipes to tenderize and remove any bitterness. Handle the plant very carefully, as its leaves are thorny and will prick your fingers. Slice off the top of the cardoon and discard the tough outer leaves, then separate the inner leaves, wash individually, and trim the leafy edges off each stalk with a carrot scraper. That's where the thorns are, but you need to remove only a thin layer, as if you were peeling celery. Cardoon may discolor as you work with it, but the color will even out as it cooks.

Preparing

The pared stalks can be sliced, diced, or juilienned, according to your recipe. To precook, put the pieces into a large quantity of boiling salted water with a little vinegar or lemon juice, and cook about 30 minutes, or until tender. Drain and discard the water, then proceed with your recipe or simply serve with a little melted butter and salt and pepper. Once cooked, cardoon turns the same grayish color as overcooked artichokes, and like artichokes, it should never be cooked in an aluminum pot. While its color isn't particularly pretty, it tastes great.

Cooked, drained cardoon is very tasty marinated in a good vinaigrette—let it stand

Cardoon

in the refrigerator overnight, then garnish with olives and capers and serve cold. For a good mixed-vegetable dish, sauté a little garlic and some onion in olive oil, add plum tomatoes, cooked cardoon, thyme, oregano, salt, and pepper, and simmer five to ten minutes. Cardoon is especially delicious pounded, breaded, and fried like cutlets or fried tempura-style and served with anchovy sauce.

Cardoon Tempura with Anchovy Sauce 4 to 8 servings

½ to 1 bunch cardoon

dash of vinegar or lemon juice

vegetable oil for frying

BATTER

1 cup ice water

1 egg

1 cup flour

pinch salt

DIPPING SAUCE

4 tablespoons sour cream

1 2½-ounce tin anchovies, including oil

2 tablespoons vegetable oil

3 tablespoons white wine vinegar

1 teaspoon minced fresh thyme

GARNISH

1 to 2 tablespoons minced fresh parsley

Half fill a large stockpot with water, add 1 teaspoon salt, and bring to a boil. Cut the cardoon into sticks about 2 inches long and ¾ inch wide. Add to the boiling salted water along with the vinegar or lemon juice, and cook for about 30 minutes, or until tender. Drain and dry thoroughly.

In a large bowl, prepare the batter by mixing the ice water and egg together. Add the flour and salt and stir until just mixed. The batter will be thin. In a skillet heat the vegetable oil until very hot. Dip the cardoon sticks into the batter and fry a few at a time until they're lightly browned. Remove from the oil with a slotted spoon and drain thoroughly on paper towels.

Prepare the sauce by thoroughly blending the sour cream, anchovies, anchovy oil, vegetable oil, vinegar, and thyme in a small bowl.

Before serving, sprinkle the cardoon with the minced parsley and serve with the dipping sauce on the side.

Carrot

Carrots used to be sold with their tops on, but most markets now carry only cello-pack carrots because, surprisingly, leaving the tops on quickly robs a carrot of moisture and sweetness. If you plan on buying fresh carrots with their tops, use them immediately.

The best carrots are grown in the soft, alkaline soil of California, which produces the sweetest carrots you can find. Although a medium-sized carrot is the sweetest, even large California carrots taste better than carrots grown elsewhere. Florida carrots tend to be bitter and become limp very fast, so steer clear. Cello-pack baby carrots, which are often already washed and trimmed, can be a good buy. These are immature carrots and usually are tender and sweet.

Season

Available year round; there is always an ample supply.

Carrot

Selecting Look for a bright, shiny carrot. If the tops are on, they should be green and fresh-looking. The crown, or top of the root, should have a slightly green, red, or purplish cast where it has been exposed to the sun. The lower part of the root should be deep orange, free of bruises and rot, with no black skin. Inspect cello carrots through the bag to make sure they have good color and haven't developed cracks or long white root hairs; those carrots have been in storage too long and will be limp, dry, and tasteless.

Carrots are grown practically everywhere—Canada, New York, Michigan—but the farther West they're grown, the sweeter they are. California carrots are by far the sweetest, so look for them. They're easy to find—the state of origin is always marked on the package.

Storing Refrigerate cello-pack carrots in the bag. If you've bought carrots with the tops on, remove them immediately; you can twist them off right at the store or ask your grocer to do it. The longer the tops stay on, the more freshness they'll rob from the roots. It's best to use these carrots right away; otherwise rinse, shake off the extra moisture, and store in a plastic bag in the refrigerator for up to 2 weeks.

Put carrots that have gone limp into ice water to revive. They'll have lost some flavor, but you can bring back the crunch. They'll crisp up faster if they're trimmed and halved lengthwise or cut into sticks.

Preparing Carrots have a lot of natural sugar in them, and the less you do to them, the better. A fresh carrot doesn't have to be pared. Just rinse and trim or give it a quick scrub with a vegetable brush and cold water. Cook carrots briefly, until they are just tender (al dente).

Carrots can be grated into salads, cut into sticks, steamed, baked, braised, creamed, pureed, or made into juice. Carrot cake is a favorite among Americans, and for good reason: carrots make a cake moist and sweet without adding a lot of sugar.

Carrot

Carrot Cake

Makes one 8- or 9-inch layer cake or one 9- by 13-inch sheet cake

1½ cups vegetable oil

2 cups sugar

4 eggs

2 cups flour

2 teaspoons baking soda

1 teaspoon ground cinnamon

½ teaspoon ground nutmeg

½ teaspoon ground cloves

½ teaspoon salt

3 cups grated carrots

1 cup chopped walnuts (optional)

Cream Cheese Icing

Preheat the oven to 350°F.

In a large bowl, blend together the oil and sugar. Beat in the eggs, then add the dry ingredients and mix well. Add the grated carrots and walnuts and mix until blended.

For a two-layer cake, pour into greased 8- or 9-inch cake pans and bake for 25 minutes. For a sheet cake, pour the batter into a greased 9- by 13-inch pan and bake for 1 hour. Cool, then cover with cream cheese icing.

(continued)

Carrot

Cream Cheese Icing

½ cup (1 stick) margarine, softened

8 ounces cream cheese, softened

1 pound confectioners' sugar

2 teaspoons vanilla extract

Cream together all the ingredients until smooth.

About Beta Carotene Beta carotene is called a precursor to vitamin A—that is, it's a substance that's converted to vitamin A by the human body. Even though your skin may temporarily turn yellow if you eat huge quantities of carrots, you won't overdose on beta carotene (there is no evidence of toxicity even in large amounts). Along with vitamins C and E, beta carotene is considered an antioxidant that helps protect the body in a number of ways, and researchers believe it to be an important anticarcinogen.

Carrot

Cauliflower

Known as the "queen of garden vegetables," cauliflower is actually a densely packed head of tiny, unopened flower buds that form clusters called florets. The name comes from the Latin *caulis,* meaning "stem" or "cabbage," and *floris,* meaning "flower." Like broccoli, cauliflower is a member of the nutritionally important crucifer family. Cauliflower has a sweet, mild taste and can be cooked in dozens of ways. Raw cauliflower is also becoming more popular; the newer varieties are crunchy and sweeter than what came off the farm years ago.

Straight off the farm, cauliflower is enclosed by large, green, edible leaves; in the field these are bundled up around the head to keep it white. Left exposed to the sun, the head turns yellow. When you see cauliflower with the leaves on, it's been grown locally. Cello-pack cauliflower, usually shipped in from California, is what you see in the store 90 percent of the time. The leaves on the commercially grown varieties are removed for two reasons: they can add as much as 50 percent to the shipping weight of the heads, and they turn an unappetizing yellow-brown after a couple of days. Cauliflower is very perishable and is shipped wrapped and chilled to preserve the flavor and texture.

There is a purple variety of cauliflower available in some markets; it has a texture more like broccoli, and it tastes like a cross between the two.

Season

California varieties are available year round, with peak supplies from September through November.

Selecting

Look for a good-sized cauliflower that is hard and heavy, with a touch of dew on the head. The florets should be compact and tightly packed. If florets have started to spread apart and the head looks very light and granular, that's called ricing, and it indicates changes in growing conditions. Ricing doesn't mean the cauliflower is spoiled, but it won't have quite the flavor or crispness of a firm, compact head. Riced cauliflower is a little softer and should be cooked for a shorter period.

Locally grown cauliflower will have its leaves on. Local varieties are almost never shipped across state lines. If the leaves are on, they should be bright green, not wilted. The leaves are edible and are similar in flavor to collard or mustard greens.

Cauliflower

Storing Cauliflower must be refrigerated. Wrap it in plastic and store in the crisper drawer of your refrigerator, where it will keep for several days.

Preparing Cook whole heads in just an inch or two of water until fork-tender—no more than ten minutes. Broken into individual florets, cauliflower takes a little less time to cook.

Cauliflower can be eaten raw, steamed or braised, or breaded and fried. It can be curried, served in a cream or cheese sauce, or sliced into vegetable salads, and it makes a terrific pickle.

Cauliflower Salad 4 to 6 servings

1 head cauliflower

½ cup sliced onions

1 teaspoon garlic powder

¼ cup wine vinegar

¼ cup vegetable oil

salt and freshly ground black pepper to taste

Break the cauliflower into florets. In a large saucepan, steam the florets until fork-tender but still firm (do not overcook). Cool and toss with the remaining ingredients.

Cauliflower

Cauliflower and Cheese Casserole   6 servings

....

1 large head cauliflower

1 pound Velveeta cheese

½ cup milk

2 tablespoons chopped onion

1½ cups Ritz cracker crumbs

3 tablespoons unsalted butter or margarine

Preheat the oven to 375°F. Rinse the cauliflower and break into florets.

In a medium-sized saucepan, steam the cauliflower until fork-tender (do not over-cook). In a small saucepan, melt the Velveeta cheese over low heat, then add the milk and onion and stir until well blended.

In a large casserole, place some of the melted cheese on the bottom and layer with cauliflower, then cracker crumbs, dot with butter or margarine, and repeat. Crumble additional cracker crumbs and place on top. Cover and bake for 20 minutes. Uncover and let stand in the oven for an additional 5 minutes.

Cauliflower

Celery

We have the Italians and the French to thank for celery as we know it. They cultivated it to a point mother nature would never have imagined. Celery is related to carrots; both are in the parsley and anise family. Its wild ancestor grew in Mediterranean wetlands, and Romans used it as an herb in cooking—and as a remedy for hangovers! The French cultivated the stringy wild variety, producing the less woody, sweeter celery that we're familiar with.

There are basically two kinds: Pascal and golden or white celery. Pascal celery is green, with thick, almost stringless ribs. It has a sweet flavor and a very long shelf life. Golden or white celery, which is grown under cover to keep it white, has a sharper flavor. It's also stringier and will go limp in just a few days. Fifty years ago nearly all celery sold was the golden variety; today Pascal is by far the more common.

Season

Celery is good almost all year round *except* in the late spring, when most of it goes to seed.

Selecting

Pascal celery should have bright green leaves on top and stiff, green, unblemished stalks. White varieties have nearly white stalks and paler green leaves. Neither variety should be limp or show brown spots. Turn the bunch over and look at the bottom (called the butt). It should be white and hard, with a touch of dew on it. A soft, dry butt indicates tough, dry, stringy celery.

Western varieties—generally from California—are probably the best buy. Michigan and parts of Canada also grow decent celery, but the quality of celery grown in Florida is only fair. It tends to be stringy, with an overgrown, ''shooty'' heart.

Storing

Celery *must* be refrigerated. Keep it in a plastic bag in the crisper, and it should stay crisp about a week.

Preparing

Celery is more than just a garnish for tuna salad. There are loads of uses: it can be stuffed, served with dips, or sliced into Spanish omelettes. Add celery to duck, chicken, or roasts, and it will help absorb excess fat in the pan. A few stalks (with the leaves on) stuffed into the cavity of poultry before roasting will add a good aroma and flavor.

Celery Root (Celeriac)

A homely looking vegetable, celery root resembles a small, knobby turnip. Many wine lovers have discovered it, though, because it's so good for clearing the palate. Raw celery root can be sliced thin into salads or served with dips. It's crunchy and sweet and has a texture similar to celery; and celery root stays crisp even after it's cooked.

Season Celery root is available practically year round, except June and July. It is most abundant during the Jewish holidays because it's a traditional holiday dish.

Selecting Look for a firm, heavy root with a little touch of dew on it. It will be dirty and stringy-looking, with stems shooting off, but don't let that worry you. What you *don't* want is a root that is shriveled and woody-looking.

Storing Store celery root as you would celery—in a plastic bag in the refrigerator. It will stay crisp for weeks, even months.

Preparing To prepare, rinse the root and trim off any shoots. Raw celery root can be sliced thinly into salad or served with a dip. When used in recipes, it's often parboiled to tenderize it before further cooking. The root can be peeled with a carrot scraper first or boiled and then peeled. Depending upon its size, a whole peeled celery root will take 20 to 30 minutes to cook. Peeled sliced celery root (cut into ¼-inch-thick strips) takes considerably less time to cook—about eight minutes.

Cherry
Sweet Cherry

Cherries have one big flaw: they have a very short season, not much more than two weeks in most places.

Although cherries originated in the Middle East and have been cultivated for centuries in Europe and the Orient, the biggest producer, consumer, and exporter of cherries is the United States. Most sweet cherries are grown on the West Coast; Washington State is the biggest producer. Except for local crops, which aren't shipped at all, the cherries you'll see on the market have been shipped from California, Oregon, and Washington State, with Idaho and British Columbia contributing to the supply.

Cherries are graded by size from 8½ to 14. The numbers indicate how many will fit side by side in a row in a cherry box. Growers place the first two layers in the box upside down by hand; then the rest of the box is filled with loose cherries.

The two most common varieties are Lamberts and Bings.

Lamberts ripen earlier and are smaller and more tender than Bings. They range in color from deep pink to red, with a soft somewhat watery flesh and a deep red or blackish-red juice. They arrive from California early in June, with later harvests coming from Oregon, Washington, and Idaho.

Bings are big, dark, heart-shaped cherries with great flavor. They are very firm, with a deep red to black skin, a white heart, and a bit of crunch when you bite into them. They last longer and ship better than Lamberts.

Royal Annes, also called Raniers and sometimes Napoleons, are occasionally seen on the market. This large, heart-shaped fruit is amber to yellow in color, with a red blush. It's an excellent cherry with an intense flavor, juicy flesh, and a white heart. Royal Annes are more fragile, easily bruised, and have a shorter shelf life than Bings. Many people shy away from Royal Annes because of their color, but one taste and they love 'em.

Season   California cherries arrive in early June and are generally out of season by mid-June, with more northern crops gradually replacing them during the summer months, ending with cherries from British Columbia in early August. That's a total of seven or eight weeks, so if you like cherries and see some good-looking ones at the fruit stand, buy them. The next time you look, they may be gone. Sweet cherries are also grown in the Midwest and in northeastern states, but I don't think the fruit compares to the size or flavor of the western cherries.

The sweet cherries that show up in January are from Chile, and although they're improving in flavor and texture, they're still not quite up to snuff. As producers continue to experiment with shipping methods, however, I expect we'll see very good cherries from Chile in the near future.

Cherry

What you see is what you get. Cherries won't ripen or improve in flavor after they're picked. They must be picked ripe, and then they'll last only a couple of days, so harvesting time is critical. A ripe cherry is heavier in the hand, meatier, sweeter, and juicier than an immature cherry. Picked too soon, cherries are pale and tasteless; too ripe, they're soft and watery. The best time to pick seems to be right before the birds start eating them—birds have an uncanny instinct for ripe cherries.

Choose firm, large, bright-colored fruit. Royal Annes should be bright colored and unblemished; Bings should be as firm and dark as possible. Pale red Bings are immature and won't be especially sweet. Also look at the stems: if the cherries have green stems, they're fresh; if the stem is missing, pass the cherries by—they've been off the tree too long. Never buy cherries if they seem to be very soft, flabby, or sticky on the outside. The should look clean and dry. When cherries go bad, they start to loose color, develop a brownish color, and leak. Once a cherry starts leaking, the fermentation process will quickly make the whole box go bad.

Sour Cherry

Although the crop of sour cherries grown in the United States is about double that of the sweet ones, fresh sour cherries are seldom seen except at farm markets and stands and fancy produce stores. Most are sold to processors for canning. Michigan probably leads the states in production, but sour cherries are grown in most parts of the country, generally coming into season in July.

Fresh sour cherries make more than wonderful pies, cobblers, and tarts: they're also excellent for syrups, jams, jellies, wines, and brandies. Sour cherries come in endless colors and color combinations—there are yellow fruits with a red blush; pink with a yellow splash; and a solid semired. Some are tart, others very sour, and some are almost semisweet. Whatever the color, the flesh is firm and juicy, and the very thin skin makes them easy to pit.

Look for fresh sour cherries at farm stands or produce markets, where they make a brief appearance usually in July. Look for bright-looking, firm fruit. Overripe fruit will have brownish flesh and a mushy texture.

Storing Sweet or Sour Cherries Whether they're sweet or sour, refrigerate cherries immediately and use them as soon as possible. They'll only stay good for a couple of days.

Betty's Cherry Cheesecake   6 to 8 servings

CRUST

1¾ cups graham cracker crumbs

¼ cup chopped walnuts

2 teaspoons ground cinnamon

½ cup unsalted butter or margarine, melted

FILLING

3 eggs

¼ teaspoon salt

1 pound cream cheese, at room temperature

1 cup sugar

2 teaspoons vanilla extract

1 teaspoon almond extract

3 cups sour cream

1½ cups fresh cherries, pitted and cut in half

Preheat the oven to 375°F.

In a bowl, mix together all the crust ingredients, then press on the bottom and sides of an 8- or 9-inch springform pan.

In a large bowl, beat the eggs, salt, cream cheese, sugar, vanilla, and almond extract until smooth. Blend in the sour cream. Pour the filling into the prepared crust and bake for 35 minutes, or until a knife inserted into the center comes out clean. Top with cherries, then chill for 3 hours.

Cherry   76

Cherry Dessert Cake   8 servings

3 eggs

1 cup sugar

1¾ cups flour

¼ teaspoon salt

2 teaspoons baking powder

2 tablespoons water

1 teaspoon vanilla extract

½ teaspoon almond extract

1½ cups pitted fresh cherries

½ cup chopped walnuts

2 cups heavy cream, whipped

Preheat the oven to 350°F.

Line two 9-inch cake pans with waxed paper and set aside.

In a large bowl, beat the eggs until light. Add the sugar gradually and beat until lemon colored. Add the dry ingredients and mix well. Add the water and vanilla and almond extracts and mix thoroughly.

Pour the batter into the cake tins and sprinkle the cherries and walnuts over the top. Bake for 30 minutes. Allow the cakes to cool on a wire rack. When the cakes are cool, spread the whipped cream between the layers and over the top of the cake.

Cherry

Coconut

Along with the date, the coconut is an indispensable member of the Palmaceae family, plants of utmost importance to hundreds of millions of people throughout the tropical areas of the world. The coconut palm has provided food, drink, oil, sugar, fuel, housing, and even clothing materials for thousands of years. It probably originated in Southeast Asia, but because coconuts (which are actually huge seeds) can stay afloat for weeks at sea, the plant spread to the islands of the Indian Ocean, throughout the Pacific, and finally to the West Coast of the Americas. Coconuts were introduced to the Caribbean and to tropical areas of the Atlantic coast in the sixteenth century.

Coconuts are very large fruits encased in elongated green husks. Inside is the fibrous brown nut familiar to most Americans. A coconut takes about a year to mature, but it can be enjoyed at several stages of development. In the tropics, coconuts are consumed at early stages. At six months they contain a milky liquid and a thin interior coating of meat that is extremely nutritious and so tender it can be eaten with a spoon. As the coconut matures, the milk is gradually absorbed by the meat.

The mature coconut is what is exported. The green husk is usually removed to expose the hard, dark brown, fibrous shell. Inside, the nutty-tasting white flesh is covered by a paper-thin brown peel.

Season Available year round but most plentiful from October to January.

Selecting When buying a coconut, look for a heavy one. Shake it and listen for a sloshing sound—the coconut should still contain some milk. There are three "eyes," or indentations, fairly close together on the shell; this is where it's softest and thinnest. There should be no sign of moisture near the eyes nor any smell of fermentation—check the coconut eyes with your nose.

Storing Coconuts keep at room temperature for three or four weeks or more. They'll last for weeks in the refrigerator, but the milk will eventually dry up. Once opened, a coconut must be wrapped and refrigerated, and it will only keep two or three days. To store longer, you can grate it, then either freeze it or dehydrate it and store tightly covered.

Here is an easy way to open a coconut: drive a screwdriver or nail into the eyes and drain the liquid, which can be chilled and added to fruit juice, then, place the whole coconut in the oven at 250° to 325°F and roast about fifteen minutes. This will make the shell easier to crack and cause the flesh to shrink away from the shell slightly. Remove from the oven and tap the shell with a hammer; it will break easily and the flesh should be easy to remove. If the flesh clings to the shell, return the pieces to the oven for five to ten more minutes.

You can eat the flesh with the thin brown skin on—I think it's good that way—or you can peel it. Grated coconut can be sprinkled over fruit salad or ice cream, added to granola, or made into macaroons, coconut cake, or cream pie. Use it in curries or tropical drinks. I love to add it to my cereal in the morning.

Coconut milk is used in a number of cuisines, including Thai and Indian. You can make coconut milk by grating the flesh by hand or using a food processor. Combine the grated meat with three or four cups of water, bring to a boil, and let it simmer a few minutes, stirring constantly. Allow to cool and strain it through a cheesecloth, squeezing the cloth to wring out all the milk. Discard the solids and store the milk in the refrigerator or freezer. Coconut milk makes a terrific rice pudding, and it can be added to the filling for coconut pie. It's a key ingredient in tropical drinks like the coco-loco (coconut milk and rum) and piña colada (pineapple juice, coconut milk, and rum).

Coconut Crisps

Preheat the oven to 250°F. Open the coconut according to the instructions above. Using a sharp knife or vegetable peeler, shave off thin strips or curls of coconut meat. Spread these on a baking sheet and bake for 1 to 2 hours, or until golden brown, turning once or twice during baking. Remove from the oven and sprinkle the crisps with salt if desired. Cool and serve as a snack. The crisps keep for weeks well stored in an airtight container at room temperature.

Coconut

Coconut Cookie Bars Makes 15 bars

8 tablespoons (1 stick) unsalted butter, melted

1½ cups graham cracker crumbs

1 small can condensed milk

6 ounces semisweet chocolate chips

¾ cup chopped walnuts

1 cup shredded coconut

Preheat oven to 350°F.

Pour melted butter into the bottom of a 9- by 13-inch baking pan. Sprinkle graham cracker crumbs evenly over the top. Pour condensed milk over the crumbs, then the chocolate chips and walnuts, making sure to spread the ingredients uniformly. Top with the shredded coconut, pressing it gently over the top of the mixture.

Bake for 35 minutes, or until golden brown.

A Taste of the Tropics

When it's cold and wintry, people enjoy eating tropical fruits and giving them as gifts. I especially like to eat a mango in the winter. Does it make me feel warmer? I don't know, but I do think tropical fruits are nice to give around the holidays—foods people might not think to buy but would enjoy if given. You can make an attractive gift by lining an inexpensive basket with a Christmas napkin and loading it with mangoes, pineapple, coconuts, kiwis, kumquats—whatever looks pretty and appealing. Almost everyone appreciates good things to eat as gifts, so when the alternative is yet another scarf or necktie, a basket of tropical fruits can be a winning choice.

Coconut

Corn

Americans seem to be the only people who understand the virtues of sweet corn on the cob. A native American grain related to wheat, barley, and rye, corn didn't reach Europe until the sixteenth century. It's still far more popular here than among Europeans, who continue to call corn by its proper name—maize.

Sweet corn is harvested young for use as a vegetable. Field corn is the variety that's dried and ground for meal, pressed for corn oil, or used as feed for livestock.

The best sweet corn is an ear that's brought from the field straight to the pot. Years ago farmers would deliver corn to our market at three o'clock in the morning. My father would wake us, and we'd have to go down to the store to unload the corn—dozens of bags with fifty ears in each bag. There was a little stove at the back of the store, and my mother would put water on to boil, husk a bunch of ears, and cook corn for us right on the spot, which made this awful middle-of-the-night chore bearable. It was so fresh coming off the truck that to this day I don't think I've ever had corn as good.

Once corn is picked, its natural sugars start turning to starch. The process is slowed by refrigeration, but by the time corn is harvested and shipped from California or Florida to the rest of the country, as much as a week may have passed. The corn will be pretty good, but not as good as corn picked locally. People with vegetable gardens literally start boiling the water before the corn is picked so they can put it in the pot as fast as they can shuck it.

Varieties

You can get white, yellow, or bicolor corn, and though lots of people have preferences, the color has little to do with the sweetness. The only thing that determines taste is how long it's been off the stalk. There are, however, two relatively new hybrids designed to make corn hold its sugar longer: sugar-enhanced varieties and the newer "supersweets." Sugar-enhanced varieties have good corn flavor and are excellent when corn is out of season and has to be shipped to market. The supersweets are very, very sweet; in fact, many corn lovers think they have an artificial taste. For my money, old-fashioned sweet corn straight out of the field is still tops.

Season   The best time to eat corn on the cob is middle to late summer. Corn is grown almost everywhere, and the best place to get it is at farm stands or produce markets where corn is delivered every day. We send someone up to Smith's Farm every morning at 6 A.M. to pick up corn from Wally, who has been supplying Napolitano's for more than thirty years.

Selecting   Look for a husk that's firm, fresh, and green-looking. Don't strip it; just look at the tassel or silk. On really fresh corn, the tassel will be pale and silky, with only a little brown at the top, where it's been discolored by the sun. Also try holding the ear in your hand: if it's warm, it's starting to turn to starch; if it's still cool, it's probably fresh. Although producers have fewer problems with worms now, don't worry if you spot a worm or two. The worms know what they're doing—they go after the sweetest ears. And since they usually eat right around the top, you can just break that part off.

Storing   The short answer is don't; just eat fresh corn right away. But if you must, store it in the refrigerator.

Preparing   A lady came in the store one day last summer and told me, "I cook corn so long it almost starts to pop, and it's still tough." I said, "That's because you're cooking it so long!" Never overcook fresh, sweet corn. It only needs a few minutes' cooking time. To boil it, bring the water to a boil before dropping in the shucked ears. If the ears are too long for the pot, don't cut them with a knife, which tends to crush the kernels; just break them in two with your hands. Let the water return to a boil, and boil hard for three to four minutes. Remove immediately and serve; don't let the corn stand in the water.

To microwave corn, shuck it, spread with butter if you wish, cover closely with plastic wrap or waxed paper, and microwave on full power (100 percent) about 2½ minutes *per ear*.

Corn is also great cooked on the grill. To prepare, pull down the husks but don't detach them and remove the silks. Spread some butter and salt on the kernels, then pull the husks back up and twist closed. Grill the ears for about fifteen minutes, turning them often.

Corn

If you've got corn that's two or three days old, you can add it to soups or use it to make creamed corn, fritters, or spoon bread. Add it to seafood chowder or other soups, or make corn relish with it—there are plenty of ways to prepare it.

Corn Fritters   4 to 6 servings

1 cup grated fresh corn

1 egg, beaten

½ teaspoon salt

1 teaspoon sugar

pinch freshly ground black pepper

¼ cup flour

1 teaspoon dried basil

¼ cup unsalted butter or shortening

confectioners' sugar for sprinkling

In a bowl, thoroughly mix the corn, beaten egg, salt, sugar, pepper, flour, and basil. (You may use an electric blender or food processor to mix these ingredients.)

In a large skillet, melt the butter or shortening. Drop the corn mixture by tablespoons into the hot butter. Fry on each side until golden brown. Sprinkle confectioners' sugar over the fritters and serve warm.

Cranberry

Cranberries have been a part of the American holiday scene for many years. Raw berries are pretty strung with popcorn to make old-fashioned garlands for the Christmas tree. They're also used during the Jewish high holy days to construct little houses used in the celebration of Succoth. And although a lot of people have become accustomed to using canned cranberry sauce, it's quick and easy to make a delicious sauce from whole fresh berries. People are also starting to discover how useful cranberries are beyond Thanksgiving and Christmas. These festive, very firm red berries add great flavor to a lot of foods.

Generally a half inch to an inch in diameter, cranberries are oval in shape, with a smooth, glossy, red to deep red skin, and contain tiny, soft, edible seeds. They are too tart for most people and require some sweetening.

Cranberries are a member of the heath family (Ericaceae), which also includes blueberries, lingonberries, and huckleberries. Their natural habitat is a swamp or bog in temperate climates, such as Wisconsin, Cape Cod, and Long Island. Native Americans used cranberries for dyes, medicines, and food, including a dish made of cranberries and dried meat. The various Indian names for cranberries translate as "sour berries," but settlers called them crane berries, possibly because they were favored by cranes or because the plant and flower look like one of these elegant birds. By the nineteenth century, American sailors and loggers were using cranberries to make a drink to prevent scurvy.

Today cranberries are cultivated in shallow bogs that are flooded with water at appropriate times during the season. They are important crops in Massachusetts and New Jersey and are also cultivated in Wisconsin, Oregon, Washington State, British Columbia, and Quebec.

Season and Selecting Fresh cranberries are available from September to January. They're usually packaged in twelve-ounce cello bags, which yield about three cups. Packaged cranberries are always sold in good condition unless there has been a problem with refrigeration. Their high acid content gives them a long shelf life.

Storing Packaged unwashed fresh cranberries will stay fresh up to four weeks in the refrigerator. You can freeze unwashed berries in doubled, well-sealed plastic bags, and they'll keep

Cranberry

for as long as a year. Rinse them briefly, pick out the stems, and use directly in recipes without thawing—they collapse when thawed.

Wash well just before using, discarding the stems and any soft, wilted, or bruised berries. Cranberries need to be sweetened with sugar, honey, maple syrup, or other fruit juices. The high pectin content in cranberries makes them an ideal fruit for jellies or fruit chutney.

Besides the popular cooked sauce and jelly used to accompany poultry and meats, cranberries can be made into an equally delicious uncooked relish. Grind or mince one package of cleaned berries with the grated zest and chopped pulp of one orange. Mix with ¾ to 1 cup of sugar, add cinnamon if desired, and let the mixture stand overnight in the refrigerator to blend the flavors. The relish will keep up to two weeks in the refrigerator.

Cranberries are excellent mixed with apples or pears in pies and tarts. Apples are delicious stuffed with sweetened cranberry sauce, or try stuffing pears with cranberry sauce, sprinkling them with orange juice and cinnamon, and baking in a 325°F oven for twenty minutes. Cranberry muffins are understandably popular, but your family will also enjoy cranberry nut loaf, cranberry upside-down cake, and cranberry cheesecake. Cranberry juice is delicious mixed with apple juice or lemonade, and cranberry sorbet is a refreshing treat.

Cranberry Chicken   4 to 6 servings

oil for frying

3- to 4-pound frying chicken, quartered

1 onion, minced

grated fresh ginger to taste

zest of 1 orange, grated

juice of 2 oranges

1 cup fresh cranberries

½ cup sugar

(continued)

Heat the oil in a deep frying pan, add the chicken, and brown on both sides. Add the onion, ginger, orange zest, and orange juice. Simmer, covered, for about 20 minutes, turning the pieces about halfway through the cooking time.

Add the cranberries and sugar and simmer, uncovered, for about 10 minutes.

Cranberry Bread   6 to 8 servings

2 cups flour

1 cup sugar

1½ teaspoons baking powder

1 teaspoon salt

½ teaspoon baking soda

2 tablespoons vegetable oil

¾ cup orange juice

1 egg, well beaten

1 tablespoon grated orange zest

1½ cups fresh or frozen cranberries, coarsely chopped

½ cup chopped nuts

Preheat the oven to 350°F. Grease a 9- by 5-inch loaf pan.

In a bowl, mix together the flour, sugar, baking powder, salt, baking soda, and oil. Stir in the orange juice, egg, and orange zest. Mix until well combined. Fold in the cranberries and nuts. Spoon into the greased pan and bake for 1 hour, or until a wooden toothpick inserted into the center comes out clean. Cool and remove from the pan.

Cucumber

There are more exotic things on the market, but nothing tastes cooler than a cucumber. Related to squash and melons, cucumbers are plentiful year round in most states. Although there are many varieties, there are basically four types: select, European seedless, kirby, and gherkin. Select cucumbers are the smooth-skinned, garden-variety cucumbers that occasionally have a knobby end. "Super select" are the top of the line of this variety—they are long, straight, and smooth, with a dark green skin.

The European seedless has great color, good size, and great shape, but I think it has very little flavor compared to regular cukes. Often called the burpless (cucumber seeds cause some people to belch), they have less flavor precisely because they *are* seedless. The seeds are what carry most of a cucumber's flavor.

The variety I think has the best flavor doesn't always look the best: the kirby, which is a small, knobby, pale green cucumber with a warty skin. Although it's considered a pickling cucumber, it is excellent eaten fresh. Crisp and crunchy, it has tiny seeds and an excellent flavor. You can usually find kirbys at produce markets and farm stands.

The fourth variety is almost never available at retail stores. The gherkin, the tinest of the cucumbers, is usually sold straight to processors and made into sweet pickles. I'm a fanatic for them, but they generally show up on the market in jars, not fresh.

Season

In winter supplies come from California, Florida, and Texas, with imports from Mexico and the Caribbean. Winter cucumbers are usually waxed to prevent moisture loss in shipping and storage. During the growing season in your area, buy locally grown unwaxed cucumbers. A good unwaxed cucumber doesn't need peeling; wash waxed ones well or peel them.

Selecting

Very simply, the darker the cuke, the better—except for the kirby, which is naturally very pale. Standard cucumbers should be long and slender. Don't buy jumbo sizes, as they will be mostly seeds. Avoid soft, withered-looking, or yellowed cukes, which are more likely to be bitter.

Preparing

When you can get cucumbers unwaxed, all you need to do is rinse them. Although waxed cucumbers are only coated with vegetable oil, I recommend peeling them. You'll never be able to remove all the oil by washing.

Daikon

Known as *daikon* to the Japanese, and *lo bok* or *lo pak* to the Chinese, this Oriental radish is a smooth, carrot-shaped root that usually reaches a foot or more in length. Although the skin can be black, pink, or even green, most varieties on the market are white. The skin is very thin; the flesh is white and very juicy, with a mild, refreshing radish taste and crunchy texture. You can use daikon all the ways you'd use a red radish: on a crudité platter, grated into coleslaw, or served with fish, poultry, or meats.

Daikon probably originated in East Asia, where it's an extremely popular vegetable. It's now grown in many parts of the world, including North America. Daikon tops or leaves are popular in Japan, but you're not likely to find them here—they're perishable and don't ship well.

Season Daikon is available year round in produce markets that sell Oriental vegetables, but its flavor is best during the fall and winter months. During the summer, it is hotter but less flavorful.

Selecting Choose firm, crisp, smooth-skinned roots. Avoid roots that look limp, dried out, or withered.

Storing Daikon will stay crisp and juicy for three to four days refrigerated in a plastic bag. If you want to keep it longer, use it cooked instead of raw.

Daikon

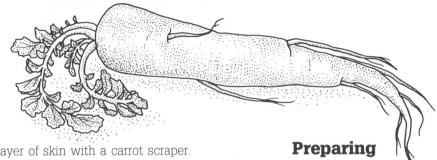

To prepare, scrub or pare off a thin layer of skin with a carrot scraper. **Preparing**

The Japanese like to use daikon grated into a salad to serve along with tempura or other fried foods. They believe it cuts the oiliness and aids the digestion. Most often eaten raw, daikon is delicious pickled and will add flavor and texture to cooked foods.

Daikon can be cut in rounds or sticks and served with a dip. Sticks or chunks tossed with watercress and other salad vegetables are delicious dressed with yogurt, lemon juice, garlic salt, and pepper. Daikon is excellent added to salads or to stir-fries. Cooked in soups and stews, it has a flavor something like that of a turnip. It's best only lightly blanched, pureed, or minced and added to cooked dishes at the last minute.

For a tastier, juicier hamburger, try shredding daikon and mixing it into the meat before grilling.

Japanese Pickles   4 servings

1 to 2 roots daikon
1 small onion
pinch chile powder
pinch sugar
salt and freshly ground black pepper to taste
juice of ½ lemon
rice wine vinegar

Clean the daikon and slice very thin into a quart jar or container suitable for refrigerator storage. Mince the onion and add it to the sliced daikon, along with chile powder, sugar, salt, and pepper. Add the lemon juice and enough rice wine vinegar to cover; mix thoroughly and let stand for 2 days in a cool place. Pickled daikon will keep about 2 weeks in the refrigerator.

Daikon

Eggplant

Eggplants got their name because eggplants used to come in only one color—white. Hanging from the plant, they looked like eggs. The problem was that when they were shipped, they tended to bruise and scar easily. So the hybridizers went to work to develop an eggplant that wouldn't scar and in the process widened the variety.

The eggplant is a member of the nightshade family. We're almost positive it originally came from India and spread to Europe by way of Africa. Italians were growing it by the fourteenth century, but you'll find that eggplant doesn't figure in northern Italian cuisine as it does in southern. That's because it needs heat to grow—heat and considerable irrigation. From Europe eggplants spread to the Americas and were being cultivated in Brazil by the mid-1600s.

In some places the eggplant is known as the "mad apple"—from *mala insana,* meaning "bad egg" or "bad apple." Legend has it that an Indian traveler ate some raw eggplant, had a fit, and people thought the eggplant had poisoned him. Some people still think eggplants are poisonous.

Early in the growing season, eggplants produce beautiful star-shaped blue-violet flowers. The eggplant is the berry that forms after the flower drops.

Varieties The most commonly available eggplant is a deep purple that's almost black. These range in size anywhere from four ounces to 1½ pounds.

Eggplant

When my father was a youngster, one of his favorite dishes was gumbroit, which is sort of like ratatouille, made with eggplant, squash, tomatoes, and other vegetables. Clean-out-the-refrigerator time. Everyone raved about Nonna's gumbroit.

My mother was Irish, but she was the best Italian cook there ever was. Basically, it was my father's mother who taught her how to cook. There were only three things in the world that would make Mom angry: if you talked about her husband, if you talked about her children, or if you talked about her cooking. Whenever my mother made gumbroit, Pop would say, "That's good, but not as good as my mother's." It drove Mom crazy. She made it just the way Nonna taught her.

For a long time she tried to figure out what she could be doing wrong. Pop was the twentieth of twenty children and the spoiled baby of the family. He was a very picky eater. My mother knew that. She also knew that with such a big family, my grandmother used to save money by buying fruits and vegetables that had spots or bruises on them. And when they were running their own store, Nonna would take home the stuff that the customers wouldn't buy. It finally dawned on Mom that this was what she was doing wrong. The spotted vegetables Nonna used were absolutely dead ripe. So Mom went down to the store, picked out all the spotted eggplants and squashes and tomatoes, and took them home to make gumbroit. My father absolutely loved it!

The problem with most Americans is that they buy with their eyes. Sure, there are things you need to look for when you're buying fresh produce, but just because something looks perfect, it won't necessarily taste good. A winter tomato can be perfectly round and uniformly colored, but it's not going to taste like anything. As often as not, your other senses—especially your *nose*—are going to tell you as much about fruits and vegetables as your eyes will.

Eggplant

The original white eggplant is now very trendy. It is generally smaller than the purple variety, and a lot of people say it's more tender, but I don't really see any difference. It's more expensive than the purple kind because it's not cultivated as widely.

All the varieties are good, but I'm particularly fond of the Spanish eggplant, which has purple and white stripes. These seem to be a little heavier in texture and taste.

Season Baby or Italian eggplants have long been popular on the East Coast; they're available in the summer months, with the peak in July through September. In sunnier climates they're available year round, but the supplies may be limited.

Other varieties are generally available year round.

Selecting Round, oval, or pear-shaped, eggplants may be white, purple, or striped. The flesh is firm and creamy white, with a lot of edible white seeds in the center. Baby or Italian eggplants are smaller, with a thinner skin.

When choosing an eggplant, look for firm, shiny fruit that's heavy in the hand for its size. The top should be green and fresh-looking; a green cap with little spikes around the stem is a sure tip that the eggplant is fresh.

Next, look at the blossom end. If it has a round mark, it's a male. If the mark is oval—slightly elongated—it's a female. The females are firmer and have fewer seeds. The fewer seeds the eggplant has, the less bitter it will be.

Now hold the eggplant in your hand. If it's large but feels light, it will be pulpy. Press the flesh gently with your thumb. If it leaves an indentation, pass that eggplant by. Unless you're making gumbroit, the eggplant should be firm, with no wrinkling or soft spots. If it's the purple variety, it should be smooth and shiny, not dull.

Storing Store at room temperatures on the cool side, or wrap loosely and store in the crisper drawer of your refrigerator. A firm eggplant will keep for several days.

Preparing Eggplant has a slightly bitter taste, especially when mature. To get rid of it, peel the eggplant (the skin is likely to be both bitter and a little tough), then slice it, sprinkle with salt, and allow it to drain in a colander for up to half an hour. In addition to purging the bitter juices, salting eggplant also helps keep it from absorbing oil when you sauté or fry it.

Eggplant

You can bread and fry eggplant or use it in dozens of different vegetable dishes. It's a good, filling substitute for meat in a vegetarian meal. Like my father, I love gumbroit, but my favorite dish is actually eggplant Parmesan, which my wife, Betty, makes with alternate layers of eggplant and zucchini. She also makes a wonderful eggplant rollatini—sliced eggplant rolled and filled and served with a tomato sauce.

Eggplant and Zucchini Parmesan   8 servings

3 large eggplants

2 large zucchini

3 eggs

¾ cup milk

3 cups bread crumbs

¼ cup vegetable oil

4 cups prepared tomato sauce

1 pound mozzarella cheese, shredded

¼ cup grated Parmesan cheese

½ teaspoon salt

Preheat the oven to 350°F.

Cut the unpeeled eggplants and zucchini into slices about ¼ inch thick. Dip the eggplant slices into the egg and milk mixture, then into the bread crumbs.

In a large skillet, heat the oil until very hot, add the breaded eggplant, and fry on both sides until golden brown. Drain on paper towels. Fry the zucchini as is; do not put into bread crumbs. Drain.

In a large baking pan, place a layer of tomato sauce in the bottom to cover and follow with a layer of eggplant slices, mozzarella cheese, Parmesan cheese, zucchini, and pinch of salt. Repeat the layers, ending with tomato sauce. Top with mozzarella and Parmesan cheese. Bake for 20 to 25 minutes.

Eggplant

Stuffed Eggplant 4 servings

                2 medium eggplants
                ¼ cup olive oil
                1 pound lean ground beef
                ½ cup chopped onion
                2 teaspoons garlic powder
                1 teaspoon dried oregano
                salt and freshly ground black pepper to taste
                1 teaspoon fresh Italian parsley
                ¼ cup grated Parmesan cheese
                2 eggs
                ½ cup bread crumbs
                2 cups tomato sauce
                1 cup shredded mozzarella cheese

Preheat the oven to 325°F. Wash the eggplants and cut in half lengthwise. Scoop out the centers as much as possible, leaving ¼-inch-thick shells; put aside. Chop the eggplant centers.

In a large skillet, heat the olive oil and brown the chopped eggplant, ground beef, onion, garlic powder, oregano, salt, and pepper. Stir and add the parsley, Parmesan cheese, eggs, and bread crumbs; mix well. Cook until the eggplant is fork tender. Spoon the eggplant mixture into the eggplant shells. Place in a baking dish and pour the tomato sauce over each eggplant. Top with shredded mozzarella cheese, and bake for approximately 30 minutes.

Eggplant

Gumbroit

4 servings

....

3 tablespoons olive oil

2 onions, diced

2 cloves fresh garlic

2 zucchini, cubed

1 eggplant, cubed

2 peppers, diced

1 pound fresh string beans, cut into pieces

2 fresh tomatoes

1 tablespoon oregano

dash of salt

In a large skillet, pour in the oil and add the diced onions and garlic. Sauté until golden brown. Add the zucchini, eggplant, peppers, and string beans and sauté until soft. Add the fresh tomatoes, oregano, and salt. Stir and sauté for 5 minutes longer.

Eggplant

Endive, Belgian

See Belgian Endive

Endive, Curly

See Lettuce: Escarole and Chicory

Exotic Fruits

The following are some exotic newcomers to the market.

For other exotic and tropical fruits and vegetables, see separate entries for *Coconut, Jicama, Kiwi, Mango, Papaya, Pineapple,* and *Prickly Pear.*

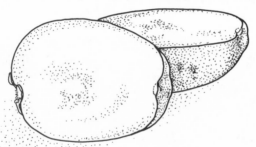

Feijoa

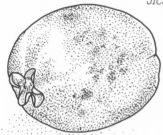

Although it is also called the pineapple guava, the feijoa is not closely related to either of those fruits. It is a delicious if rather innocuous-looking fruit, about 2½ to 3 inches long and shaped like a football with flattened ends. The thin skin ranges from pale lime green to dark olive in color and may be smooth or bumpy. Inside, the dense, juicy, slightly gritty yellow-tan flesh is similar in texture to that of a very ripe guava and has a spunky, minty pineapple flavor. Feijoas from California are on the market in the autumn and winter, and those from New Zealand appear in the spring and summer.

Storing and Preparing If the fruit is not completely ripe when you buy it, it will ripen on the counter, out of direct sunlight. To speed the process, place the feijoas in a paper bag with a ripe apple.

When a feijoa feels like a soft, ripe pear and smells wonderfully fragrant, you'll know it's ripe. Once ripened, feijoas can be refrigerated, uncovered, on a tray lined with paper towels for up to two days.

Feijoas darken quickly once they're cut, so if you want to serve them sliced in a fruit salad or on pancakes or waffles, squeeze on some lemon juice to help them keep their color. For a delicious dessert, serve poached feijoa halves with unwhipped heavy cream. If you are feeling extravagant or are lucky enough to be able to buy feijoas inexpensively, scoop the flesh out of several feijoas, puree them, and serve over sliced bananas, strawberries, and oranges. Sprinkle with minced crystallized ginger, and you have the dessert of a lifetime.

Kiwano

The kiwano, also called the horned melon, is often described as looking like a hand grenade, with a flesh that has the taste and texture of a mild crunchy melon. To me, it looks like a big punk Easter egg—bright orange and covered with spikes. The skin color actually ranges from deep yellow to golden orange, with a bright green flesh almost the color of kiwi. It really is gorgeous.

The horned melon was discovered by a New Zealander on holiday. He was smart: he took the fruit home with him, grew acres and acres of it, and started shipping it around the world, marketing it as a brand-new fruit. I've read that the horned melon is a favorite of the African hippopotamus. Maybe it's popular among hippos because they don't have to pay for it. It's one of the most expensive of all the exotic fruits on the market.

Inside, the soft-textured, brilliant green flesh is packed with edible white seeds. You think you're going to taste something wild when you bite into it, but to me the flavor is like cucumber jelly. Cucumber jelly inside one of the most beautiful packages nature ever designed.

Season

Harvested from February to April, available late February to June.

Selecting

As long as a horned melon shows yellow or orange color in its skin, it will ripen properly. It should feel firm and have unblemished skin. Perfectly ripe horned melons are bright deep orange, without spots or bruises.

Storing

Do not, do not refrigerate.

Exotic Fruits

Preparing Use in a centerpiece or fruit basket.

Use the pulp to create salad dressing for seafood, poultry, or vegetable salad.

Horned melon flesh and melon balls, macerated in a mixture of liqueur, citrus zest and a little squeeze, served in the half shell, looks and tastes good.

Make a drink, blend pulp and strain it, add a squeeze of lemon or lime juice, and sugar to taste. (Melt the sugar in a little hot water.) Add a little orange or melon liqueur, if desired, and serve in a tall glass filled with ice.

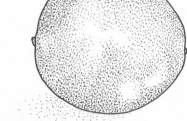
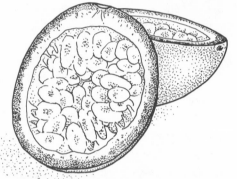

Passionfruit

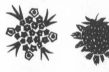

The outside of a passionfruit may be purple, shriveled, moldy, and generally awful-looking, but that just means that the pulp inside is ripe and juicy, with a taste that's sweet, sour, and lemony. In a family all its own, passionfruit is produced by just a few of several hundred species of tropical passionflower native to South America. Their beautiful blooms were named passionflower by early Spanish missionaries in their attempt to explain the mysteries of Christ's passion to the native tribes they were sent to convert. Passionfruit is now grown in most tropical areas throughout the world—New Zealand, Australia, Southeast Asia, Thailand, India, the Mediterranean and Caribbean, and almost every Central and South American country. Hawaii is a large producer, and there are small crops grown in California and Florida.

Only about thirty of the four hundred species of the genus *Passiflora* produce edible fruit, and only a few of these are cultivated commercially. The most common varieties have yellow, orange, or purple skin and range in size from an egg to an apple. Some are known as Maracuya; some as granadilla or grenadilla, so named because their color and many seeds reminded the Spaniards of little pomegranates. A number of hybrids now exist as well.

Exotic Fruits

The hard, leathery, inedible shell encloses a juicy, almost gelatinous flesh that's tart and aromatic. The flesh may be white, pinkish, green, yellow, yellow-orange, or nearly colorless, but whatever the color, it will contain dozens of small, black, crunchy, edible seeds.

The *Maracuya* variety is sweeter than the others. It is large and has a yellow-orange skin and white or grayish white flesh. Unlike other varieties, it's usually eaten while the skin is still smooth. The *curuba,* also called taxo—banana passionfruit—is imported from Colombia and Venezuela. This variety is shaped like a short, squat cucumber and has a white, yellow, green, or red skin and yellow flesh. The "Jamaican honeysuckle," a sweet white-fleshed passionfruit, and the maypop, a variety grown in southeastern states, are other varieties seen in North American markets.

Season

Because it's cultivated all over the world, passionfruit is available year round, although it is most plentiful here from March through September. California passionfruit is available most of the year, with imports from Thailand, Brazil, and New Zealand coming on the market in different seasons.

Selecting and Storing

Generally, the worse a passionfruit looks, the better it tastes. With the exception of the Maracuya, a smooth-skinned passionfruit will need ripening; simply keep it at room temperature until the skin becomes wrinkled and shriveled. When it looks like it's ready to be thrown out, it's ready to eat; then it can be refrigerated. A little mold on the surface won't hurt if the skin isn't cracked, but it means the fruit needs to be consumed immediately. You can also scoop the pulp into freezer containers and freeze it for as long as several months.

Preparing

To eat as is, cut in half with a sharp knife and scoop out the flesh with a spoon. Some people like to sprinkle a little sugar on passionfruit. The juice is good if you briefly blend the pulp and seeds with a little water or fruit juice, strain out the seeds, and chill. Sweeten as desired and serve plain or add to tropical cocktails such as daiquiris, drizzle over ice cream, or use to top yogurt. One or two passionfruit are enough to add flavor to a fruit salad, a punch, or fruit sauce. The tart flavor is well suited to sorbet or frozen desserts; the juice or puree can also be mixed into salad dressings or used as a glaze for poultry.

Exotic Fruits

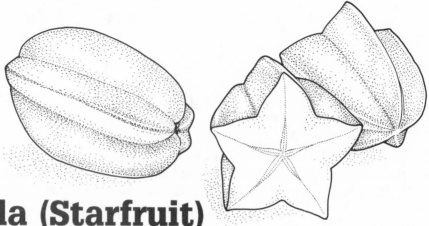

Carambola (Starfruit)

The carambola is the exotic-looking, succulent fruit of the ornamental carambola tree. More commonly called starfruit, the carambola is bright yellow and oval in shape, with four to six ribs running down its length. These give the fruit a unique star shape when it's sliced crosswise. The starfruit's waxy, translucent skin is edible, and its yellow flesh is firm, tender, sweet-tart, and juicy. It's a great complement to other fruits in both flavor and appearance: nothing could be prettier than a platter of bright green kiwi slices, golden starfruit, and ripe red strawberries.

Most starfruit comes from Malaysia, but it is also grown in Israel, tropical Africa, Taiwan, the Carribean, and throughout South America, as well as in California and Florida. The most common variety here is called the Golden Star. Green starfruit is merely unripe starfruit.

Season Starfruit is available from January to May and then again from July to October.

Selecting It's not always easy to tell whether a starfruit is going to be pleasantly sweet-tart or unpleasantly sour. Generally, the deeper gold the color, the sweeter it will be. Another clue is the thickness of the ribs: those with thicker ribs tend to be sweeter. A bit of brown on the ribs is another good indication that a starfruit is ripe. A really ripe one will give off a wonderful fruity, floral aroma, telling you that you should eat it soon.

Choose firm fruit with shiny, smooth skin. It is perfectly all right to buy a green starfruit because it will ripen and turn yellow after a few days if you leave it out at room temperature. Handle it carefully, though; it's quite fragile.

Exotic Fruits 100

White starfruit, if you can find it, is a different variety from the Golden Star. It is almost always good and sweet.

A ripe starfruit will keep for three days at room temperature. If you need to keep a ripe one longer than that, wrap and store it in the warmest part of the refrigerator. It doesn't take cold well. Freezing is not recommended. **Storing**

Wash in cold water before using. Trim off the top and bottom, then slice the fruit **Preparing** horizontally to show off the star shape. The fruit contains a few tiny seeds, which should be removed.

Starfruit will brighten many dishes with its tart flavor and star shape. Use it in place of pineapple rings to decorate a glazed ham—either raw or sautéed briefly in butter. Use it to decorate trays of hors d'oeuvres. Float stars in your punch bowl, or use a slice as an eye-catching replacement for an orange or lemon slice on the edge of a juice glass or cocktail. Use stars to decorate lemon- or orange-flavored cakes or chilled cheesecakes and chiffon pies. For a children's party, insert a birthday candle in the center of each star and use them to top cupcakes. Stars are delicious in mixed fruit or tossed green salads and go well with Chinese-style recipes. Starfruit on the tart side add a good flavor to grilled fish and are a lovely treat sautéed with shrimp. Cook them only briefly, however—they'll fall apart if overcooked. Add a squeeze of lemon if desired.

Spinach Salad with Stars   4 servings

4 ounces fresh spinach, washed

4 ounces cooked chicken breast, cut in strips

1 cup cubed ripe avocado

1 large tomato, cut into 8 wedges

2 scallions, thinly sliced

1 starfruit, sliced into stars

1 recipe Raspberry Vinaigrette (see page 43)

Place all ingredients in a large salad bowl and toss gently with the vinaigrette.

Exotic Fruits

Tamarillo

This bright red or golden yellow tree tomato is grown in California and New Zealand. The tamarillo has a smooth skin and is shaped rather like a pointed egg—it's as perfectly formed as its cousin, the eggplant. The flesh is like that of a meaty plum and is a beautiful deep yellow to orange color, with two deep red swirls of tiny edible seeds. When you slice a tamarillo, it will remind you of a tomato, but the similarity ends there. The unusual flavor is somewhat tart, although the yellow variety is a bit sweeter than the red.

Season Tamarillos are available from March to October but are most plentiful during the summer months. Because they hold up wonderfully through shipping and storing, nine times out of ten you'll find them in perfect condition at the market.

Selecting A ripe tamarillo yields to gentle pressure like a firm ripe red plum. It will also develop a fragrance somewhere between that of an apricot and a tomato.

Storing Unripe fruit will ripen at home on the counter, out of direct sunlight. Ripe fruit will keep in the refrigerator in a plastic bag for up to three weeks.

Preparing No matter how you plan to use them, tamarillos must be peeled first. Either use a vegetable peeler or blanch in boiling water for about one minute, then plunge briefly into ice water. When you pull it out of the water, pierce the skin with the tip of a knife and the skin should slip right off.

Tamarillos can be served as a vegetable—peeled, sliced, and marinated in dressing, then added to salad. They can also be served as a fruit—slice them and let them sit in honey for a minute or two, then serve on yogurt or ice cream.

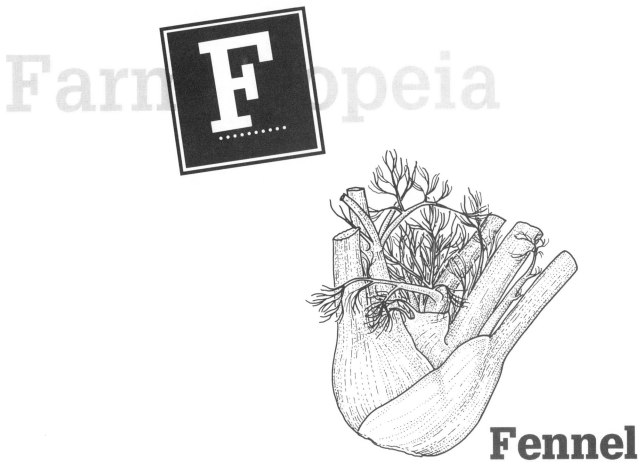

Fennel

Sweet or Florence fennel, also known as *finocchio* ("finook" among Italians here), is related to parsley. It looks something like a pale, very fat celery bunch topped with fine leaves that resemble dill. The fennel bulb has a crisp texture and a slightly sweet flavor that is faintly reminiscent of anise or licorice. The fennel grown in California is often labeled anise or sweet anise, and although it is related, it's not what Europeans know as anise, which is a stronger-tasting, weedy relative generally used as an herb. Fennel has a much more delicate flavor that's very refreshing in salads or added to vegetables and seafood. It's also simply delicious braised.

103

Fennel has been popular in Mediterranean countries since ancient times. The Greeks prized it as a medicine as well as a food; the Romans, who cultivated it extensively, prized it more for the fine-leafed tops, which they used as an herb. They also made an extract of fennel to treat eye diseases, especially cataracts. Italian immigrants introduced the plant to the United States, where it's now grown for export. The bulb size of California fennel is about the size of a grapefruit, while imports from Belgium and Italy are a bit smaller.

Season Imports make fennel available all year, but its main season is October through April, when fennel grown in California is plentiful.

Selecting Choose firm, pale bulbs with a good appearance. The tops of fresh fennel should be green and sprightly. Avoid fennel displayed with the tops cut off—it's usually old.

Storing Fennel should be used within a few days of purchase because it dries out and the flavor fades as it gets older. Cut off the tops and discard or use them right away, since they spoil faster than the bulb. The tops or thin part of the stalks can be used in salads or in pastas. If you're not using it right away, wrap the bulb in plastic and refrigerate. If fennel gets limp, you can restore its crispness by putting it in ice water for half an hour to an hour.

Preparing To prepare the bulb, trim off the stalk and the base. Then wash the fennel very well in cold water. Some people use a vegetable peeler to pare off the thin outer layer, but I don't think that's necessary. In my family we usually slice the bulb thin and use it raw in salads, but it can also be baked, braised, grilled, creamed, or cooked with butter and dusted with Parmesan cheese for an excellent side dish. It can be stir-fried with other vegetables, made into tempura, or added to soups. Fennel is especially good with seafood and fish; simply slice it thin over the top of the fish before cooking, and it will add a great flavor.

In the fall, when fennel is at its peak, Italians use the green tops in pasta. With their delicate, ferny leaves, the tops are also decorative as a garnish. My mother used to decorate pumpkins with vegetables and use fennel tops for the hair. It certainly made an out-of-the-ordinary jack o'lantern.

Fennel

Fennel Salad Niçoise   6 servings

2 bulbs fennel (approximately 1 pound each)

3 tablespoons olive oil

2 tablespoons lemon juice

½ teaspoon sugar

½ teaspoon chopped fresh basil

2 tablespoons sliced scallions

1 tomato, seeded and coarsely chopped

⅓ cup pitted ripe olives, halved

Discard the fennel stalks and cut the bulbs in half lengthwise, then thinly slice crosswise. Place the fennel in a saucepan with enough water to cover and boil until tender. Drain and set aside.

In a small bowl, combine the olive oil, lemon juice, sugar, and basil, whisking until well combined.

When you're ready to assemble the salad, place the fennel and scallions in a bowl and toss with the marinade. Cover and refrigerate for at least 30 minutes. Just before you're ready to serve, stir in the chopped tomato and olives.

Fennel Parmesan   6 servings

2 large bulbs fennel

2 cups water

3 tablespoons chicken bouillon granules

3 tablespoons unsalted butter or margarine

½ cup bread crumbs

1 teaspoon dried oregano

pinch freshly ground black pepper

3 tablespoons grated Parmesan cheese

½ cup light cream or milk

3 tablespoons cornstarch

pinch paprika

¼ cup dry white wine

Preheat the oven to 350°F. Trim the fennel stalks and discard. Reserve the leaves for garnish. Cut a thin slice from the fennel base; cut each fennel into quarters lengthwise.

In a medium-sized saucepan, mix the water and chicken bouillon granules. Bring to a boil, add the fennel, cover, and simmer 10 minutes.

In a skillet, melt the butter or margarine, add the bread crumbs, oregano, and pepper, and stir until the bread crumbs are browned. Add the cheese, stir, and put aside.

Drain the fennel, reserving ½ cup of the liquid, and place in a baking dish. In a medium-sized saucepan, combine the reserved liquid, cream, cornstarch, and paprika. Cook and stir until thickened and bubbly, then cook 2 minutes longer. Stir in the wine and spoon over the fennel. Top with the toasted crumbs. Bake for 15 minutes. Garnish with fennel leaves.

Fennel

Fennel and Tomato Salad

4 servings

DRESSING

2 tablespoons olive oil

2 tablespoons white wine vinegar

1 clove garlic, finely minced

1 teaspoon finely chopped fresh mint

salt and freshly ground black pepper to taste

2 medium-sized fennel bulbs, thinly sliced

1 medium-sized sweet onion, thinly sliced

2 tomatoes, cut into wedges

8 whole lettuce leaves

In a salad bowl, mix the ingredients for the dressing. Add the fennel, onion, and tomato wedges and toss. Serve on a bed of lettuce leaves.

Fig

Many people have never had a fresh fig, since so much of this perishable crop is dried rather than shipped fresh. Fresh figs can be round, flat, oval, or elongated, with a white, green, purple, or black skin, depending on the variety. The flesh, which ranges in color from yellowish-white to a deep reddish pink, has a very delicate flavor and soft texture. This is one of the most fragile fresh fruits you'll find at your produce store and must be handled with extreme care both by the shippers and by the consumer.

Although there are some seedless varieties, most figs are full of tiny crunchy seeds that are eaten along with the flesh. The three most popular figs on the market are the saclike Breba, the flat green Kadota, and the round black Mission fig, so called because it was first cultivated by monks in California. Of these three, I think the Mission is the best of all.

Fig

The very best figs in the world, however, are the ones that are ripened right on the tree—and for that you have to grow your own or become friends with someone who does. My wife's grandfather had a fig tree in his backyard that required loving care. By the time Betty and I started dating, her grandfather was already getting on in years, and every fall, around October, I'd help him prepare the tree for winter. The tree was probably fifteen feet tall, but together we'd tie a rope near the top of its trunk, then pull on the rope until the tree was bent almost double. Then we'd lash it down and wrap the whole thing in tarpaper to protect it from the weather. In the spring we'd remove the tarpaper and untie the tree, which would gradually straighten up again as the growing season progressed. Come summer, I'd help him harvest those figs, eating quite a few myself along the way. They were sweet as honey.

Historians argue about whether the Greeks sent figs to Egypt and beyond or whether figs traveled the other way. In any event, figs are grown extensively in India and are also cultivated in Iran, Turkey, Greece, and Sicily. I may be biased, but I think that Sicilian figs are especially wonderful. In the United States, figs are grown in many home gardens as far north as New York, but almost all the fresh figs on the market here are grown in California, with a smaller crop from Texas that is primarily sold to canners.

California figs are cell-packed to protect the delicate flesh—that is, they're packed individually in separate compartments within cardboard or wooden boxes, then shipped by air to the rest of the country. Because they're so perishable and hard to handle, they tend to be one of the more expensive items you'll find at the produce market.

Season   The California season is from June through September.

Selecting   Avoid figs with brown or grayish spots on the skin, which indicates that the fruit has started to ferment. Because packers handle them so carefully, figs usually arrive at the market in good shape. If the fruit doesn't show signs of fermentation or damage, it will almost certainly be good. Firm fruit can be ripened at home at room temperature, but even firm fruit must be handled with great care.

Fig

Perfectly ripe figs are soft to the touch and secrete a sweet sap from the opening at the blossom end. At this stage they're extremely fragile and perishable and need to be handled *very* gently. Because they will quickly ferment, they need to be eaten right away. If you must store them, lay them on a paper towel, cover with plastic wrap, and store in the refrigerator for no more than three days.

A ripe fresh fig is delicious simply eaten out of hand. You can eat the skin if you wish or nibble the flesh from the skin. In place of melon, try wrapping fig halves in prosciutto as an appetizer. Figs can also be poached with sugar, used in baking, or made into jam or preserves.

Flowers, Edible

Flowers and herbs have been used since ancient times, both for their unique flavor and appearance and for their medicinal properties. Certain flowers have been used for centuries in confections and liqueurs. Today in California edible flowers are becoming popular as a gourmet treat, and that influence is spreading throughout North America. Bergamot, borage, chive flowers, chrysanthemums, daisies, hibiscus, honeysuckle, impatiens, jasmine, lavender, lime blossoms, marigolds, magnolias, mimosa, mustard flowers, nasturtiums, pansies, petunias, primroses, red poppies, roses, sweet William, tagetes, violas, and violets are all now being grown for culinary uses. Each has a slightly different flavor. As if the list weren't long enough, you can expect to see additional varieties on the market in the coming years.

Some flowers are available year round; some have seasons.

Season

Flowers grown for human consumption are chemical-free and safe to eat. They are sold at specialty counters in fancy produce departments, usually packaged in small plastic containers. Although there are many edible flowers in the world, there are also many toxic ones. Flowers purchased from florists have chemicals used on them in all phases of their growth, and you should never eat them. Nor should you eat flowers from your own garden unless you have an organic garden and have done research into which flowers are edible.

Selecting

The production of edible flowers is still very new, and supplies may be scarce in your area because the restaurant trade uses most of what's available. Growers are currently increasing production, and we can expect that edible flowers will be more widely and readily available in the future.

Storing You can keep edible flowers in the refrigerator for a few days if necessary, but they should be eaten as soon as possible.

Preparing Flowers supplied to the market as food are hydroponically grown and very clean. Do not wash them. Use them as is or separate the petals for specific uses such as floral butters or crystallized petals. Remember to add the flowers right at the end of any preparation to preserve their appearance. If you're adding them to salad, add them *after* you've tossed the salad with dressing so that the petals won't absorb any liquid.

Edible flowers make any salad gorgeous. Garnish meat, poultry, or fish dishes with edible flowers to turn them into something special. Float two or three nasturtiums in a delicate soup, a few violet petals in champagne cocktails, some red poppies in fruit punch. Rose petals added to apple or peach pie give off a wonderful appetizing aroma. Edible flowers can be used plain or crystallized in sugar for an elegant final touch to desserts.

Flowers, Edible

Salad with Edible Flowers   2 to 4 servings

· ·

4 ounces mache

3 kumquats, sliced into thin rounds

8 to 12 edible flowers (use different varieties)

DRESSING

2 tablespoons hazelnut or walnut oil

2 tablespoons fresh orange juice

1 tablespoon fresh lemon juice

½ teaspoon honey

pinch salt

pinch freshly ground black pepper

Arrange the salad ingredients on individual plates or on a platter, with the mache on the bottom, the kumquat slices surrounding the mache, and the flowers sprinkled over the top.

In a small bowl, whisk the dressing ingredients together. Serve the dressing separately to preserve the beautiful appearance of the salad until the last moment.

Flowers, Edible

Garlic

Garlic is the most pungent member of the onion family. It is an essential ingredient in Italian cooking and as far as I'm concerned, no kitchen should be without it.

The garlic plant grows to a height of about 12 inches, with a bulb made up of 8 to 12 sections or cloves, forming underground. The cloves are well protected by a papery white skin that may be streaked with red or purple. Garlic is believed to be a native of central Asia and is the oldest member of the allium family. In the Dark Ages, people believed a garland of garlic would ward off evil spirits and the plague. Over the years it's been prescribed for everything from athlete's foot to baldness. In fact, the concentration of organic sulfur compounds in garlic is now recognized to have anti-bacterial properties; many people today swear it will stave off the common cold. Garlic is grown everywhere, but the largest U.S. supplier is California, with Mexico also supplying the market. Aromatic garlic is used to season meats, poultry, fish, vegetables, breads, marinades, sauces, and pasta—just about everything except desserts.

Elephant garlic is big—bulbs can reach a pound apiece. It always fetches a high price in stores, but its flavor is rather mild. I prefer the potency of regular garlic—it's richer and goes a long way.

Garlic

Available year round.

Choose garlic as you would onions: the bulbs should be fat and very firm with no spongy areas and no green sprouts. Sprouts indicate the bulbs have been in storage too long.

Stored in a cool, dry, well-ventilated place, garlic should keep for a month. Avoid refrigeration or plastic wrap; dampness quickly deteriorates the bulbs.

Raw garlic has a pungent flavor that adds depth and zip to salad dressings and marinades. It mellows as it's cooked. Long, slow cooking makes garlic especially mellow and sweet. Leg of lamb is traditionally roasted with slivers of garlic pressed into the flesh. Try surrounding poultry or meats with whole cloves—peeled or unpeeled—before roasting, or toss the cloves with new potatoes, olive oil, and salt and roast in a covered pan. Roasted garlic cloves nearly liquefy inside, and the paste is delicious spread on toasted Italian bread. Simmer whole, peeled cloves gently in milk until tender. Drain. Serve them alongside steaks or chops. Use garlic to make bean or fish dishes richer. My mother made aioli by simmering garlic in olive oil until tender, adding salt, herbs, and often crushed hot peppers, and drizzling the mixture over pasta for a simple but satisfying dish.

Ginger

Although it's often called gingerroot, fresh ginger is actually a rhizome—an underground stem with roots and shoots that are removed after harvesting. Its spicy taste is brighter and fresher than ground ginger and adds big flavor to many dishes—not just desserts and sweets.

A hand of ginger is irregularly shaped and has small irregular nobs protruding from it. It has a thin, very light brown skin and beige flesh with a spicy, characteristic flavor. Depending on the mineral content of the soil, ginger can be tinged blue, green, or gold.

Young ginger is tender and very pretty, with pale pink and green shoots. It's so mild you can chew on a piece of it, something you wouldn't dare do with a mature piece.

Ginger

Ginger has been cultivated in southern China and India for thousands of years, where it's long been held in high esteem for its medicinal properties. Thirteenth-century Arab traders brought it to their settlements in East Africa; about three centuries later the Portuguese introduced it to West Africa and began trading it back into Europe, where it became very popular, especially in England. Before refrigeration, ginger was considered to be essential as a preservative. Today Hawaii, Fiji, Brazil, Puerto Rico, Florida, Jamaica, and New Zealand are the largest producers for the North American market.

Season   Ginger is available year round.

Selecting   Mature ginger: Look for a very firm, heavy piece with a smooth skin and a plump, full hand with as few protruding knobs as possible—these are very woody and won't grate well. Avoid pieces that look wrinkled or feel spongy. Young ginger should have delicately colored shoots and a translucent skin.

Storing   There are a number of ways to store fresh ginger, depending on how long you need to keep it. It can be covered and stored in the refrigerator for a week or two. Some people put it in the freezer and break off pieces as they need it. Others cut it into pieces, place them in a jar, cover with sherry, and refrigerate.

You can also keep ginger by burying it in a small pot of damp sand. Keep the sand lightly moist, and the ginger will keep for months.

Preparing   Depending on the recipe, the root may be sliced, minced, or grated. Peeling is optional. Substitute about 1 tablespoon of freshly grated ginger for ⅛ teaspoon of powdered ginger.

Ginger is used in scores of recipes: gingerbread or ginger cake, ginger muffins, gingersnaps, ginger puddings, and candied ginger. Beef, chicken, and vegetables such as carrots, winter squash, and pumpkin are delicious prepared with grated ginger. It is delicious in chutney, curries, spicy Mandarin dishes, and in barbecue sauce and salad dressings. A hot honey and ginger drink is a great home remedy for sore throats.

Ginger

Pureed Carrot and Ginger Soup   **4 servings**

2 tablespoons butter or oil, or as needed

2 large onions, chopped

2 pounds carrots, chopped

2 to 3 tablespoons grated ginger

2 cloves garlic, chopped

4 cups chicken or vegetable stock

salt and freshly ground black pepper to taste

fresh parsley or chives for garnish

In a large saucepan, heat the butter or oil, then sauté the onions, carrots, ginger, and garlic until the onions are soft and translucent, about 10 minutes. Add the chicken stock and simmer until the carrots are very tender. Remove from the stove and puree the mixture until smooth, then return to the pan to reheat, but do not boil. Add salt and pepper to taste. Garnish with chopped parsley or chives.

Grape

Grapes symbolize the good life. Commercially grown mainly in California, this late spring to early fall crop is now also available throughout the winter at good prices, thanks to imports from Chile, which has a season opposite to our own. Despite some negative press, Chilean grapes, in my experience, are high in quality and offer a welcome way to add fresh fruit to the table during the winter months.

Seedless Grape

There are basically three types of seedless grapes—white, red, and black. *California Pearlettes* usually arrive in early May. They're round, very light green, and have a firm

Grape

and crisp texture. Look for grapes that have a golden-yellow undertone to the green—they're sweeter. The ones that are very green are very, very tart—they'll make your mouth pucker. The season is six to eight weeks long; wait a week or two after they first arrive before you buy them.

The familiar *California Thompson* seedless, another pale green grape, is America's favorite. Thompsons are larger, more oval than round, and have a sweeter taste and more tender skin and flesh than Pearlettes. Here, too, you should look for a grape that has a golden glow, which indicates ripeness. The Thompsons start coming in about a month later than the Pearlettes and stay on the market a couple of months longer.

White grapes from Chile start arriving in December. They tend to have a more raisiny look compared to California varieties. Some people pass them up because they think they're overripe, but they're not. That golden color is a sign that they're good and sweet.

Red seedless grapes, which come on the market after Thompsons, are becoming one of the most popular grapes around. The Red Flame variety is relatively new, but it may soon surpass Thompsons in popularity. A cross between the Tokay (a seeded grape) and a round seedless, Red Flames are firm and sweet, with a very good crisp texture.

The *ruby seedless* has a richer, deeper color than the Flame, but the grapes are smaller, with a shape like a Pearlette. They have a tougher skin and less flavor than Flames. They're the last of the season for seedless grapes.

Black Beauty is a new variety of seedless grape with a relatively short season. It doesn't have quite the flavor that the other varieties do. The Chilean black seedless grapes are better than those we get from California. Domestic black grapes are available in June and July, while Black Beauties from Chile are available in mid-winter.

Champagne grapes are probably the sweetest of all. These tiny red grapes are available virtually year round because they are cultivated everywhere, mainly for restaurant use. You're most likely to find them in gourmet or specialty markets. They're so tiny you eat them by putting a small branchful into your mouth, then pulling the stem out between your teeth to remove the grapes—sort of like eating an artichoke leaf.

Grape

Seeded Grape

The best-known seeded grapes are the Tokay and Concord, but other hybrid varieties are available in many markets. Although they're not as popular as the seedless varieties, seeded grapes have a much fuller flavor. They also tend to be meatier and juicier.

The *Tokay* is a large, round, red grape that's primarily grown in California. Available in the fall, it's a tender grape with a very good flavor. The huge *Red Globe* is a variety of Tokay grape, as is the *Christmas Rose,* which comes out in November and December. The Christmas Rose has a slightly thicker skin and is a little firmer than the Tokay.

Ribier grapes are large, very deep blue, almost black grapes that range from about the size of a nickel to the size of a quarter. They have an excellent flavor that is just slightly tart. Ribier grapes from California start to arrive in September, with the season finishing at the end of December. Fortunately, Ribier grapes from Chile arrive to extend the season.

The *Concord* is another blue-black grape that's smaller and tarter than the Ribier. It's the grape our grandmothers used for jelly-making—one a lot of people now associate with Welch's. The Concord remains popular in the Northeast for eating out of hand. It has a very tart skin with a sweet flesh—a combination that makes it a very tasty, refreshing grape to serve at the table. Domestic Concords are available in the fall.

Season

Grapes are available year round, with the California grapes available from late spring through fall, followed by grapes from Chile, which begin in December and end in May.

Selecting

Look for plump, smooth grapes with good color. They should be firmly attached to a fresh-looking green stem, with no evidence of wrinkling or withering. There should be a dusty bloom on the skin of the grape itself. Like the dusty bloom on blueberries, it's a naturally occurring substance that helps protect the grapes and is a good indication of freshness. Green or white grapes will have a golden glow when they're ripe; red grapes will be a soft, rich red, and black grapes will have a full, deep, blue-black color.

Storing Grapes don't ripen off the vine, so what you buy is what you get. They're very delicate and need to be handled carefully. Refrigerate them dry in a plastic bag. Never wash them until you're ready to eat—moisture will make them deteriorate very quickly. Grapes will last up to a week properly stored in the refrigerator, but it's best to eat them as soon as possible.

Grape Pie 6 to 8 servings

3 cups red seedless grapes

¾ cup sugar

¼ cup water

1 tablespoon lemon juice

3 tablespoons cornstarch, dissolved in ¼ cup water

1 tablespoon butter

pastry for 2-crust 9-inch pie

Preheat the oven to 350°F.

In a medium-sized saucepan, bring the grapes, sugar, and water to a boil over high heat for 1 minute. Add the lemon juice and dissolved cornstarch and continue to cook, stirring constantly, until thickened. Add the butter.

Pour the grape filling into the pie shell and top with the remaining pie crust. Carefully crimp the edges of the pie to seal. Prick the top crust with a fork. Bake for 50 minutes.

Oriental Chicken and Grapes

6 servings

- **3 pounds fryer chicken pieces**
- **3 tablespoons Dijon mustard**
- **3 tablespoons soy sauce**
- **2 tablespoons honey**
- **¼ teaspoon garlic powder**
- **1½ tablespoons sesame seeds**
- **2 cups red or green seedless grapes, halved**

Preheat the oven to 400°F.

Arrange the chicken, skin side down, in a large, shallow baking pan. Bake for 20 minutes, remove from the oven, and drain off the excess fat.

In a small bowl, combine the mustard, soy sauce, honey, and garlic powder, then brush the mixture onto the chicken. Sprinkle the chicken with sesame seeds and bake 20 to 25 minutes longer, or until golden brown, basting once or twice during baking. Add the grapes to the chicken and return to the oven for another 10 minutes. Pour any pan juices over the chicken before serving.

Grapefruit

Have you ever wondered where grapefruit got its name? Our best guess is that the name comes from the way grapefruit grows—in clusters just like grapes, sometimes as many as twenty-five fruits in a cluster hanging from a tree.

Hybrid grapefruit are wonderfully different from the original grapefruit, which can still be found occasionally in Oriental markets. Called pomelos or shaddocks, these tend to be larger than grapefruit, with rough, puffy, thick rinds and lots of seeds. In most cases they're also quite sour and have very little juice. For my money, today's hybrid grapefruit is a vast improvement.

Grapefruit

Grapefruit are grown in many parts of the world, but the United States is the main producer and consumer. Florida produces 75 percent of the domestic crop, with Texas a distant second, followed by California and Arizona.

Grapefruit was introduced to Florida in the early 1800s. For a hundred years it was sold chiefly to tourists as a curiosity. Not until the turn of the century were the first limited supplies shipped to northern cities. Grapefruit are now shipped to all parts of the United States and Canada, as well as to Europe and the Near and Far East.

Florida grapefruit are grown in two areas: in central Florida and in the Indian River area on the eastern coast, where the soil and climate are perfect for grapefruit. The Indian River valley runs parallel to the Gulf Stream, and the warm ocean current shields the groves from temperature changes and spares them from frost even when groves much farther south are damaged.

There is a difference between California and Florida grapefruit. Florida grapefruit have a thinner rind and are sweeter and less pulpy than the California varieties. California grapefruit, which are in the stores in late summer and fall, are easier to peel and segment, but their flavor is only fair—the flesh just isn't as heavy with sweet juice as the Florida fruit.

Grapefruit with a clear yellow rind are called goldens; those with some bronzing are bronzes, and those with heavy bronzing are called russets. Flesh color runs from yellow-white to pink to nearly red. Although their colors vary, there's not much difference in their flavor and juiciness. Those qualities are determined by the lateness of the season, the specific variety, and how the fruit has been handled. *Duncans* and *Orchids*—old top-of-the-line varieties—are juicy and sweet; they are excellent for segmenting and make a great juice. The Duncan is now grown only in limited supplies and sold to canners and processors, but a descendant of the Duncan—the *Marsh seedless*—has taken its place. It's not quite as juicy as the Duncan, but it has a fine flavor and texture. From the Marsh seedless, hybridizers have developed a pink Marsh, and from that a darker pink strain called the *Ruby Red,* a very good grapefruit now primarily grown in Texas. The large Marsh rubies from Florida are now called Star Rubies, and they're probably the sweetest of all—great for segmenting, juicing, or eating with a spoon. Red grapefruit has twenty-five times more vitamin A than Golden, but otherwise they are almost nutritionally equal.

Grapefruit

Grapefruit are available year round, but the best fruit—from Florida and Texas—are found between November and June, with the peak starting around Christmas and continuing through April. Small early golden and pink grapefruit are the first to show up on the market in October. They're very juicy but not as sweet as they are later in the season. Don't be afraid to buy a small grapefruit; even in the fall they make good juice, and as the season progresses into winter and early spring, the smaller varieties get sweeter even as they maintain their high juice content. Whether they're large or small, the Florida and Texas crops improve in quality from October to December and are at their sweetest and juiciest in late winter and early spring.

Season

In late July, California and Arizona grapefruit start to arrive and continue through October, but at best they're only pretty good—not as high in quality as the fruit from Florida and Texas. During the midsummer months, grapefruit also become pretty costly. Here again the old rule of thumb applies: the higher the price, the lower the quality. In the summer months, forgo that breakfast grapefruit and replace it with seasonal berries and fruits.

Look for smooth, thin-skinned fruits that are either round or slightly flattened at each end. Like other citrus fruits, grapefruit should be firm, shiny, and *heavy in the hand for its size*. Fruit that's heavy for its size promises the most juice, and because grapefruits are almost three-quarters liquid, juiciness always means flavor. Avoid coarse, rough-looking, or puffy fruit or any that have a puffy or protruding end, which indicates that the fruit is dry and flavorless.

Selecting

Leave grapefruit on the counter if you're going to consume it in less than a week; for longer storage, refrigerate.

Storing

Grapefruit is great on its own, but if you want to sweeten a particularly tart fruit, sprinkle the halves with a little brown or white sugar and a dot of butter and put them in a shallow baking dish under the broiler for a minute or two, until the tops glaze and start to bubble.

Peeled and sectioned grapefruit is excellent in a salad of mixed mild and bitter greens with a light dressing.

Preparing

Grapefruit

Pete's Broiled Grapefruit **2 servings**

1 grapefruit

2 tablespoons brown sugar

1 tablespoon granulated sugar

2 tablespoons honey

Preheat the broiler.

Cut the grapefruit in half and place on a baking sheet. Sprinkle the brown and white sugars equally on both halves. Add the honey and place under the broiler for 3 minutes, or until the tops become bubbly and brown.

Grapefruit Salad **6 servings**

2 roasted red bell peppers

3 pink grapefruit

½ small red onion

3 tablespoons olive oil

1 tablespoon lemon juice

1 tablespoon lime juice

1 tablespoon grapefruit juice

⅛ teaspoon salt

3 drops Tabasco sauce

6 cups mixed lettuce (Bibb, red leaf, radicchio, and romaine)

18 black olives

freshly ground black pepper to taste

Cut the peppers into wide strips. Section the grapefruit. Slice the onion very thin. Put the peppers, grapefruit sections, and onion into a large bowl. In another

Grapefruit **122**

bowl, whisk together the olive oil, citrus juices, salt, and Tabasco and pour over the grapefruit mix. Let the mixture stand for 2 hours. Add the mixture to the lettuce, toss, and garnish with olives and black pepper.

Greens

Beet greens, collards and kale, dandelion greens, mustard greens, spinach, Swiss chard, and turnip greens are collectively called greens. They are gaining popularity throughout the country—and for good reasons. Along with being delicious, versatile, and low in calories, greens are packed with vitamins and minerals. An important component of southern soul food, greens are creeping into other cuisines as well. Many of the greens complement each other and can be exchanged in recipes, but each has its own distinctive taste.

Beet greens are the leaves of ordinary beets. They are often left attached to the beet roots, especially early in the season when the beets are small and the leaves are especially tender and young. Cooked beet greens have a wonderfully delicate, buttery flavor and tender texture. They may be cooked like spinach, but they usually require less cooking time. (*See also* Beet.)

Collard greens and *kale* originated in eastern Europe and western Asia and have been eaten for thousands of years. *Kale,* also called borecole, has long been considered a healthy, hearty winter vegetable in Europe. The Scots are probably the biggest fans, followed by the Germans and Scandinavians. Kale was among the first European plants brought to North America by the colonists. Resembling a giant specimen of curly parsley, kale may be light, dark, or bluish green. It has a mild cabbage taste that is sweetest when the plant is harvested after the first frost. Even if kale actually freezes, the texture holds up.

Collards have a taste similar to that of kale but milder. This dark green vegetable has a large, smooth leaf with a slightly ruffled edge and a relatively tough central rib that's usually discarded. Collards spread from Africa to Europe centuries ago and were brought to North America by slaves. They've been popular ever since in the American South. Collards and kale can be cooked like spinach, but they normally require a longer cooking time. Southern cooks often add a bit of bacon, ham, or salt pork to the greens for flavoring, sometimes serving them with pepper sauce or vinegar. Collards and kale

may also be added to soups and stews, especially those that contain beans and spicy sausages.

Dandelion greens are thought to have originated in western Asia and the Middle East. For centuries they've been used as a diuretic and remedy for kidney problems; during the Renaissance they were considered to be beneficial to the complexion.

It is only in recent years that dandelions have been cultivated for specialty markets. We don't see too many wild dandelions on the market anymore, and the two are easily distinguished: cultivated varieties have a broader leaf, while wild ones have a jagged, chopped leaf like chicory. In fact, the name *dandelion* comes from the French *dent de lion,* meaning ''lion's tooth.'' Cultivated varieties tend to be a bit sweeter, while wild dandelions have a tangier, more robust taste.

As long as your lawn is free of dangerous weed killers and pesticides, you can keep your wild dandelion population in check by harvesting them. The younger leaves are more tender and a little more bitter than older leaves. Young dandelion leaves (cultivated or wild) are excellent raw in salads, where they add a refreshingly tangy, slightly bitter flavor. Although the leaves are not as peppery, dandelions can be substituted for arugula in many salad recipes.

Greens **124**

Mustard greens look a bit like a lighter, more delicate kale, but the flavor is entirely different. Mustard greens are one of the tangiest of the greens and are very good mixed with milder greens such as spinach to give them some oomph. The very young greens (four inches long or less) are good raw in salads; leaves six inches long or longer are best cooked. They can be cooked like spinach; in the South they are often served mixed with turnip greens.

Spinach is generally found in two varieties: smooth-leafed, which has relatively small, bright green leaves, and Savoy, which has large, crinkled, dark green leaves. Spinach should be washed very thoroughly because it harbors sand—the crinkly Savoy type especially. Tender young spinach is delicious added to salads of mixed greens or dressed with bacon bits and a warm vinegar and oil dressing. (*See also* entry for Spinach.)

Swiss chard is the stem and leaf of a hard beet. Prepare the leaves as you would spinach, cooking them a bit longer to tenderize the tougher leaves. (*See also* entry for Swiss Chard.)

Turnip greens are the leafy tops of turnips. They have a pleasant, slightly bittersweet taste with a hint of turnip flavor. In the South they're often cooked with a bit of smoked meat and sometimes served mixed with mustard greens or with the turnips themselves. (*See also* entry for Turnip.)

Season

Except for dandelions, which tolerate heat, most greens are cool-weather crops.

Kale: available year round but most abundant from December to April

Collards: most plentiful from October to May, although sometimes found at other times of the year

Dandelion greens: in season from March to December

Spinach, turnip, and beet greens: generally available year round—especially spinach. All are most plentiful in the spring

Mustard greens: generally easier to find in the spring

Selecting

Except for dandelion greens, whose younger leaves are tangier, the rule of thumb is that the smaller and younger the greens, the milder and tastier they are. Always choose leaves that have good fresh color with no signs of limpness or wilting. Yellowed leaves or leaves that show traces of wet, dark slime on the edges are old.

Greens

Storing   Greens still attached to their roots will keep better than cut greens. Never wash greens until you're ready to use them; washing causes them to break down more quickly. To store, wrap the *unwashed* greens in a dampened paper towel, place in a plastic bag, and refrigerate, preferably in the crisper drawer. Greens are best used within two days of purchase, while they're still fresh and at the peak of flavor.

Preparing   Greens—especially kale, collards, and spinach—must be washed carefully because their crinkled leaves can hide a lot of sand. Soak in tepid water, then either run under the tap, or use a salad spinner. Pick over the leaves and discard any that are wilted or yellow. Unless they're very young and tender, strip out and discard the central rib from kale and collard leaves.

Remember that raw greens cook down to a fourth of their volume—so get lots of them. And remember that tender, delicate leaves cook more quickly than large, coarse leaves.

To sauté collards or kale, blanch them first in boiling water, remove, drain, and dry with paper towels; they should be completely dry before sautéing. Sauté them in a bit of oil, then add a small quantity of water or chicken or vegetable stock, cover, and simmer until tender. Collards are most appetizing when cooked in seasoned broth for ten to twelve minutes, while kale will cook in half the time. Kale and collards can be treated like spinach—lightly cooking and using them as a bed for shepherd's pie or poached eggs or as a filling for omelettes and crepes.

Dandelion greens are often used in salads or cooked like spinach. Some people like to slice, cook, and serve them in a little chicken broth. Blanched or coarsely chopped raw dandelion greens are excellent in cheese omelettes, and they can be substituted for spinach in a variety of dishes, including eggs Florentine, quiches, and frittatas.

To steam spinach or other tender greens, place them in a pot, cover, and put on very low heat. Don't add water—the moisture that clings to the freshly rinsed leaves is enough. Spinach and beet greens cook very quickly, so they must be watched carefully. After the leaves have steamed for a minute or so, turn them so that they will cook evenly (use tongs or a pair of forks). Replace the lid for another minute, then turn the greens again. Continue to check and turn the greens frequently to avoid burning and to cook the leaves evenly; if desired, season them with salt, a little sprinkle at a time, each time you turn them. Spinach and beet greens are done when all the leaves are wilted but are still nice and green; depending on the quantity, it should take less than five minutes. Check and adjust the seasonings and add a squeeze of lemon juice or a dab of butter and a grating of nutmeg if desired.

Small quantities of greens are easily sautéed in a bit of butter or oil.

Jimi Quick's Mixed Greens   6 to 8 servings

7 pounds mixed greens (collard, kale, or turnip)

12 ounces lean slab bacon, cut into ¼-inch cubes

1 cup finely chopped onions

½ cup finely chopped celery

1 green bell pepper, finely chopped (about ¾ cup)

2 ham hocks (about 12 ounces each)

salt and freshly ground black pepper to taste

2 tablespoons red wine vinegar

1 tablespoon hot pepper flakes

2 cups water

Remove the stems from the greens, leaving only tender leaves.

In a large saucepan, cook the bacon over moderate heat, stirring, until browned. Add the onions, celery, and bell pepper. Cook for 5 minutes, stirring constantly. Add the greens and stir. Cover the saucepan tightly and cook until the greens are wilted. Add the ham hocks, salt, pepper, vinegar, and hot pepper flakes. Stir, cover the pan, and cook for 15 minutes. Add the water, cover, and simmer slowly for 1½ hours.

Mixed Green Salad with Dandelion

Toss together coarsely chopped dandelion greens, arugula, watercress, and Bibb lettuce. Add thinly sliced sweet onion rings. Dress with a mixture of olive oil, red wine vinegar, minced garlic, a touch of Dijon mustard, a pinch of sugar, salt, and freshly ground black pepper. Add anchovies, croutons, or slivered sweet peppers if desired.

127

Herbs

There's a powerful difference between fresh herbs and packaged dried varieties. With the exception of oregano, which may be more flavorful dried, fresh green herbs have an aroma and flavor that make their dried counterparts seem bland by comparison. Just brushing your hand across a bunch of fresh thyme or pinching a leaf of basil or rosemary will release their rich fragrances—one whiff and you'll be in the mood to cook. Many home cooks grow a pot or two of herbs even if all they have is a sunny windowsill for a garden, but there are a number of fresh herbs that are widely available in good produce markets. The following are the most commonly available—and to my mind, the most important. Most of them are quite perishable and should be used as quickly as possible after purchase. (For other seasonings, *see also* Daikon, Fennel, Ginger, Horseradish, Shallot.)

Most herbs are available year round, either grown outside or hothouse grown. Most are grown in Israel under the Carmel brand and shipped to the United States; Israel grows the best herbs.

Basil

Basil is an aromatic herb that has been a favorite in the Mediterranean for centuries. Basil, garlic, and tomatoes seem to have been made for one another, and the combination is the backbone of a lot of Italian cooking.

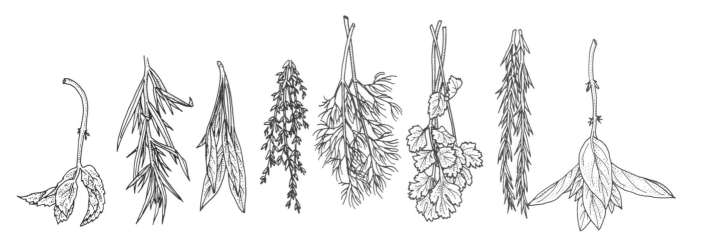

There are two general types: bush basil and leaf basil. Bush basil has smallish pointed leaves and grows on a small, round, bushlike plant. Leaf basil, which is more common in produce markets, grows on long stems with oval leaves that may grow to two inches or longer. In addition to the green varieties, basil is also found in purple and variegated versions, but the flavor is essentially the same.

If you're growing basil yourself, pinch back the growing tip of the stalk, which will force the plant to grow thicker rather than taller and inhibit flowering. Stop pinching it back about two weeks before the first frost is expected and allow the plant to flower before pulling it up by the roots for preserving.

Season

Basil is a summer herb; out of season it's very expensive and usually not of the highest quality. It's best when bought from local sources from June to the first frost. It is available year round.

Selecting

Buy basil with the roots still attached; it's susceptible to cold, so late in the season you're likely to see it with blackened edges and spots. The flavor is acceptable, but cold-damaged basil should be used immediately because it will deteriorate very quickly.

Storing

Rinse basil well, especially the roots, then gently pat dry with a towel and refrigerate in an *unsealed* plastic bag. Or put it in a vase of water as you would cut flowers. Basil

in good condition may last for a week or more at room temperature this way, but only if you're careful to change the water at least once a day.

Fresh basil can be preserved by drying, freezing, or packing in oil. To dry it, rinse off the roots and hang the whole plant, roots and all, upside down in a warm, dry, airy spot out of direct sunlight. When you're ready to use it, just brush the leaves off into your hand. Once it's completely dry, store basil in a capped jar.

To freeze basil, cut off the root end and discard, wash, and put the leafy stalks into a plastic bag. Do not defrost before using (the leaves will be darker); just chop or throw right into the pot. Some cooks coarsely chop or tear fresh basil leaves into ice cube trays, cover with water and freeze, then add the cubes to tomato or pasta sauces as desired.

Using Basil can be used to flavor poultry, lamb, pork, or seafood. It's especially good snipped into salads or used in pasta and is the basic ingredient in pesto sauce. I think it's in its full glory in a simple salad of tomatoes, basil, garlic, and olive oil.

Flavored Olive Oil   2 to 4 cups
....

Flavored oils are great for stir-fries, salads, or on bread. Use any jar or bottle with a tight-fitting lid.

2 to 4 cups olive oil (depending upon size of jar)
3 to 4 whole cloves garlic
3 to 4 sprigs fresh rosemary

Place the oil, garlic, and rosemary in a clean pint or quart jar, pouring oil to within 2 inches of the rim. Allow the oil to stand for at least a few hours and strain before using.

VARIATIONS:
fresh thyme
fresh oregano
1 or 2 jalapeño peppers

Herbs

Gabby's Pesto

This dish brings back especially fond memories for me. Gabby Garbarino was a close friend who used to own a restaurant called Club Gabby in Tenafly, New Jersey. He was one of those people who is always kind and generous to young people. He'd take us to his summer house on the Jersey shore when we were kids, let us enjoy the beach, and cook for us. When you're young and an adult shares his time, interest, home, and table with you, you never forget him. His wife, Tess, was kind enough to pass along Gabby's pesto recipe.

Gabby's Pesto Sauce   4 servings

1 bunch fresh Italian parsley, washed and stems removed

3 bunches fresh basil, leaves only

1 head garlic, peeled and separated into cloves

½ cup olive oil

8 ounces cream cheese

1 teaspoon salt

1 teaspoon freshly ground black pepper

⅓ cup grated Parmesan cheese

Chop the parsley, basil, and garlic in a food processor fitted with the metal blade. With the motor running, slowly add the olive oil to make a smooth paste, about 30 seconds. Transfer the mixture to a small bowl and set aside.

Place the cream cheese, salt, pepper, and Parmesan in the food processor and pulse 3 or 4 times to blend. Add 4 to 5 tablespoons of the herb-garlic mixture and process for 2 minutes. The sauce can be thinned with a little olive oil if necessary. Place the remaining mixture into a sealed container, which can be frozen or refrigerated for future use.

Toss with cooked pasta.

Herbs

Chives

Like garlic and shallots, chives are in the onion family, and they do have a mild oniony taste, but the flavor is fresher and much more delicate.

Season   Available year round.

Selecting   Choose fresh-colored leaves without dark edges or signs of rot.

You can grow chives indoors on a sunny windowsill or under fluorescent lighting. Snip off leaves as you need them, leaving at least half an inch of green to keep more chives coming.

Storing   Chives in good condition can last up to three weeks if they're placed unwashed in an airtight jar and refrigerated. If you feel compelled to wash them first, dry them carefully before storing.

Using   Snip fresh chives directly onto baked or boiled potatoes and into potato soup. Chopped chives are good added to cooked carrots, cottage or cream cheese, green salads, cold soups, omelettes, and scrambled eggs.

Cilantro (Fresh Coriander)

Fresh coriander, also called Chinese parsley, is the leafy part of the plant that produces the coriander seeds on your spice rack. The Latin American name, *cilantro*, has been widely adopted in the United States, and that's how you'll most often see it labeled.

Cilantro has a flat lime-green to medium green leaf and thin stems and is usually sold with the roots on.

It is widely used in Mexican and Asian cooking, including Indian and Thai. Related to parsley, it closely resembles it as well. If you're ever in doubt, pinch a leaf and smell: a distinctive aroma will tell you immediately that you're holding a bunch of cilantro.

Season   Available year round.

Selecting   Smaller leaves are usually tastier than larger ones. Look for fresh-looking bunches without excessive moisture or any signs of yellowing. Although cilantro is not as crisp as parsley, the leaves shouldn't be limp.

Herbs

Cilantro can be refrigerated wrapped in plastic, but some cooks suggest standing it in a glass of water and putting a plastic bag over the tops. Store the whole "bouquet" in the refrigerator, change the water from time to time, and break off leaves as needed.

Cilantro adds a characteristic pungency to Mexican foods such as salsa and gazpacho, as well as to Thai seafood dishes and Indian curries. Use it sparingly, as it's highly aromatic. Don't put a lot of cilantro into a dish that's going to sit in the refrigerator for more than a day because its fresh flavor can turn sharp and slightly bitter.

Dill

Fresh dill has tiny, feathery, bright green leaves, a tangy aroma, and a flavor that is more delicate and less pungent than dill seed.

Season

Available year round. Grown thoughout the U.S. and hothouse grown.

Selecting

Dill is usually sold cut and bundled. The feathery leaves should be bright green and sprightly, not dark or wet.

Storing

Fresh dill is highly perishable, but it will keep a day or two in the refrigerator if it's stored dry (unwashed) in an unsealed plastic bag. Use it as soon as possible after purchase.

Using

Fresh dill leaves are excellent snipped into cucumber salad, chicken salad, potato salad, and deviled eggs. Scatter snipped sprigs over sliced tomatoes as a change of pace from basil, or toss them with boiled new potatoes. Use dill in marinades and sauces, as a seasoning for fish, and in omelettes. Along with dill seed, the leaves are a primary ingredient in pickles and are essential for making salmon gravlax.

Mint

There are dozens of different kinds of mint—some varieties even taste like lemon, chocolate, or licorice. The most familiar and the one you're most likely to find at the market is the common spearmint, a bright green plant with slightly crinkled, pointed

leaves that are generally about an inch long. Mint is a reliable herb that tolerates fairly cool temperatures and comes back year after year; in the home garden it can become as invasive as a weed.

Season Available year round, either fresh (outside) or hothouse grown. Israel grows great mint and ships it to the U.S.

Selecting Choose bright green, unwilted leaves. Stems of mint are generally sold with the roots off.

Storing Wrap dry in an unsealed plastic bag, and mint will stay in reasonably good condition for several days.

Using Mint is most commonly seen garnishing summer drinks like iced tea or turned into sauce for lamb. It is also refreshing snipped over peas, fruit, or lettuce salads.

Parsley

The most widely used of all the herbs, parsley grows wild on the shores of the Mediterranean and is as old as ancient Rome. Although there are four or five varieties, the most commonly available are curly (or American) parsley and plain flat-leafed parsley, also called Italian parsley.

The curly American type is decorative. It turns dark when cooked, so it's best used raw in salads, for dressings or dips, or as a garnish. Flat-leafed or Italian parsley has longer stems and a better, richer flavor. It also retains its green color during cooking.

Parsley is a perennial plant with a better than average tolerance of chilly temperatures. A healthy plant in the garden can stay green well into November or beyond.

Season Available year round, either grown outside or hothouse grown.

Selecting Curly parsley should be bright green and especially crisp; flat-leafed varieties are a little more tender but they shouldn't be limp. There should be no yellow leaves or black edges, which indicate the parsley is old.

Wash the parsley and pat dry with a towel, then refrigerate in an *un*sealed plastic bag. **Storing** Parsley needs to breathe, but it should not be allowed to dry out.

Italians use flat-leafed parsley for everything. It can be added to pasta sauces, including **Using** pesto; it can be stuffed into poultry; and it adds zip when snipped into salads, especially cucumber salads. It's the seasoning of choice, of course, for boiled new potatoes.

Rosemary

Rosemary is a tender evergreen that can grow into a good-sized bush. The gray-green needlelike leaves are somewhat similar to the needles of a fir tree. Rich in aromatic oils, rosemary has a strong sweet flavor.

Available year round, either grown outside or hothouse grown. **Season**

Rosemary is generally sold in sprigs. The needles should be relatively soft, dry, and **Selecting** fresh in color.

Rosemary will keep several days if it's wrapped and stored in the refrigerator. **Storing**

Rosemary is primarily used to season roast lamb, pork, veal, and poultry—it imparts a **Using** wonderful aroma and flavor. It's also excellent roasted with potatoes and with leeks.

Sage

Sage is a flavorful member of the ornamental salvia family. It has pebbly-textured gray-green leaves that are generally an inch to an inch-and-a-half long and either oval or pointed. The leaves of some varieties have reddish undersides.

Available year round, either grown outside or hothouse grown. **Season**

Sage is usually sold cut in bundles. Look for fresh unwilted leaves that are on the green **Selecting** side; the older the leaf, the grayer—and the more likely it is to be bitter.

Storing Sage will keep a day or two if it's kept dry and stored like dill, but it should be used as soon as possible.

Using Sage is traditionally used to flavor meats, poultry, and cheese dishes. New potatoes are also excellent roasted with a handful of fresh sage leaves, a little garlic and olive oil, and salt and pepper to taste.

Tarragon

If the Italians perfected the culinary uses of basil, the French did the same with tarragon. A delicate annual, tarragon has slender stems; small, narrow, opposite leaves; and a sweet, nearly floral aroma. There are two basic varieties—French and Russian; the French variety is by far the more flavorful.

Season Available year round, either grown outside or hothouse grown.

Selecting and Storing Fresh tarragon is probably the most perishable herb. Look for sprightly, unwilted green leaves and stems. Use tarragon immediately if possible. Refrigerate, wrapped, if necessary, but it won't last long.

Using Fresh tarragon is used to flavor white wine vinegars and is a key ingredient in béarnaise sauce. It's excellent in salad dressings, vinaigrettes, and marinades or snipped over fresh tomatoes or English peas. It also adds a subtle, aromatic flavor to chicken, fish, and sauces.

Thyme

The classic seasoning for poultry, thyme has thin, sometimes woody stems, very thin oval leaves, and a fragrant aroma. The two most common varieties are English thyme and lemon thyme, which often has a yellow edging on the leaves and is a bit more fragile than English thyme. Lemon thyme is exactly what it sounds like: thyme with a lemony scent and flavor.

Herbs

Available year round, either grown outside or hothouse grown.

Thyme is sold in sprigs. Look for fresh green leaves with no traces of black. Refrigerate unwashed and loosely wrapped in an unsealed plastic bag.

If the stems are still tender and green, they can be eaten; if they're brittle and woody, pull the leaves off and discard the stems. The drier and woodier the stem, the more easily the leaves will rub off.

Use thyme on poultry and fish and in stuffings. Whole sprigs can be placed in the cavity of poultry before the bird is put in the oven for roasting—either alone or combined with other aromatics such as celery, onion, and parsley (remove before serving). Lemon thyme is especially nice with grilled fish and shellfish. Either sprinkle the freshly rubbed leaves over the cooked fish or, better yet, add a generous quantity to a simple olive oil marinade with just a squeeze of lemon juice and marinate the fish for ten or fifteen minutes before grilling; moisten the fish with a bit more of the marinade when you turn it on the grill.

Horseradish

Horseradish root is very hard, with a coarse, light yellowish brown skin and pale flesh. Shaped something like a carrot, it usually grows to about a foot long. When scraped or grated, it releases a volatile oil and a pungent, sharp aroma that can bring tears to the eyes. Fresh horseradish has a sharper flavor than prepared horseradish.

Horseradish is one of the bitter herbs mentioned in the Exodus story of the Old Testament. It originated in the vast region that spans eastern Europe and western Asia. It was known to many ancient civilizations and was used as a remedy for ills ranging from coughs to gout. Horseradish eventually made its way into Scandinavia and England, where it became popular as a sauce for beef.

Horseradish now grows abundantly in North America and many parts of the world.

Although it's available year round, fresh horseradish is sometimes hard to find because prepared horseradish has become so common. It's most abundant during the spring and again in the late fall, and is nearly always available during the Jewish holidays, when observers want it with the tops on for the Seder table.

 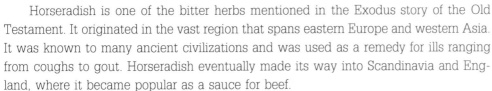

Horseradish root should be very hard, not limp, with no signs of withering or soft spots. **Selecting**

Wrap the root in a slightly damp paper towel, place in a paper bag, and refrigerate in **Storing** the crisper, where it will keep for several weeks. Always use paper instead of plastic bags to avoid condensation, which will encourage rot. If the roots look like they are beginning to shrivel or go soft in spots, prepare them immediately. Prepared horseradish will keep a long time, but it will gradually lose its pungency—even if frozen.

Wash the root thoroughly and peel. If any green flesh lies immediately under the skin, **Preparing** peel it off because it will be very bitter. If the center of the root appears hard and woody, cut out and discard it as well.

A small amount of horseradish can be grated by hand over food just before serving. Larger amounts are more easily prepared in a food processor or blender. First, using a knife, chop the root into small pieces, then process until finely chopped but not liquefied. Immediately add lemon juice or vinegar to keep it from turning brown (which will happen quickly once it's exposed to the air). Add some grated beet, if you wish, to give the horseradish a more attractive color. For a touch of sweetness, add some apple or grated turnip along with a pinch of sugar. For extra pungency, add a touch of mustard or garlic.

Grated raw horseradish combines well with cream, sour cream, yogurt, or mayonnaise for sauces. It is excellent in a tomato-based sauce—catsup will do—to accompany shrimp, crab, raw oysters, or other seafood cocktails.

Horseradish is also wonderful in mashed potatoes and in tuna and chopped-egg salads. It is great with beef and with a variety of meats, and delicious mixed with mayonnaise and spread on roast beef or turkey sandwiches. Horseradish is an interesting addition to vinaigrettes, and it adds zip when sprinkled over soups, especially borscht and creamed soups such as potato or leek.

For a juicy, great-tasting hamburger, mix grated fresh horseradish into the meat before grilling.

Horseradish

Smoked Trout With Horseradish Sauce

4 servings

1 cup grated horseradish

½ cup white wine vinegar

3 to 4 tablespoons mayonnaise

pinch salt

4 medium-sized or 8 small tomatoes

4 whole lettuce leaves

4 fillets of smoked trout

1 cucumber, cut into sticks

8 to 12 slices bell pepper

Grate the horseradish into a bowl, then add the vinegar. (Don't let the grated horseradish sit before adding vinegar or it will turn brown.) Add the mayonnaise and salt and blend well; taste and adjust seasoning.

Slice the tops off the tomatoes, scoop out the flesh, and fill the shells with the horseradish sauce. Place the lettuce leaves on four individual plates or on one large platter and lay the trout fillets on top; add cucumber sticks and sliced bell peppers to make an attractive arrangement. Use different-colored peppers for a brighter plate.

Store any remaining horseradish sauce in the refrigerator or freeze for later use.

Horseradish

Jerusalem Artichoke

Native to North America, Jerusalem artichokes—also called sunchokes—have nothing to do with Jerusalem or with artichokes. They are a tuber from a plant related to the sunflower.

These tubers are usually quite dirty and must be cleaned carefully before using, but underneath the dirt some varieties have a pale, whitish skin and are rounded in shape, while others are more elongated and have a reddish skin. Raw, Jerusalem artichokes are crunchy and spicy without being hot; cooked, they are mild and sweet and can be used like potatoes.

Long cultivated by Native Americans, they quickly became popular among colonial settlers, who called them sunroots. Today they are grown in many parts of North and South America, Europe, and Africa.

Season   Jerusalem artichokes are most plentiful between October and May and are sweetest in the fall and winter.

Selecting   Choose small, firm tubers that have a smooth, dry skin with no tinge of green.

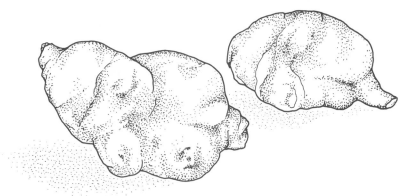

Storing

Wrap in a piece of paper towel to absorb excess moisture and place in a plastic bag in the refrigerator. Use within a week or two of purchase. Jerusalem artichokes do not freeze well, even after cooking.

Preparing

Scrub very well to remove dirt. Peel if desired, but the skins are very nutritious. Raw sunchokes make a very good juice when combined with carrots; they may be thinly sliced and tossed into salads or grated into coleslaw, and they make delicious pickles. They can be steamed and served with cream sauce or battered and fried like tempura. It's important not to overcook them—even one or two minutes too long robs them of flavor and turns them to mush. They are good added to soups and stews, but add them during the last twenty minutes of cooking.

Depending on the size, boil or steam whole, cleaned sunchokes with a squeeze of lemon for twelve to twenty minutes, or until tender. They can be served whole or mashed with butter or other seasonings. Leftovers can be combined with minced onions to make hashed browns.

Jerusalem Artichoke

Jerusalem Artichoke Salad

4 servings

DRESSING

2 to 3 tablespoons olive oil

2 tablespoons white wine vinegar

1 tablespoon Dijon mustard

½ teaspoon Worcestershire sauce

salt and freshly ground black pepper to taste

4 to 6 Jerusalem artichokes

1 green apple, such as Granny Smith, diced

1 orange, segmented, seeded, and chopped

2 stalks celery, chopped

2 cooked beets, peeled and julienned

8 whole lettuce leaves

1 carrot, grated

Prepare the dressing first, mixing all ingredients in a small bowl.

Peel and coarsely grate the Jerusalem artichokes; place in a bowl and toss immediately with two-thirds of the dressing to prevent discoloration. Add the apple, orange, and celery to the Jerusalem artichokes. Toss the beets with the remaining dressing.

Place lettuce leaves on four salad plates and arrange the beets in a ring on the lettuce. Place the Jerusalem artichoke mixture in the center and sprinkle grated carrot over the top.

Jerusalem Artichoke

Pickled Jerusalem Artichokes 6 to 8 servings

- 1 pound Jerusalem artichokes, peeled and sliced into rounds
- juice of ½ lemon
- ½ cup white wine vinegar
- 1 cup water
- grated zest of ½ lemon
- ¼ cup sugar
- 2 to 3 tablespoons coarse salt
- 1 tablespoon celery salt
- 1 teaspoon turmeric
- 2 tablespoons pickling spice
- 1 teaspoon dry mustard
- 1 large bunch fresh dill
- 2 red bell peppers, cut into strips
- 1 cup pearl onions, peeled
- 1 or 2 cups fresh cauliflower florets (optional)
- 6 cloves garlic, peeled
- 1 or 2 whole chile peppers
- 2 teaspoons capers (optional)

Peel the Jerusalem artichokes and slice into rounds; place in a bowl of cold water with the lemon juice until ready to use.

Combine the vinegar and water in a saucepan. Add the lemon zest, sugar, salt, celery salt, turmeric, pickling spice, and dry mustard and stir until the sugar dissolves. Bring to a boil, then reduce the heat to a simmer while you ready the vegetables for pickling.

Remove the Jerusalem artichoke slices from the lemon water, reserving the liquid. In a 1-gallon pickling jar, layer whole sprigs of dill, Jerusalem artichoke slices,

(continued)

Jerusalem Artichoke

bell peppers, pearl onions, and cauliflower if desired, sprinkling garlic, chile peppers, and capers if desired between each layer.

Pour the hot vinegar mixture over the vegetables, then add enough reserved lemon water to completely cover the top layer. Place a plate on top of the jar and weight it with a stone or other object, but do not seal.

Allow to stand for 2 to 3 weeks in a cool, ventilated place before capping and refrigerating.

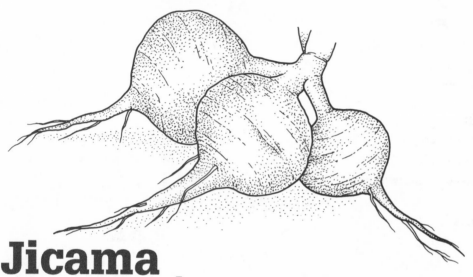

Jicama

Jicama (*hick*-ah-mah), also known as Mexican turnip, is a tuber from a plant indigenous to Mexico and the Amazon regions of South America. Its seeds were used medicinally by the Aztecs. After Spanish explorers introduced it into the Philippines in the seventeenth century, it gradually spread through the Pacific islands into Asia. Mexico remains a major exporter today.

Jicama looks like a turnip that has been slightly flattened at both ends. It has a thin, light brown skin and white flesh that tastes a bit like water chestnut: juicy, crisp, and slightly sweet. It can be used raw or lightly cooked.

Season   Jicama is available year round but is most plentiful from December through April.

A jicama can weigh anywhere from one-half pound to five pounds, but the small to medium-sized ones are juicier and less fibrous than the larger ones. Select clean-looking, firm jicamas, avoiding those with cuts or dark spots.

Selecting

Store jicamas as you would store potatoes—in a cool, dry place. They will stay fresh for as long as several weeks. If you want to use only part of a tuber, wrap the remainder in plastic and store in the refrigerator, where it will keep for up to a week.

Storing

Simply peel off the inedible skin, and jicama is ready to use.

Preparing

Jicama is delicious raw or cooked. For a refreshing low-calorie snack, try it Mexican style—sliced thinly in rounds, with a squeeze of lemon or lime juice and a sprinkle of salt and chile powder. Jicama is a great vegetable for your favorite dip and is good in both vegetable and fruit salads.

Jicama is also an excellent substitute for water chestnuts in stir-fries and a wonderful addition to sweet-and-sour dishes. To preserve its crisp texture, cook it only briefly.

Jicama

Jicama and Mango Salad   4 servings

DRESSING

3 tablespoons sunflower seed oil

2 tablespoons fresh lime juice

2 tablespoons fresh orange juice

1 to 2 teaspoons honey

salt and ground white pepper to taste

1 head romaine lettuce, washed, dried, and cut into strips

1 small to medium-sized jicama, peeled and cut into matchstick strips

2 small mangoes, peeled and diced

2 to 3 tablespoons toasted sesame seeds

To make the dressing, whisk the ingredients together in a small bowl.

Place the romaine in a salad bowl and top with the jicama and mangoes. Add the dressing and toss well. Garnish with sesame seeds and serve immediately.

Kiwi

Although the first kiwis didn't arrive in the United States until relatively recently, they've been cultivated in China for nearly seven hundred years. This small, brown-skinned fruit was prized by the great khans for its flavor and brilliant emerald green flesh. Kiwis have a mild, sweet-tart, strawberry-pineapple flavor and a texture something like a firm peach, with tiny, crunchy, edible seeds about the size and texture of poppyseeds.

Called Chinese gooseberries in an earlier day, kiwis were introduced here in 1904 but received no agricultural testing until 1935. The first commercial planting didn't occur for another twenty-five years, when a man named Smith was asked to plant some kiwi vines next to his grapevines. Smith passed seeds along to George Tanimoto in Gridley, California, who produced a crop of 1,200 pounds in 1970. Although kiwis imported from New Zealand were served in 1961 at Trader Vic's in San Francisco, U.S. growers and consumers were still catching up. It wasn't until the 1980s that kiwi fruit became widely popular. *The Packer*, a newspaper for the produce industry, pronounced it the hot produce of 1984—eighty years after kiwis first showed up, they took off. Today California produces about 95 percent of what we consume in the United States, with imports from New Zealand available when California kiwis are out of season.

Although the rest of the world has been slow to catch on, the Chinese gooseberry is now also grown in Spain, Italy, Greece, France, Israel, India, South Africa, Russia, Vietnam, and elsewhere. At our market they're as popular as oranges.

Season Available year round: from New Zealand, May through November; from California, October through May; from Chile, April through October.

Selecting A ripe kiwi will give to gentle pressure from your thumb. To hasten the ripening process, put kiwis in a paper bag with an apple or a banana and let stand at room temperature; in one to three days they'll be ripe.

Storing Kiwis are a very undemanding fruit. A ripe kiwi will stay good for several days in your fruit bowl at room temperature. In the refrigerator it will keep as long as four weeks. An unripe kiwi will ripen nicely at room temperature, or you can refrigerate it to retard ripening. An unripe kiwi may stay good in the refrigerator for months. When you're ready for it, bring it out and allow it to ripen.

Preparing Contrary to popular perception, you don't have to peel a kiwi—just wash it. The thin brown skin does *not* taste bitter, and it holds the fruit together for eating out of hand.

Kiwis have a beautiful, bright green flesh that looks great when combined with blueberries, oranges, and other fruits. They're terrific pureed—use the puree to sweeten strawberries or raspberries, drizzle it over ice cream, or put it in ice cube trays, freeze, and eat like sorbet (there's no need to add sugar).

Kiwi   148

Kiwi Chiffon Pudding

4 to 6 servings

5 to 6 kiwi, peeled

water

1¼ cups sugar

3 tablespoons cornstarch

¼ teaspoon salt

2 tablespoons lime juice

3 eggs, separated

1 teaspoon grated lime zest

Place 3 of the kiwis in a blender or food processor fitted with the metal blade and puree the fruit. Add enough water to make 1 cup of liquid.

In a saucepan, combine the sugar, cornstarch, puree, lime juice and salt and bring to a boil over medium heat. When the mixtures boils, turn off the heat but leave the pan on the stove.

In a small bowl, beat the egg yolks. Add ¼ of the puree to the yolks, stir, and then add this mixture to the puree. Stirring constantly, cook over medium heat until the mixture has thickened. Stir in the lime zest, and set aside to cool for 20 minutes.

In a medium-sized bowl, beat the egg whites until stiff, then fold them into the kiwi puree until just blended.

Pour into individual serving dishes and slice the remaining kiwi over the top for garnish. Serve at room temperature or chilled.

Kiwi

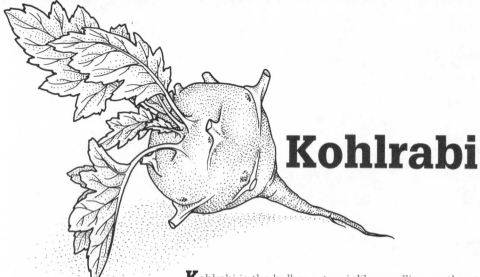

Kohlrabi

Kohlrabi is the bulbous, turniplike swelling on the stem of a cruciferous plant from which leaves shoot off in all directions. The name is a German word meaning "cabbage-turnip," and although kohlrabi is not a cross between the two plants, its flavor is reminiscent of both. The skin of the bulb is either pale green or purple; the purple variety has a slightly more pronounced flavor than the green. Some large varieties have been developed, but most people prefer smaller kohlrabi because they are less fibrous and more mellow than the stronger-flavored large globes. Young kohlrabi is sweet and mild, with a hint of radish flavor. Kohlrabi leaves, which taste something like kale or collards, can also be cooked and eaten.

Season The crop peaks in June and July, with good supplies also available from August through October. Although kohlrabi is available all year, it may be hard to find. Look for it in German, Austrian, Italian, or Russian neighborhoods.

Selecting For best results, choose smooth, unblemished globes that are no more than two or three inches in diameter. If the leaves are still attached, they should be firm, very green, and fresh-looking.

Storing Remove the leaves if attached and cook or store them in a plastic bag in the refrigerator; they'll keep a day or two. Refrigerate the globes in a separate bag; they'll keep up to a week.

Kohlrabi

Eaten raw, kohlrabi is crisp, sweet, and tastes a bit like a mild radish. Simply wash and peel the bulb, removing any fibers that may be visible just under the skin. Then grate, cube, julienne, or slice into thin rounds. Raw kohlrabi can be salted and served as a snack with a dip or added to salads. Some people also eat the thin stems—raw or cooked—that join the leaves to the kohlrabi.

Cooked kohlrabi has a mild flavor that is complemented by many herbs and spices. To cook, boil or steam the whole kohlrabi until tender—about twenty to thirty minutes, depending on its size. You can peel *after* cooking—the skin will come off easily. This keeps the nutrients and flavor in and wastes less of the vegetable. Try kohlrabi glazed with a little sugar, butter, lemon, garlic, and ginger; served with sour cream and dill or chives; or prepared au gratin. For stir-fries, stewing, braising, roasting, or baking, peel it before cooking. Many recipes from the Middle East recommend hollowing out cooked kohlrabi bulbs, stuffing them with a sautéed meat and vegetable filling, topping them with sautéed bread crumbs, then baking them briefly in a 325°F oven.

The leaves are tasty when they're young and fresh. Strip out and discard the central ribs, wash the leaves well, and steam or braise with very little water for two or three minutes, or until tender. Season with a touch of butter, salt, pepper, and a squeeze of lemon if desired.

All parts of a kohlrabi are good in soup. The bulb itself, when pureed, is a good thickener for soups, stews, and sauces.

Kohlrabi

Kohlrabi Chinese Style   4 servings

2 to 3 tablespoons peanut oil

2 medium-sized or 4 small kohlrabi, peeled and cut into sticks

8 small or 4 large fresh shiitake mushrooms, sliced

½ red or yellow bell pepper, cut into thin strips

2 or 3 shallots, minced

1 or 2 cloves garlic, minced

2 teaspoons grated fresh ginger

2 tablespoons rice wine

1 tablespoon soy sauce

1 teaspoon sesame oil

1 tablespoon water

1 teaspoon cornstarch

pinch sugar

pinch salt

handful of cashews or pine nuts, toasted

In a wok or large, heavy, nonstick skillet, heat the peanut oil until moderately hot. Add the kohlrabi, mushrooms, pepper, shallots, garlic, and ginger, and stir-fry for a minute or two. Then add the rice wine, soy sauce, and sesame oil. Cover and cook 5 to 6 minutes, or until tender, stirring occasionally.

Meanwhile, in a small bowl, combine the water and cornstarch and mix until smooth. Add to the wok and stir another minute or two, until the juices thicken. Add the sugar and salt and garnish with the toasted nuts. Serve as a vegetable side dish with rice and meat, chicken, or fish.

Kohlrabi

Kumquat

Frequently mistaken for miniature oranges, kumquats have a thin, sweet rind and a very tart flesh, a combination that I love. They're very pretty added to a fruit bowl or used as a garnish. Kids like their tiny size. Let them try them in the spring, when domestic kumquats are at their sweetest.

Kumquats have been known to China and Japan for thousands of years and were finally introduced to Europe by the British horticulturalist Robert Fortune in the mid-nineteenth century. Called the golden orange by the Chinese, kumquats were introduced to Florida and later to California, where they are now cultivated. Kumquats are also grown in Brazil, Peru, southern Europe, Israel, and parts of Africa, as well as in the Far East.

In the past kumquats grown here were mainly sold to canners and processors, but now the fresh fruit is showing up in retail markets in increasing quantities. There are three basic varieties, but all are bright golden yellow to orange in color and entirely edible, although most people prefer to discard the pair of white seeds inside.

Season

Florida and California kumquats are usually on the market from October to April. Fall kumquats are tarter than those found at the end of the season; in March and April the domestic crops are at their sweetest. Imports ensure that kumquats are available year round.

Selecting

Look for firm fruit with brightly colored rinds and no blemishes. They are often sold in pint containers, with stems and leaves still attached.

Storing

Kumquats will keep five or six days at room temperature and up to two or three weeks refrigerated. Store them either in their pint containers or loosely wrapped.

Preparing

Kumquats are ordinarily eaten rinds and all. If you like, you can blanch them in boiling water to make the rinds more tender. Kumquats make a beautiful tart, delicious marmalade, and unusual brandy preserves. They're excellent poached in sugar syrup and add a decorative and tasty garnish surrounding a roast turkey, duck, or chicken. Kumquats can be thinly sliced and added to fruit salad, fruit punches, or cocktails. They are delicious finely sliced into fruitcake or muffin batter and add great flavor to a sweet-and-sour sauce. Seeded and pureed, kumquats make a refreshing sorbet and can be used to flavor icings for cakes.

Kumquat and Broccoli Salad 4 to 6 servings

1 head broccoli, trimmed and cut into bite-sized pieces

10 kumquats

5 tablespoons olive oil

1 teaspoon minced garlic

3 tablespoons lemon juice

1 teaspoon sugar

½ teaspoon salt

freshly ground black pepper to taste

10 oil-cured black olives, pitted and sliced

Steam broccoli until fork-tender, drain, and place in a serving bowl in the refrigerator to cool.

Place the kumquats in a saucepan with enough water to cover. Bring to a boil and allow to boil for approximately 20 seconds. Drain in a colander, and when cool enough to handle, cut the kumquats into quarters and remove the seeds.

Heat the oil and garlic in a small skillet for about 5 minutes, being careful that the garlic does not brown. Remove from the heat and set aside.

In a blender or food processor fitted with the metal blade, puree the lemon juice, sugar, salt, pepper, and kumquats. Retrieve the broccoli from the refrigerator and toss with the pureed mixture and the warm garlic oil. Garnish with sliced olives and serve.

**Kumquat**

Kumquat Tart   6 servings

....

FILLING

3 tablespoons butter

½ cup sugar

juice of 3 oranges

squeeze of lemon juice

grated zest of 1 orange

3 eggs, beaten well

TOPPING

10 to 12 kumquats

¼ cup sugar

3 tablespoons orange liqueur such as Grand Marnier (optional)

1 tart shell, baked until golden

Prepare the filling. In the top of a double boiler over moderate heat, melt the butter. Add the sugar, orange and lemon juices, and orange zest, whisking continuously until the sugar is dissolved. Very slowly, add the beaten eggs to the mixture, continuing to whisk until it is thickened. Do not boil. Remove the thickened cream from the heat and allow it to cool.

While the cream is cooling, prepare the topping. Slice the kumquats thinly and remove all the seeds. Place them in a large skillet with just enough water to cover the fruit. Add the sugar and orange liqueur; heat until the sugar dissolves, then simmer about 5 minutes, or until the kumquats are tender. Drain the fruit in a colander (save the syrup for a later use) and set aside.

When the cream is cool, pour it into the tart shell. Then arrange the kumquats in a decorative pattern on top. Chill before serving.

Use the cooking syrup in fruit salad or reduce it for a sweet glaze.

Kumquat

Leek

Leeks have never played as big a role in American cooking as they have in European—especially French—cuisines, and that's a shame. They look like enormous scallions, and they're the sweetest and mildest of all the onions. Cream of leek soup is delicious (my mother made one I still remember vividly), and leeks also add a wonderful flavor to other soup stocks and stews. They are delicious braised and served almost as you'd serve asparagus. I love them.

Season Because they're grown in various parts of the country—California, Florida, and Texas are major producers—leeks are available nearly year round. They're best and most plentiful from late fall until early spring.

Selecting Look for leeks with crisp, green tops. The lower two or three inches should be white. Avoid leeks that have soft spots or are yellowed or fibrous-looking. The smaller leeks are usually the most tender.

Storing Trim the roots but don't cut them off entirely; if you do, the leek will fall apart. Remove any limp or discolored leaves, trim the tops a little, and store in a plastic bag in the

refrigerator. Don't leave unwrapped leeks near other foods. Like onions, they readily transmit their odor and flavor to milk and other foods in the refrigerator.

Preparing

Leeks are grown in sandy soil, and a fair amount of sand can get worked up into the stalk. Getting them clean may take some time and patience, but don't take shortcuts here—nothing is worse than biting down on a leek that's still got sand in it. First, cut the leeks lengthwise about halfway through, leaving enough of the stalk whole to keep the leek from falling apart. Wash under cold running water, separating the leaves with your fingers so that water can pour through all the layers. If you're planning to use the leeks sliced instead of whole, slice them first and wash as you would sandy greens, then drain in a colander.

If you're using them in soups, use the whole leek without trimming. If you're serving leeks as a vegetable, trim the green ends, but save them for soup stock. The white lower portions are good sliced raw into salads. Leeks are especially sweet and delicious braised whole in water or chicken stock, then served warm with a bit of butter and seasonings or cold in a vinaigrette.

Lemon

From broiled fish and raw oysters to desserts and drinks, there are scores of dishes that wouldn't be the same without fresh lemon. And for all the many kinds of cold drinks on the market now, homemade lemonade is still one of the best summer refreshers. My mom used to make the most delicious lemonade in the world. She'd take the softer lemons—there would always be ten or twelve left in each crate at the farm stand—and roll them on the counter, then squeeze them by hand into a big glass pitcher. She knew exactly how much water and sugar and lemon juice to use and never had to adjust the quantities, whether she was making one pitcher or a bucketful. It's a great way to use up ripe lemons that aren't going to keep much longer.

Lemons are available year round, although during a period in midsummer they tend to be both expensive and inferior in quality. Lemons are grown in Florida and Texas, but the best ones come from California. Lemons are one fruit that is improved by human intervention: they're picked green, then ripened artificially. If a lemon is allowed to turn yellow on the tree, it becomes very soft and will easily rot.

Selecting Look for a bright-colored lemon that has a very shiny rind and feels heavy in the hand for its size. Avoid puffy-looking, soft, or dull-looking lemons or lemons with white or rusty patches. Unless you want to use them for garnishes or for the zest, avoid very large lemons because they're likely to be more rind than pulp.

Storing Lemons keep well for as long as two weeks in your refrigerator crisper.

Preparing To get the most juice out of a lemon, roll it back and forth on the counter, pressing firmly with the palm of your hand, before cutting it. This breaks up the cells and helps release the juice. Grate the yellow part of the rind—the zest—which is full of fragrant oils, and add it to dishes that call for lemon. Avoid the white pith just under the yellow—it's bitter.

Lettuce

The most ubiquitous of vegetables, lettuce is also the most indispensable. In many parts of the country, iceberg is still synonymous with lettuce, but there are many other varieties worth trying. A salad made of nothing but several different kinds of greens dressed with a simple olive oil and vinegar dressing is something every gourmet appreciates. If you've continued to toss the same old iceberg lettuce and tomato salad, you've been missing out on a wide range of great fresh tastes.

Buttery Boston lettuce, colorful red leaf, sharp-tasting chicory, and crunchy romaine are all widely available. This list is just the beginning. (*See also* Greens *for other salad bowl treats.*)

Iceberg Lettuce

The original name for iceberg was crisphead lettuce. It was renamed in the 1920s when a load of crisphead lettuce was packed in ice and shipped from the Midwest to the East Coast by rail. That's when producers determined that crisphead had good staying power shipped chilled, and iceberg was born. It remains the most abundant and widely used lettuce; Americans seem to like its crunchy texture, mild taste, and keeping qualities. It's easy to work with. It can be shredded, torn, or cut into wedges, and for most people it's the lettuce of choice for sandwiches.

Many people tend to look for a head that's hard as a baseball. Don't make that mistake. A leafy, green, springy head—one that has a little give to it when gently pressed—is going to be a lot sweeter and more tender than a very hard head, which will have less flavor and paler, more bitter inner leaves.

A head lettuce that forms large, round, compact heads with large leaves, iceberg is a local crop in most temperate parts of the country (although about 70 percent of what's on the market is shipped from California). Even though it's usually picked early in the day, it comes out of the field warm and on the point of wilting. To give it staying power for shipment, some of the leaf moisture is removed from California iceberg before the heads are chilled; then they're vacuum packed. Iceberg is generally seven days old when it arrives on the market; by the time you buy a head it may be two weeks old, but the vacuum packing keeps it in pretty good shape.

Season

Iceberg is available year round, but different regions have different peak seasons. The peak months for California, which supplies the lion's share of the country's iceberg, are April to October. Arizona supplies lettuce to the marketplace between October and June, with the peak in December and January. Colorado supplies lettuce between July and September—the same season as local lettuces in the Northeast. Florida ships lettuce between January and April.

Practically every state produces its own lettuce crops. Local iceberg lettuce tends to be dirtier than California iceberg, but it is more likely to be particularly sweet and tender. Local growers usually cut lettuce very early in the morning, then quickly submerge the heads in ice-cold water, which gives the lettuce sufficient staying power to remain crisp for delivery to local markets.

Selecting

Choose a full, springy head with fresh green color. The butt (the cut stem end of the lettuce) should be milky white or *light* brown; the browning is simply a bit of oxidation that happens very quickly after the lettuce is cut. Avoid heads with outer ribs that have taken on a pinkish color or are speckled with rust—the whole head will rust and deteriorate quickly. This happens when growing conditions are too wet. If growing conditions are too hot and dry, on the other hand, there may be some black discoloration on the inner leaves.

159

Storing Store iceberg at about 34°F—the coldest part of the refrigerator—preferably in the crisper or humidifier drawer, or refrigerate in a plastic bag. Keep it away from the refrigerator fan, which will dry it out, and keep it away from ethylene-producing fruits and vegetables.

Preparing To core iceberg lettuce, hold it in two hands, core end down, and hit the butt hard against a table or countertop. Then just turn the head over and pull out the core, which should lift straight out. Pour water directly into the core hole to clean, then drain and chill.

Either tear the lettuce by hand or cut with a stainless steel knife to keep the edges from discoloring.

Finally, remember that lettuce leaves have to be dry if you want a good salad. Salad dressings won't be evenly distributed if the lettuce leaves have a lot of moisture on them, and a puddle of water in the bottom of the salad bowl is never very appetizing. A salad spinner works quickly and gives good results; the basket and bowl also serve as a container in which to wash and drain lettuces and greens. The softer and more fragile the lettuce, the more gently you have to handle it. Don't jam tender greens into the spinner, and spin the most fragile greens slowly and gently to prevent bruising. You can also drain the leaves and blot gently with a clean kitchen towel or paper towels. Or layer the leaves in toweling and hold them in the refrigerator for an hour or so, just until the excess moisture has evaporated.

Romaine (Cos) Lettuce

To my way of thinking, romaine is probably the best of the lettuces. Its elongated leaves are crisp and flavorful, and its deep green color is a tip-off to its nutritional value, which is the highest of the true lettuces.

Romaine dates back to the days of the Roman Empire; its name was coined because each leaf is shaped something like a Roman tablespoon. I like its extra-tender, crisp inner leaves the best.

Season Although it's available year round, romaine is essentially a cold-weather lettuce that in most regions has its peak seasons in early spring and midautumn. All lettuces tend to

bolt—send up a seed head—in hot weather, and romaine is particularly susceptible. Don't buy it if it has a stalk protruding from the center; it has bolted and will be bitter.

Selecting

Good romaine usually has very green outer leaves that should curl away from the center. A smaller head of romaine isn't necessarily a more tender lettuce—a big one can be just as tender and tasty. Look for a crisp leaf and a fresh green color; avoid tired-looking, limp, yellow, or discolored heads and any heads that have bolted.

California and Florida are the biggest shippers. Florida romaine is usually greener than romaine from California, but my personal preference is for California romaine—I think it's sweeter.

Storing

Like iceberg, romaine should be kept in the coldest part of the refrigerator, either in the crisper drawer or in a plastic bag. It also should not be exposed to apples or other fruits and vegetables that produce ethylene gas.

Preparing Pull off individual leaves as needed and wash well in cold water—especially the lower inside surfaces of the ribs, which usually retain traces of soil.

Romaine is the backbone of Caesar salad, is good mixed with other lettuces or greens, and can be used nearly any way you'd use iceberg lettuce.

Arturo's Caesar Salad   4 servings

1 head romaine lettuce

2 cloves garlic

3 anchovies

¼ cup olive oil

¼ cup vinegar of your choice

juice of ½ lemon

2 dashes Worcestershire sauce

2 egg yolks

1 tablespoon Dijon mustard

½ cup grated Parmesan cheese

1 teaspoon freshly ground black pepper

1 cup croutons

Break the romaine lettuce into large pieces; rinse, drain and pat dry, and place in a large salad bowl. In an electric blender, puree the garlic, anchovies, oil, vinegar, lemon juice, and Worcestershire sauce. Add the egg yolks, mustard, Parmesan cheese, and pepper and blend for 30 seconds. Pour over the romaine lettuce, and the croutons, and toss together until the lettuce is well coated.

Lettuce

Boston Lettuce

A soft, bright green, round ball lettuce, Boston is one of the sweetest of the lettuces. The leaf texture is more tender, and it forms a looser, generally smaller head than iceberg. Like most lettuces, the leaves get whiter and whiter as you get toward the heart, but unlike iceberg, the inner leaves of Boston lettuce tend to be sweet and soft. When you get to the middle of a good head of Boston lettuce, its leaves are very pale and crisp.

There is a red leaf Boston that's popular at our market. It looks the same as the green except for a little red at the tip. It's pretty and I think even sweeter than the green.

Season

Boston lettuce is available year round from California and Florida, which are the two main producers. Local crops are available in May, June, and occasionally in July, but Boston lettuce particularly hates the heat.

Selecting

Look for crisp-looking heads with outer leaves that are bright green, especially toward the edges. Around the base the color should be nearly white.

Storing

Tender Boston lettuce won't keep long—generally three to five days. Unlike leaf lettuces, however, Boston wilts from the outside in. You can peel off any wilted or slimy outside leaves and find good, usable leaves inside. With leaf lettuces, once you discard everything that has deteriorated, all that is left is the ribs.

Preparing

Boston grows in very black soil, and because it's a loose head, a lot of that soil finds its way inside. Peel off leaves as needed and wash them carefully, especially toward the base of the ribs.

Boston makes a great tossed salad and is becoming more and more popular as the public discovers its virtues. As a result, it's also becoming less expensive than it was just a few years ago. Boston makes an attractive bed for tuna or fruit salad and is fine on sandwiches. It can't be cut into wedges as iceberg can, but other than that you can use it any way you'd use iceberg.

Bibb (Limestone) Lettuce

A cousin of Boston lettuce, Bibb lettuce is smaller, crisper, a bit greener, and very sweet. Bibb begins to form a head as it matures, and the leaf begins to look a bit like romaine. Bibb lettuce is more expensive than Boston and other lettuces because it's not in such demand—nor do producers get a big yield out of Bibb lettuce crops. A large proportion of what's produced is supplied to the restaurant trade; at the retail level you'll most often see it in high-end supermarkets and produce stores, not in regular chain supermarkets.

Season Bibb lettuce is generally available in June and July.

Selecting Look for green small heads; make sure it's crisper than most leaf lettuces. Tends to wilt or have black spots, so check carefully. If slimy, pass it by.

Storing Store as you would other lettuces.

Preparing Grown in very sandy soil, Bibb lettuce needs lots of washing. Tear the leaves and mix into salads or use the small heads whole. If you're going to use the heads whole (they make a good container for fancy crab salads and the like), submerge the whole head in cold water and carefully separate the leaves with your fingers, moving the head around as you do so to dislodge sand. Then turn the head upside down and stir it around a bit more. Drain and shake it out. Repeat until you can no longer see any traces of sand, then drain upside down on a clean towel.

Leaf Lettuce

Red and green leaf lettuces are the most popular leaf lettuces, and the ones you'll readily find at the market. Both have very soft, curly leaves and a semisweet taste. Red leaf lettuce is softer, sweeter, and also more fragile than the green. It makes a good salad, but it wilts and turns black very quickly, especially at the red tips of the leaves.

Green leaf lettuce is a little coarser and not quite as sweet, but it's a bit crisper. I love it on sandwiches.

Lettuce

Supplies from California and Florida are available year round. Local leaf lettuces are usually in season in May and June.

You don't want to see any dark green or brown slime on leaf lettuces—a sign that the head will deteriorate very quickly. Look at the rib to make sure it's not discolored. As with iceberg and other head lettuces, the butt should be white to light brown, and there should be no pink color on the ribs, which indicates the lettuce has had too much rain and will rot quickly in your refrigerator.

Red leaf lettuce is probably the most fragile of all the lettuces. The tender red edges of the leaves deteriorate rapidly and should be used as soon as possible after purchase. Storage presents a challenge. You can store it as you would other lettuces, but for better keeping try washing the leaves carefully in cool water, draining, then layering them in paper towels or clean dish towels to absorb the excess moisture. Gently roll or fold them loosely, then either store in the crisper drawer or seal in a plastic bag. Some people claim that tender greens like leaf lettuce keep better if you put the leaves in a plastic bag and capture as much air as possible before sealing the top tight, making a sort of balloon. I've also had good success putting chopped ice in the bag before sealing. A deep plastic bowl with a snap-on lid works well for leaf as well as head lettuces; the new perforated plastic storage bags also work well. Whichever method you use, don't count on more than two or three days for red leaf lettuce, four or five for green leaf.

Escarole and Chicory

Escarole and chicory are two varieties of basically the same plant, but they have different shapes and uses. Although they're not true lettuces, they are in the same broad family—Asteraceae—and their leafy heads are usually found alongside lettuces at the market. Chicory, sometimes called curly endive, is simply called endive in Europe, and although it's related, it's not the same thing as Belgian endive. Chicory is a wild-looking, spreading head, with long, slender, very curly notched leaves. Escarole leaves are a bit broader and flatter than chicory leaves and have a smoother edge. The outer leaves are a fairly dark green but get paler toward the inside of the head. The heart is nearly white and has a semisweet flavor.

Both escarole and chicory are zesty, bitter greens. Chicory is almost always used raw, while escarole can be used cooked *or* raw. Escarole is very popular among Italians. One of my all-time favorite dishes is a simple combination of escarole, beans, and seasonings. When I was a kid, we got to choose whatever we wanted for our birthday dinners. My brother David would choose steak or leg of lamb, but no matter what, I *always* chose escarole and beans. Mom said she loved to feed me because I was the cheap date in the family.

Season   Available year round: from Florida and California during the winter months, fall, and spring; in May and June locally.

Selecting   **Escarole:** Look for green outer leaves with a white to yellow center. The butt end should be white to light brown. The leaves should be free of wilt and decay.

Chicory: Exactly the same as escarole, but the outer leaves should be very crispy and sharp.

Storing   Store escarole and chicory as you would lettuce. Both keep reasonably well—up to a week—when properly refrigerated.

Preparing   Both escarole and chicory can be sandy, so wash the leaves well before using.

The outer leaves of escarole, which are relatively bitter, are the ones to use for cooking. They're excellent in my favorite dish and delicious added to soups, cooked with noodles, or mixed with lettuce to top Mexican dishes like tacos and burritos. The sweeter inner leaves are very good in salads.

Chicory is a zesty, attractive addition to other greens, including bitter greens, for salad.

Pop's Escarole Salad

My father didn't get really interested in cooking until he was a bit older and wanted to re-create some of the dishes my mother used to make. He makes an escarole salad

Lettuce   **166**

based on my mother's method, and it's excellent. Just use the yellow-white leaves at the center, which are a bit bitter but very tender. Put them in a bowl, squeeze a little lemon juice over them, add some onions, a little olive oil, and salt and pepper to taste. It's that simple, and just as good as it is easy.

Mom's Escarole and Beans   6 servings

2 heads escarole

¼ cup olive oil

5 cloves garlic, chopped

2 19-ounce cans cannellini beans, drained

1 teaspoon salt

1 teaspoon freshly ground black pepper

1 teaspoon hot red crushed pepper flakes

Cut off 1 inch from the bottoms of the escarole; discard. Break off the escarole leaves and rinse well. Fill a large saucepan about one-third with water. Place the escarole leaves in the pan, cover, and steam until tender. Drain in a colander and set aside.

Heat the oil in the saucepan and sauté the garlic until well browned. Add the escarole and remaining ingredients and stir. Cover and simmer for 5 minutes.

Lime

Grown in warm climates around the world, limes are slightly less acidic than lemons and have a slightly different, more exotic fragrance and taste. They add flavor to any number of dishes and are an excellent substitute for lemons during the summer months, when good lemons are scarce.

Most people rarely use limes except for garnishing cocktails, but limes add wonderful flavor to a lot of different foods. They're great squeezed on other fruits—I like to squeeze them on mangoes, tropical fruits, any kind of melon—or used as a marinade

for seafood and poultry. Terrific added to iced tea and punches, lime juice can be frozen in ice cube trays and dropped into drinks to add zest. And desserts like lime mousse, lime sorbet, and Key lime pie are all excellent.

Indigenous to the Asian tropics, limes were introduced to the Middle East by Arab traders, then spread into the Roman Empire. After the fall of Rome, they disappeared from Europe until the eleventh century, when they were brought back by Crusaders returning from war. Limes were grown in Florida as early as the sixteenth century, and although California grows them too, in my opinion Florida limes are the best. A lot of different local conditions determine the quality of any fruit or vegetable.

There are two basic varieties of lime: the Florida Key lime, also known as the Mexican lime, is a small round fruit not much larger than a Ping-Pong ball. It has a rind that ranges in color from yellow to light yellow-green, pale yellow-green flesh, and many seeds. The other variety is the Persian or Tahitian lime. Larger and more oval, with a slightly pointed stem end and a thicker, greener, more fragrant rind, this lime contains fewer seeds and is a bit more acidic than the Key lime.

Hybridizers are now experimenting with a sweet lime that's a cross between a kumquat and a lime; this hybrid can sometimes be found in Hispanic markets.

Season   Limes are available year round, but they're most plentiful in June, July, and August—just when lemons tend to be scarce.

Selecting   Like lemon, lime should be firm, shiny, heavy in the hand for its size, and free from rust. Key limes can be yellowish or green, but Persians should be bright lime green. Too much yellow in a Persian lime indicates a lack of acidity.

Storing   Limes will keep a few days at room temperature, a week under refrigeration. Don't let them get too warm.

Preparing   For juice or grated zest, treat as you would lemons.

Lime

Mache

Also called lamb's lettuce, field salad, or corn salad, mache is a tender, small-leafed salad green with a mild, nutty taste and a very soft, delicate texture. An annual plant native to the Mediterranean region, mache has been regarded as a delicacy by Europeans since early Roman times. It's become popular in the United States only in the last decade or so and is found here mainly in high-end markets and on the menus of French and new-wave Italian restaurants. Its sweet, nutty-tasting, tongue-shaped leaves grow in clusters and range from medium to dark green. The long-leafed variety is called blond or green mache; the short-leafed, known as shell mache, is darker, firmer, and stronger-tasting. Today France and Holland are the major producers of mache, although Canada and the United States have recently increased production.

Season

The natural season for wild mache is in the spring, but mache is cultivated hydroponically or in greenhouses and therefore is available year round. Look for it in stores that feature fancy produce.

Selecting

Mache should look fresh, green, and dewy. It is usually sold in small plastic trays with the roots still attached—often with small clumps of dirt still clinging to them. Extremely perishable, mache will wilt within hours if its roots are cut.

Mache

Storing   Mache should be eaten as soon as possible after purchase—when it's at its freshest. Refrigerate it unwashed, with the roots still on, wrapped in the new perforated plastic storage bags. Use within a few days—it spoils quickly.

Preparing   Its small leaves are often sandy, so mache needs to be washed very well. Cut off and discard the tiny roots before washing. Handle the tender leaves very gently, and dry with care.

Mache makes a delicious salad either alone or combined with another soft, mild lettuce such as Boston or Bibb. Try dressing it with a squeeze of lemon combined with an oil such as walnut, hazelnut, or pumpkin seed to complement the nutty flavor of mache. Do not add the salad dressing until the moment you're ready to eat, or the mache will get soggy.

Cut mache into bite-sized pieces and use it to garnish cream soups. If you like delicate tea sandwiches made with cucumber or watercress, try them made with mache. Use very thinly sliced fresh bread, spread with a little butter or cream cheese, and top with mache leaves.

Mache

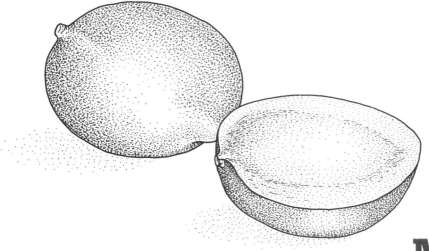

Mango

People in India call mangoes the fruit of the gods, and I think they're right. Few foods are as sweet and fragrant, as full of juice, and as wonderfully tropical-tasting as a good ripe mango. Whenever I visit the Caribbean, one of the first things I do is go out and look for mangoes. A mango can be a mess to eat, but who cares? I'll show you how to do it with the least mess, but to tell the truth, I think the best way to eat it is in your swimsuit. In fact, this is my private recipe for the blues: Put on your swimsuit, grab a towel, go outside and sit in the sun and eat a mango. If you're discreet, you can probably eat two before your mate starts wondering where you are. Better yet, share them with your mate. Mangoes are really *very* sexy.

Not only does a mango taste like paradise; it's one of the richest sources of beta carotene around.

Mangoes are as common as apples to better than half the world. Asia produces three-quarters of the world's mangoes, with India producing and consuming the most of all. Mangoes grow on huge trees, and the fruit hangs down like lollipops on very long stems. Mangoes in U.S. markets are generally from Florida or imported from Mexico, Haiti, and other parts of the Caribbean. They come in all shapes and colors—from green-gold to rich gold, orange, or nearly red. They come in all sizes too, from four ounces to five pounds. Look for medium-sized mangoes, a pound to a pound and a half.

Mango

Varieties The following are the mangoes you'll see most often in the market. I've given a few hints about how to distinguish one variety from another, which gets easier with practice. You can always ask your produce manager where the fruit comes from when you're in doubt.

Mexican Mangoes I like the mangoes imported from Mexico a lot. Basically kidney-shaped, they're big and greenish yellow, with a red-orange blush in May. Those on the market in March and April tend to be greenish yellow and not quite as large or as plump.

Florida Mangoes Also excellent and of very high quality, the crop from Florida starts in May and continues through September. The most popular variety is the *Tommy Atkins*, probably because it's so colorful, with orange to orange-red skin. Oval in shape, it averages about a pound in size and has a bright yellow, fine-textured flesh. Tommy Atkins are sweet and juicy, but a little more fibrous than other varieties.

The *Haden* usually runs less than a pound, is rounder than most varieties, and has a green to yellow skin with a red blush. The flesh is firm and bright orange and has a good, rich flavor.

The *Keith* is round and very fat and is the largest of the Florida mangoes, running from two to three pounds. Its green skin may or may not have a touch of red. Because it has less color and less aroma than the Haden, Kent, or Tommy Atkins, people often pass it by because they think it's not ripe when it actually is. The pit is smaller than that of most mangoes, and the flesh is yellow-gold. Although it's not quite as fragrant or sweet as other varieties, the Keith has a full flavor, tart and lemony, and a smooth, fiber-free flesh.

The *Kent* is fairly large, fat, and not as oval or as flat as the others. It has a green skin with a reddish cheek and averages a pound to a pound and a half in size. Its yellow-gold flesh is very juicy and fiber-free.

The *Palmer* is a long, oval-shaped fruit that usually runs about a pound in size. It has rosy, speckled skin with an orange-yellow—almost apricot-colored—flesh. It's not as fragrant as some, but it's very sweet and is fibrous only around the pit. The Palmer has a little less of the tropical taste of most mangoes, with a flavor more like that of a nectarine or peach.

Mango 172

Haitian Mangoes Although they're always underrated, Haitian mangoes are my favorite. At our store we sell fifty crates of Tommy Atkins for every one we sell from Haiti. A Haitian mango is very flat and elongated, with a skin that starts out lime green and ripens to yellow. It doesn't look pretty, and the flesh is a little more fibrous, but I think it has the best flavor—an intense, tropical taste. It's a great winter treat in January, when the season begins, and it ripens very well at home.

Season

You can usually find good mangoes on the market from January through September. The poorest time is toward the end of the year—November and December. Mangoes are good early in the season, but like oranges, they're at the peak of flavor toward the end of the season.

Mexican mangoes: peak season begins in late March and lasts through September

Florida mangoes: May through September

Haitian mangoes: January through September

Selecting

Handle a mango very gently, as it bruises easily. Pick it up and very *gently* press your thumb against the flesh—it should have a little give and a really sweet smell. A very ripe mango will often have some black speckling outside; don't worry about that or about a little bruising, but avoid mangoes that are black all over—they're past the point of no return. I think mangoes that are a pound to a pound and a half have the sweetest taste.

Always use your nose when you're choosing mangoes. Ninety-nine percent of the time, a mango that smells wonderful tastes wonderful. If the stem end smells sour or acidic, reject it. If a mango is firm and green, it won't have any smell, but if it looks good, bring it home and ripen it yourself.

Storing

Leave a firm, unripe mango out on the counter a few days, until it colors, develops a sweet aroma, and "gives" when you press it very gently. *Never* refrigerate a mango. If you must have it chilled, put it in the refrigerator for a few minutes, but I think mangoes taste best at room temperature. In any event, storing a mango below 50°F for any length of time will take the flavor out.

Preparing   Mangoes are great simply peeled and eaten as is or with a squeeze of lime juice. (Don't eat the peel—it's bitter.) Unlike some fruits, they're slow to discolor when they're sliced. They make a beautiful tropical salad sliced with pineapple chunks, kiwi, papaya, banana—just about any tropical fruit. I like to add a little squeeze of lime and some shredded coconut too. For a refreshing and very nutritious tropical drink, puree some sliced mango with banana, pineapple, and a squeeze of lime.

How to Eat a Mango   Mangoes are *not* freestone. They have a large stone right in the center of the fruit that is difficult to remove. Here's the best way to deal with it. Make two lengthwise cuts on either side of where you figure the pit is; if it's a flattish mango, turn it up so a narrow side is facing you. The pit is large but fairly flat, so make the cuts no more than half an inch on either side of an imaginary center line. You'll have three slices—the center one with the pit in it.

Now take the two outside slices and score the flesh with the tip of a knife, as if you were drawing a tic-tac-toe game. Get as close to the skin as you can without breaking it. Hold the scored slice in two hands and gently push up from the skin side, which will pop inside out. The segments of mango will separate and can easily be scooped off the skin with a spoon or table knife. Add a sprinkle of lime juice if you like.

As for the slice with the pit, you can discard it if you have the willpower. I personally find the flesh around the pit to be the tastiest part. All I can say is that the best way to eat it is to remove the strip of skin around it, pick it up with your fingers—and stand over the sink. Enjoy, enjoy!

Mango   174

Mango Fruit Salad   4 to 6 servings

1 mango, peeled and cut into chunks

½ pound seedless grapes

2 cups watermelon chunks

¼ pound cherries, washed, stemmed, and pitted

1 cantaloupe, seeded and cut into chunks

1 small honeydew melon, seeded and cut into chunks

Mix all the ingredients in a large serving bowl. Chill for at least ½ hour before serving.

Melon: Cantaloupe and Muskmelon

Great fragrance is the hallmark of a good ripe cantaloupe or muskmelon. If I've got a crate or two of them in the truck, it doesn't matter what other produce is in there. When I open the door to unload, the warm, rich, sweet summer smell of melons is the first thing that hits me.

Usually the least expensive and probably the most popular melons on the market, cantaloupes and muskmelons are sweet, fragrant, and juicy, with a pinkish orange to bright orange flesh. Both are varieties of the same species with a similar flavor, but they have other very different characteristics. Grown primarily in California and other western states, cantaloupes are round, with a golden, tightly netted skin. Muskmelons are more oval or oblong, with a loose netting and deep grooves running along the length of the melon—almost as if it were already marked with cutting lines.

175   Melon

Cantaloupe

Although good cantaloupes from the West are available from June through December, they are best between June and September. That's when the California crop is at its peak, and I think that state grows the best cantaloupes. Arizona is next, with a brand known as Kandy that's not picked until it has a sugar content of 20 to 25 percent, which makes a very sweet melon. New Mexico and Texas also grow big cantaloupe crops. See under Muskmelon for Season, Selecting, Storing, and Preparing.

Muskmelon

Muskmelons are grown almost everywhere, and most are sold locally because they are much more fragile and have a softer texture and more juice than cantaloupes and therefore don't ship well. Muskmelons are generally larger than cantaloupes, some reaching eight to ten pounds. They have large, wet seed pockets with larger seeds than cantaloupes. Some people shake them to see if the seeds inside will rattle, and in fact, loose seeds are a pretty good indication that a muskmelon is ripe.

Season The best time to buy western cantaloupes is between June and September, when the California melons are at their peak. During December, January, and February, we get cantaloupes imported from Central America. Although you'll occasionally get lucky and find a good one, most of these are both overpriced *and* lousy. In February, March, April, and May we start to see Mexican cantaloupes. They aren't as good as summer cantaloupes from the States, but over the last few years the quality has improved and the price has become more reasonable.

Muskmelons are available in almost every state that has reasonably warm, long summers, but they're in season only briefly—generally in August and September. Look for them at farm and produce stands in your area. I like locals because they're usually picked ripe and are very sweet. Some people think the flesh is mushy, but there are varieties that are almost as crisp as a western cantaloupe.

Selecting Color and, more important, fragrance—not softness at the stem end—indicate ripeness. A cantaloupe or muskmelon with a golden color and ripe, sweet aroma is going to be

Melon

a ripe, sweet melon. Don't push the stem end—if your neighbor presses a thumb there, and I press mine there, you're going to feel something soft even if the melon is grass green. For some reason, cantaloupes with tighter netting seem to have a firmer, crisper texture and cut better than those with the looser, more open netting.

A cantaloupe or muskmelon on the green side will ripen if you leave it out at room temperature until any green undertones in the rind have turned golden and the melon has a rich smell. But in season, during the summer, there's no excuse for taking home a green melon. In-season melons should have been picked fully mature and fully ripe, with little or no green showing.

Storing

I think both of these melons taste better and have a better texture at room temperature, but if you like your melon chilled, refrigerate it right before you're going to eat it. Cut melons, of course, have to be refrigerated, but wrap them tightly in plastic to preserve moisture. If you don't want everything in your refrigerator to smell and taste like cantaloupe (and vice-versa), it's a good idea to put the melon in a heavy plastic or glass container with a tight-fitting lid.

Preparing

Cantaloupes and muskmelons are fine eaten as is for breakfast or dessert or cut up with other melons and fruits in a salad.

Watermelon

You ought to see all the ways people try to test whether watermelon is ripe. They thump them. They twist the stem to see if it will twist back. I've seen people balance a straw on a melon to see if the straw will rotate. People have even brought buckets of water into the store to see if a melon will float. Everybody has some magical way to see if a watermelon is ripe, but there's one simple, sure way to tell. Look at the stem end: if the stem is shrunken and shriveled, the melon is ripe.

African in origin, watermelons are actually edible gourds in the same family as cucumbers and squash. The top three producers in the United States are Florida, Texas, and California, with Florida providing up to 90 percent of those we get on the East Coast.

There are many varieties, many different shapes and sizes—a few with yellow

Melon

flesh, most of them with red. Some people avoid watermelons because they're so big, but a lot of small varieties have been developed that are terrific, and most markets sell large melons cut into halves or quarters. The average weight of a watermelon is twenty-five to thirty pounds, with some varieties as small as two pounds.

Varieties The two most familiar watermelon varieties are probably the Charleston Gray and the Jubilee. *Charleston Grays* are the first ones out in the summer. They have a pale gray-green rind and red flesh. The earliest ones are sometimes rushed to market before they're mature, however, and some people assume the Gray is a poor melon because of it. Wait a bit. Late in June and into July, they're really sweet.

The *Jubilee* is the striped one. Another red-fleshed melon, it's one of our most popular varieties. There's one problem I've found with Jubilees: they often have a bruised end, which makes the flesh mealy.

Newer varieties include the *Sangria*, a dark-skinned watermelon with red flesh and very dark seeds. *Allsweet*, which looks a lot like the Sangria, has a dark green rind, black seeds, and very rich red flesh. I like the Allsweets a lot—they have good texture, are very sweet, and hold their flavor well.

Smaller melons include the *Sugarbaby*—round in shape, with a dark green rind; the *Cannonball*, which is a bit larger but otherwise very similar; and a melon with a light green rind striped in darker green, usually called an *Icebox* melon. These melons range in size from a little bigger than a softball to the size of a basketball.

My personal favorite is the *Crimson Sweet*. On the East Coast we get them in late July, August, and early September. Because they're grown in the area, they're left on the vine longer, so they've got a very high sugar content. I think they're excellent. At fifteen to eighteen pounds, one of these melons is the perfect size for a small family.

Yellow-fleshed varieties come in a standard (Jubilee) size and a smaller variety called the *Golden Doll*. Although they're sweet in the middle of the summer, they're not as sweet early or late in the season as the red varieties are, and the flesh tends to be mealy.

A few years ago the seedless variety was popular, but the flavor wasn't very good. Thanks to improvements in the hybrid, it's very good now, but it costs about three times what the varieties with seeds cost. In midsummer, when watermelons are ten to twenty cents a pound, the seedless are forty to fifty cents. You should understand that "seedless" watermelons do have some seeds, but they are very pale, very small, and edible.

Seventy-five percent of the crop is produced in June, July, and August, but watermelons **Season** are available year round—imported from Mexico and Central America in the hard winter months, although in December and January they're very expensive and in limited supply. As with most fruits, you should buy watermelons when the domestic crop is in season.

Although a watermelon will ripen after it's picked, if you want it ripe when you buy it, **Selecting** look for a stem that's shrunken and discolored. If the stem is missing, the watermelon is *too* ripe; it will be mealy and dark and not taste fresh.

Cut melons are usually more expensive per pound than those bought whole, but they may be a better buy because you see exactly what you're getting. The blossom end of the watermelon is usually the ripest and therefore the sweetest part. If you're buying a cut melon, look for the blossom end. Make sure the flesh is dark red and firm. A yellow melon should be a rich gold color and firm. If the color is pale, the watermelon is green—not sweet. If the flesh looks dark and wet, it's soft and overripe.

Store a whole watermelon in a cool place, not in direct sunlight. Don't refrigerate it **Storing** unless it's cut or you want to chill it a few hours before serving.

Slice and serve or combine chunks or balls with other fruits for fruit salad; serve in the **Preparing** watermelon shell. Puree watermelon for a delicious drink or freeze the puree to make ice pops or sorbet.

179 Melon

Melon: Late-Season and Winter Varieties

There are four basic attributes I look for in a good melon: flavor, sugar content, juice, and aroma. I have distinct preferences among the varieties of melon, but the best variety in the world isn't going to be worth a nickel if it isn't ripe. Here's where you need to use your common sense—and all your senses. Different varieties offer different clues for ripeness, but in general you want to look for good color, good smell, and a little give to the melon—not soft but not brick hard. Most late melons are in season from August through October, with only one—the Galia—likely to be worth buying in the dead of winter. When you get that winter hunger for fresh fruit, I suggest you pass up most melons in favor of late pears and tropical fruits that *are* in season.

Here is the pick of the crop among late-season melons—and a list of those I recommend you steer clear of.

Honeydew

After cantaloupes and watermelons, probably the most familiar melons to Americans are honeydews, which are available into the winter months. The rind is very smooth, greenish white to yellow in color, and the flesh is a cool lime green. An unripe honeydew is terrible, but a ripe one is probably the sweetest melon of all—and the prettiest. Honeydew is definitely one of my favorite melons.

All too often it's difficult to find a ripe honeydew, but it's not difficult to pick out a ripe one. The rind will develop a golden color and will actually become sticky outside. Never be afraid of a honeydew that has developed a bit of brown freckling on the rind—that's where it's tacky with sugar. The other clue to a ripe honeydew is a sweet, heady aroma. People tend to check the stem end of the melon to see if it's soft, but that's not going to tell you a thing. Good aroma, color, freckles, and a sticky feel are the telltale signs of a sweet honeydew.

In season, honeydews from California are the best. Unless you live in California, however, a ripe honeydew before August or after October is as rare as a blue moon.

Because ripe ones are fragile and hard to ship, 99 percent of those you see most of the year have been picked green, and they'll never ripen. From August through October, however, a new crop of honeydews is ripening in California, and they become ready so quickly the growers can't pick them fast enough. Lucky for you, because most of the honeydews end up staying on the vine until they're ripe and full of sugar. Honeydews from Arizona, Texas, and Mexico are in season at the same time, but in my opinion they range from decent (Arizona honeydews) to lackluster (those from Texas and Mexico). There are a couple of consistently good California brands you may want to watch for—Pony Boys and Sycamores. Start looking in August, and you'll rarely be disappointed.

Orange-fleshed honeydews are fairly new on the market. The rind has a more golden color that turns to orange as the melon ripens, so it's a bit easier to tell a mature one by looking at it. I don't think the orange-fleshed variety is quite as sweet as a regular honeydew that's mature and really ripe, but in the winter, when the orange-fleshed variety is shipped in from Chile and other growers south of the equator, it is a better melon and a better buy than any domestic honeydew you're likely to find.

Crenshaw Melon

Another smooth-skinned melon and another favorite of mine, the Crenshaw is a very large melon with a green rind speckled golden—the more golden the color, the riper it is. Crenshaws have dense, golden-orange flesh and a smaller seed pocket than a honeydew; you'll get more yield out of a Crenshaw than out of a honeydew the same size. Usually picked vine ripe, the Crenshaw is an excellent melon—sweet and juicy. The peak season is almost the same as for the honeydew but a little longer—from July through December. There are two varieties: the golden Crenshaw from California, and a white variety grown in various states as well as in Chile and parts of Europe. I think the golden variety is the best.

If it's not ripe, a Crenshaw will taste like squash, but unlike the honeydew, a firm Crenshaw will ripen at room temperature, provided it's not grass green. If it has a little break of yellow on the rind, leave it out until the speckling on the rind turns a deep golden bronze color.

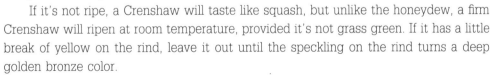

Because Crenshaws may weigh up to ten pounds, most farm stands and many supermarkets sell it cut. Even if the flesh is a good orange color, the melon may not be mature, so if you want to buy a half, turn it over and look at the rind: it should be a golden bronze color. If it's not, it won't be sweet.

As a rule, however, Crenshaws are picked ripe and they're very sweet. They're also expensive. When I was a kid, my father used to buy rejects that showed a few spots of mold. A little mold on a Crenshaw (unlike other melons) won't penetrate the flesh or affect the taste—just cut the spot off. My mother used to station herself at the fruit stand with a pile of spotted Crenshaws, cutting them and giving the customers a taste. We sold hundreds and hundreds of Crenshaws that way. If you can find one that's been marked down because it has a little spot of mold on it, grab it.

Galia Melon

The Galia is one exception to the rule that good melons only come in the late summer and fall. This import is fairly new to Americans, introduced to us by Israel. Galias are now grown in California, Chile, and a few other places, and while they are good, to my mind Galias from Israel are still by far the best. The Israelis have the culture down to a science, and growers there won't pick the melons unless they're mature and have a high sugar content. They are shipped from Israel beginning in November and ending as late as March, with the peak from November through February—just when local melons are out of season, substandard, or simply not available.

Galias basically look like cantaloupes, but the rind is much more golden and the flesh, which is an appealing pale green, has a texture more like that of a honeydew. Galias are very sweet, very juicy, and have a smooth texture. They're also very costly— a Galia the size of a cantaloupe goes for $3.50 to $4.00 in most markets. But I figure you have two choices: you can spend $1.99 and get a tasteless, out-of-season melon or you can spend $4.00 and get something that's good to eat.

Persian Melon

The Persian is a very old variety—one of the oldest of all melons—and although it's not very plentiful anymore, it's very good. Like the Sharlyns (below), Persians have

a tight netting that goes from gray-green to golden beige. The flesh is fragrant, deep orange, and very firm, with a high juice content. The melon is said to have originated in Persia—hence the name—and botanists are still arguing about whether the cantaloupe descended from the Persian or vice-versa.

Persians have a wonderful aroma, and when you're in the vicinity of a ripe one, you'll know it. To me they smell like a field of flowers on a hot summer night. On evenings when I've got a load of produce in, if I've got a case of ripe Persians on the truck, the fragrance of those Persians flies right out at me the moment I open the door.

You want to eat only fully ripe Persians, so look first at the color. As on a cantaloupe, the gray-green rind turns a more golden beige as the melon ripens. The melon will have a little give to it instead of being rock hard, and it will smell wonderful.

Late August and September are the best times to buy Persian melons. Eat them at room temperature for the best flavor.

Sharlyn Melon

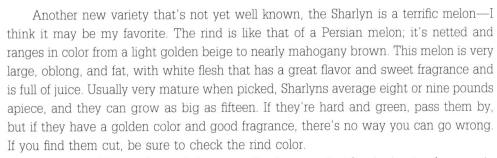

Another new variety that's not yet well known, the Sharlyn is a terrific melon—I think it may be my favorite. The rind is like that of a Persian melon; it's netted and ranges in color from a light golden beige to nearly mahogany brown. This melon is very large, oblong, and fat, with white flesh that has a great flavor and sweet fragrance and is full of juice. Usually very mature when picked, Sharlyns average eight or nine pounds apiece, and they can grow as big as fifteen. If they're hard and green, pass them by, but if they have a golden color and good fragrance, there's no way you can go wrong. If you find them cut, be sure to check the rind color.

Mainly available in fancy fruit stores, Sharlyns are just beginning to show up in supermarkets. I predict they are going to become very popular and we'll start to see them all over the place. And I suspect that as they get more popular, growers will develop a smaller hybrid.

Sharlyns are available from late July through September.

Storing Melons

Left whole, a ripe melon will keep several days at room temperature. I think winter melons have the best flavor at room temperature, although a lot of people like them

chilled. A whole *ripe* melon will keep in the refrigerator, but only for two or three days. A cut melon should always be wrapped tightly, refrigerated, and eaten as soon as possible—the tender flesh tends to absorb odors and will easily dry out.

Preparing Melons

A good ripe melon is delicious as is, but when I have a lot of melons and want something a little different, I make a tropical fruit salad. I slice up melon and add mango, kiwi, pineapple, papaya, and fresh coconut, and sprinkle a little orange or lime juice on top. It's simple, very tropical-tasting, and delicious.

Melons to Avoid

The following list includes melons that have their fans, but in my experience they have less to offer than other melons. One of the biggest problems with them is finding them *ripe*.

Canary Melon

Canary melons have a lemon-yellow rind and a white flesh. At best they're sweet and juicy, but it's hard to find a good one. Grown locally in many areas, they have a season that generally extends from July through November. If you like Canary melons, your best bet is to look for melons grown locally—in New Jersey the season is July and August. There's a much better chance a local Canary melon has been allowed to ripen on the vine, but even at that I think Canaries are only decent. It's very hard to find a ripe Canary melon shipped out of California.

Casaba

When it's good, it's pretty good, but when it's bad, it's horrid. The problem is finding a good one.

Casabas are named after Kasaba, Turkey, where they were first identified. They have a very hard, ridged rind that's white to yellow in color, with white flesh and seeds that make the melon look a bit like a big cucumber. In my opinion even a ripe one *tastes* something like cucumber. Casabas generally have very little fragrance, if any, unless you stumble on a vine-ripe one, which will have a floral aroma and a little give to it. Some melons can be pretty good eating even if they have only two or three of the important attributes of a melon—flavor, sugar, aroma, and juice—but to my mind Casabas have to score high in every category to be worth eating.

Casabas are in season beginning in late August or early fall and continue through December.

Spanish Melon

The Spanish melon basically looks like a green football, with a very hard green rind and no aroma whatsoever. It has a sweet, firm, juicy, greenish white flesh that takes on a yellow-orange tint when it's ripe. The Spanish melon is sometimes called the Christmas melon because it's usually found in stores in late December. But like most winter melons—Galias excepted—this one is very difficult to select because it's almost never mature. Look for a slight overall softness—a little give—which usually indicates a ripe Spanish melon. Most of the time it's going to be hard as a brick. If you like the flavor of Spanish melons, your best bet is to look for those that are imported from Spain. They cost a lot more, but they are much better than those currently shipped from Chile and California.

Watermelon Basket   6 to 8 servings

1 whole watermelon

2 cantaloupe, seeded and cut into chunks

1 honeydew melon, seeded and cut into chunks

½ pound seedless grapes

1 pint blueberries (optional)

1 pineapple, cored and cut into chunks

2 pints strawberries, washed, hulled, and halved

About 2 inches from the top, slice the watermelon along its length to form the basket and discard the slice. Using a melon baller, scoop out all the watermelon into a large bowl. Add all of the fruit except the strawberries and mix well. Transfer the fruit salad to the watermelon basket and top with strawberries. Chill before serving.

Mesclun

Also called gourmet salad or baby salad mix, mesclun is simply a mix of lettuces harvested at a very immature stage, when the leaves are very small and tender. Although it's expensive, mesclun has a superior taste and a more delicate texture than most ordinary salad greens and is of consistently high quality year round. According to the Department of Agriculture, it is six times as nutritious as iceberg lettuce and has fewer chemical residues than mature greens because it's harvested so young. Mesclun is a colorful, tasty, instant salad that requires no more than the addition of a good dressing before serving.

Mesclun seldom contains fewer than a dozen different kinds of lettuces. Depending on availability, typical mesclun mixes are likely to include red oak leaf, a dark red lettuce with narrow leaves that resemble oak leaves; red romaine, which has oval, bronze-red leaves and a crunchy texture; lallarosa—small, round, ruffled red leaves with frosty green interiors and a soft texture; frisee—pencil-thin, feathery leaves of ivory-yellow that add both body and depth to the salad; as well as arugula, mache and radicchio. It may also include mizuna, minoya, bronze leaf, red butter, and red iceberg lettuces—the list goes on, and it sometimes includes edible flowers.

Mesclun is sold at good produce markets. The price can be steep, but a quarter of a pound goes a long way. As mesclun becomes more popular and supplies increase, prices will doubtless decline.

Season Year round.

Selecting Choose unbroken leaves with a soft-crisp texture; avoid mesclun that is wilted, wet, or discolored. Everything in the mix should be usable—with no waste.

Storing Do not wash; simply refrigerate in an unsealed or perforated plastic storage bag and use as soon as possible.

Preparing Used alone, a quarter pound will serve three people; it can easily be extended by mixing it with a less costly soft lettuce such as Boston or red leaf. Mesclun is washed three times before it reaches the market, so it needs no washing, nor does it need trimming or tearing—the leaves are all bite-sized. Wait until the last minute to add a mild vinegar and oil dressing; because the leaves are very tender, they'll absorb salad dressing fairly quickly and will become limp otherwise.

Mushrooms

Mushrooms have probably been the most resistant to our attempts to cultivate the foods we eat. It's hard to say where any particular species originated: all grow from spores, which are easily transported on the wind, and the same varieties exist in many different parts of the world. They have been gathered in the wild since ancient times, but none were cultivated until the eighteenth century. Some varieties, such as truffles, are still gathered using the same techniques our ancestors used. In fact, the elusive flavor of certain exotic mushrooms is so highly prized that some Oriental varieties, for example, are worth twice their weight in gold and have been at the center of murderous intrigues between rival mushroom hunters.

White button mushrooms have been around for years, but more exotic varieties are showing up on the market in increasing quantities. Once available only at certain times of the year, they're now cultivated indoors in climate-controlled conditions, and if you have a taste for chanterelle, shiitake, or enoki mushrooms, you are likely to find them at the high-end produce stores in your area.

What you do *not* want to do is imitate your ancestors and go into the woods to pick mushrooms yourself. A lot of people I know who think of themselves as experts have ended up being rushed to the hospital after dining on a batch of freshly gathered mushrooms. You have to have real expertise to know which are good because so many bad ones look just like good ones, even to an experienced eye. Certain mushrooms are deadly. Why risk getting sick, or worse?

White-cap (Button) Mushroom

The common white-cap mushroom, which I'll call the cultivated mushroom even though so many "wild" ones are now being cultivated, has been around for a long time. It has been bred to be uniform and, in many cases, very white. California and

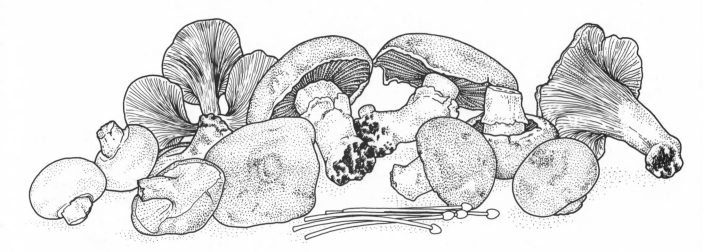

Michigan are big producers, but Pennsylvania grows about 50 percent of what's on the American market. They are raised in cellars, caves, specially constructed mushroom houses—even in abandoned mines.

The perfect white mushroom is white, firm, and dry to the touch, with no sticky or tacky feel. Some varieties have a tan tinge or slight scale, so a white-white color is not always the key indicator of freshness. A closed cap is. When you turn a button mushroom over, the underside of the cap should be attached to the stem by a thin veil of flesh. Caps that have opened to reveal the dark gills underneath show age. Button mushrooms start to open after three or four days; after a couple of more days, they are fully opened, discolored, and starting to get sticky.

Simply handling mushrooms makes them discolor. That's why white mushrooms are often packaged in small cello-packs. Larger quantities are often sold in three-pound wooden baskets or lugs. These should be bought only when you know you'll be using them quickly. Button mushrooms refrigerate well, but wrap them in paper towels. Like other mushrooms, they should never be immersed in water when cleaned.

Button mushrooms can be eaten in dozens of ways: raw, sautéed, batter-dipped and fried, stuffed, marinated, pickled. They can be used in soups, in sauces, in meat or poultry dishes—the list is endless.

Mushrooms

Chanterelle Mushroom

Chanterelles have been cultivated with only limited success to date, but this highly prized mushroom continues to be gathered wild in the cooler forests of the Northwest, as well as in a few places on the eastern seaboard, as soon as the snow melts. The most commonly available chanterelles are shaped like a flared horn or trumpet and are golden orange in color, although white and black varieties are also available (the black one is quite rare and costly). Chanterelles have a fragrance that ranges from delicate to intense, and they retain their aroma after cooking. Feature them in simple, delicately flavored or bland dishes of pasta, rice, chicken, or other white meat so that their flavor—which ranges from nutty to spicy to nearly floral—won't be overwhelmed.

Chanterelles usually arrive on the market in late spring. Like other mushrooms, they should be neither wet nor dried out. Gently touch the edges, which should be plump and firm. Select the cleanest ones you can, and store as you would other mushrooms. To prepare, clean with a very soft brush or, if absolutely necessary, rinse briefly in cold water and quickly blot dry. Trim off a bit at the base of the stem and use immediately.

Crimini Mushroom

Crimini (crih-*mee*-nee) mushrooms, also known as Romans, have been a favorite ingredient among European chefs for years. Now that criminis are being cultivated in Pennsylvania and nearby regions, we're able to enjoy their distinctive flavor in the United States. The crimini has a natural brown to dark brown exterior and a beige interior. The stems are fairly thick, and the caps are opened, not closed like conventional mushrooms.

This is an excellent variety that I recommend highly. Criminis are dense and meaty, yet tender, with a rich, earthy flavor—and they're less costly than other exotic mushrooms. Their special flavor enhances any sauce in which the mushroom can be used. They can be sautéed, grilled, broiled, or baked. Because of their size and firmness, they are especially suited to stuffing. Available year round because they're grown in climate-controlled conditions, criminis are harvested with their roots intact so that their flavor and nutrition are not so quickly diminished during storage.

Mushrooms

Enoki Mushroom

Enoki (ee-*no*-kee) mushrooms, sometimes called golden needle or straw mushrooms, are a Japanese species now grown here commercially in environmentally controlled conditions. Topped with tiny white caps that are about the size of large pearls, they are tall, thin, very fragile, and creamy white to beige in color. Enokis have been described as slightly fruity-tasting and crunchy. Great in salads or used as a garnish, they can be added to a dish of Chinese vegetables just before serving. Use uncooked enokis on sandwiches or to garnish soup. They are excellent in a clear broth or combined with thin slices of boneless beef or chicken and stir-fried Japanese style.

Enokis must be used within a few days of purchase. To prepare, discard the clump at the bottom of the stalks and separate the mushrooms. There is no need to wash them. Be very careful not to overcook, or they will become tough and fibrous.

Oyster Mushroom

Also called tree mushrooms or pleurottes (the proper name is *pleurotus*), oyster mushrooms have an unusual shape. They have short stems, are more or less fan-shaped—like their namesake—and grow on top of one other on the bark of old trees. Usually fairly large in size, oyster mushrooms range from beige to gray in color and have pronounced gills on the underside. They're in great demand for use in Chinese restaurants and are especially suited to seafood dishes.

Oyster mushrooms are the easiest of the wild mushrooms to cultivate, so they're not as expensive as many other exotics. They are being grown in ever-increasing quantities both in Pennsylvania and on the West Coast.

Oyster mushrooms are highly perishable. Store them as you would other mushrooms, but not for more than a few days, and keep them away from any strong-flavored foods in the refrigerator—they readily absorb odors.

Oyster mushrooms should never be washed. Clean with a soft cloth and discard any stems that seem dense or tough. Oyster mushrooms are fairly chewy and much tougher than other wild varieties. Their worst fault is that they tend to get sticky and gummy when even slightly overcooked. Prepare them as you would familiar varieties, but do not overcook. They are delicious added to pasta or rice dishes, are an excellent complement to seafood, and are equally good in omelettes, sauces, and soups. *Do not eat them raw.*

Portobello Mushroom

Considered the grown-up brother of the crimini mushroom, the portobello has a longer growing cycle and produces a mushroom with a very substantial texture and a deep, meaty flavor. Portobellos are harvested year round in environmentally controlled facilities and packaged with roots intact, so that during storage the flavor and nutrition are not diminished. Their tops resemble pancakes both in shape and size, and the stems are long and thick, frequently with a fair amount of black soil clinging to the base that may be difficult to remove completely.

Long, thin slices are a delicious addition to stir-fried dishes, or the mushroom can be breaded and deep-fried as an unusual entree. The portobello's impressive appearance lends itself well to interesting innovations by different chefs. Some people think portobellos taste more like filet mignon than mushrooms, and I agree. This is a great mushroom for cooking—fine, tender, and flavorful.

Shiitake Mushroom

Up until a few years ago fresh shiitake (she-*tah*-keh) mushrooms were found only in Asia, but because they're so popular in nouvelle cuisine here, they're now grown in a number of states, particularly in Pennsylvania. These brown to black, umbrella-shaped mushrooms, also called golden oak or Chinese black mushrooms, grow wild on certain species of oak trees and are commercially cultivated in climate controlled conditions.

Shiitakes range in size from two to eight inches long and have a thick, fleshy cap. They have a distinct, woodsy aroma, a meaty texture, and a full-bodied, delicious flavor. When selecting, look for shiitakes that are firm and dryish but not leathery, with meaty-looking domed tops that curl under. Avoid those that have flattened caps and no fragrance—they'll have little taste.

Shiitakes store longer than most mushrooms—when properly refrigerated, they'll keep up to two weeks—but they gradually lose their special scent and texture. It helps to sprinkle a few drops of water on a cloth and cover the shiitakes before refrigerating so they don't dry out. Don't store them in plastic, however.

To prepare, trim the stems at the base, then clean the caps with a towel or soft brush. Shiitakes may be sliced raw into salads, but they are especially good cooked. Separate the stems from the caps and cook the stems slowly in a soup or stew to make them tender. The caps should be cooked only lightly—overcooking makes them tough. Grilled shiitakes are excellent as an appetizer, and add excellent flavor to soups, salads, and Western and Oriental dishes that call for mushrooms.

Other Mushroom Varieties

Other exotic mushrooms are available in increasing varieties, but only a few have been successfully cultivated. Some, like the wonderful *morel,* continue to resist cultivation, and are gathered wild in the Northwest and parts of the Upper Midwest and East Coast. The caps are thumb-shaped, slightly tapered, and honeycombed with pits and ridges that are difficult to get clean. The stems are straight and hollow. When selecting morels, look for spongy, dry mushrooms that are as clean as possible. They should not smell sour but have a good, earthy aroma.

Morels are great delicacies that should be used in relatively bland foods so that their flavor can be fully appreciated. Never eat them raw; they can make you sick. If they are speckled with dirt, you may have to wash them before using; if so, briefly toss them under cold running water, quickly blot dry, and use immediately. Store morels in a single layer, either covered with a dry paper towel or, if they seem quite dry, with a slightly moistened towel or cloth. Don't clean them until you're ready to use.

Porcini, also called cèpes or boletus, are another prized mushroom still gathered in the wild. They come in a broad range of sizes, but look like an ordinary mushroom with a swollen, bulbous stem and a tan to brownish top. The stems are a paler cream color, as is the interior. Instead of gills underneath the caps, porcini have a spongy mass of tubes with tiny holes. Those gathered in the American Rockies are clean, while those imported from Europe—which are especially tasty and pungent—often bring insects with them, so check the base of the stems and trim away any parts that may harbor bugs. Store porcini as you would other mushrooms, but use them as quickly as possible—they lose their own flavor, pick up unwanted flavors from other foods, and spoil quickly. Add porcini to bland, mild foods to showcase their famous taste. They are particularly good grilled, sautéd, or broiled and can be served as a main dish cooked with nothing but some olive oil—which may, at the cook's discretion, be flavored with a little garlic.

Hen-of-the-woods is an Oriental delicacy that's called *maitake,* meaning "dancing mushroom," in Japan, where it originated. There it is found growing wild on tree stumps. It has a silvery color and a unique taste and smell, although the aroma disappears in cooking. Store as you would other mushrooms. To prepare, simply rinse quickly and blot dry. The maitake is a delicate mushroom that requires only brief cooking; it's best used in soups or sautéed.

The *Chinese wood ear* mushroom used to be available only in dried form, imported from China. It is now beginning to be grown in California, although fresh ones are still fairly difficult to come by. Also called tree ear, cloud ear, or elephant ear mushrooms, they grow on the bark of decayed trees. The mushroom is nearly stemless, glossy, and dark brown to black. Its meaty, somewhat rubbery texture is familiar to lovers of Chinese food. The wood ear has a damper appearance than most other mushrooms but should never feel mushy.

Store Chinese wood ears as you would other mushrooms. Unlike other varieties, they should be washed well before you use them. They need a longer cooking time than other mushrooms and are best added to dishes that include other ingredients rather than served on their own. They add good texture and are ideal for stir-frying and for soups. They absorb the flavor of sauces wonderfully, and are the mushroom of choice for Chinese dishes.

The *truffle* is the Rolls-Royce of the mushroom family. Unlike other mushrooms, truffles grow underneath the soil, making them extremely difficult to find. Truffle hunters use specially trained pigs or dogs to sniff out the aroma that these treasures give off even through the soil. No American species of the truffle is considered edible, so the truffles available here are all imported. The red truffle, which grows in various parts of Europe, is not as prized as white or black truffles. The white truffle of Italy is held in great esteem, but the coal-black truffle—gathered primarily in France and on a smaller scale in Spain, Italy, and Germany—is probably the most highly prized and most expensive.

Truffles are a costly delicacy that ranks right up there with good caviar, so fresh truffles are found only in high-end specialty markets—likely under lock and key. To showcase their extraordinary flavor and aroma, they are prepared in the simplest ways: usually shaved or finely slivered over a delicately flavored or bland food such as risotto or pasta, or added to a simple omelette.

Season Mushrooms do best in cool weather; they do not thrive when the temperature gets above 65° or 70°F. Before the advent of air-conditioning, they were out of season during the summer, as wild mushrooms still are. Cultivated varieties are available year round.

Selecting Whatever variety you choose, look for firm mushrooms that appear to be in good condition and avoid any that look dry and withered, have a lot of broken caps, or show signs of molding, dampness, or stickiness. And *smell* them. A good mushroom will smell good.

Storing Never store mushrooms in a plastic bag. Handle them gently, depending upon their delicacy, and either refrigerate in a paper bag or layer them in dry paper toweling (if they seem damp) or in slightly dampened toweling. Keep them away from strong-flavored foods and use the more delicate varieties right away. Clean only when you're ready to use, preferably with a *soft* brush or damp paper towel. Wash only if absolutely necessary, then quickly blot dry and use immediately.

Mushrooms

Sautéed Mushrooms   4 servings

olive oil

4 cloves garlic, peeled and thinly sliced

1 pound fresh mushrooms, wiped and thinly sliced

1 tablespoon chopped fresh oregano

1 teaspoon chopped fresh basil

salt and freshly ground black pepper to taste

2 ripe tomatoes, cut into wedges (optional)

In a medium-sized skillet, pour in enough oil to cover the bottom of the pan. Add the garlic and sauté over medium heat until golden. Add the mushrooms, oregano, basil, salt, and pepper, and sauté for approximately 10 minutes, or until the mushrooms begin to soften. Add the optional tomato wedges, cover, and simmer for 10 minutes, stirring occasionally.

Portobello Mushrooms and Pasta   4 to 6 servings

1½ pounds portobello mushrooms

¼ cup olive oil

3 cloves fresh garlic, chopped

3 tablespoons chopped fresh Italian parsley

½ teaspoon salt

1 teaspoon freshly ground black pepper

1 pound pasta, cooked

Rinse the portobello mushrooms well; drain, dry, and cut off the stems. Cut the mushrooms into thick strips and then into medium chunks. In a large skillet, heat the oil and sauté the garlic until golden brown. Add the mushrooms and sauté until well browned. Add the parsley, salt, and pepper and stir together. Serve over hot pasta.

Mushrooms

Ken Otto's Stuffed
Mushrooms with Crabmeat

6 to 8 servings

¼ cup butter or margarine

2 tablespoons minced garlic

2 tablespoons white wine

4 mushrooms, wiped and minced

1 pound crabmeat

1½ cups Ritz cracker crumbs

1 egg

cayenne pepper to taste (optional)

2 pounds mushrooms, wiped and stems removed

Preheat the oven to 350°F.

In a small skillet, melt the butter over medium heat. Add the garlic, wine, and minced mushrooms and sauté until the garlic is golden. Remove from the heat.

In a large bowl, combine the crabmeat, cracker crumbs, egg, cayenne, and sautéed mixture. Stir until well mixed.

Spoon the mixture into the mushroom caps, packing well. Place in a buttered ovenproof dish and bake for 20 to 25 minutes, or until the tops are crisp.

Mushrooms

Marinated Portobello Mushrooms

1 pound portobello mushrooms, wiped and thickly sliced
salt and freshly ground white pepper to season
extra virgin olive oil

MARINADE

6 tablespoons extra virgin olive oil
1 teaspoon chopped fresh Italian parsley
1 sprig fresh rosemary, chopped
1 small shallot, chopped
1 clove garlic, minced
juice of 2 limes

Preheat the broiler.

Lay the mushrooms on a baking sheet and season with salt and pepper to taste. Drizzle with olive oil and place the pan under the broiler. Cook the mushrooms for about 4 minutes, giving them a stir once while they're broiling. Remove from the oven and allow to cool.

In the meantime, prepare the marinade by mixing all of the ingredients in a small bowl. When the mushrooms are cool, transfer them to a serving bowl and toss with the marinade. Marinate in the refrigerator for at least 1 hour before serving.

Mushrooms

Nappa (Chinese Cabbage)

Also called celery cabbage, *pet-sai*, *tientsin*, *sui choy*, *chow choy*, and *won bok*, nappa is a long-leafed cabbage that's shaped more like romaine than like head cabbage; it grows to about ten inches long. If you don't like cabbage, try nappa; mild and sweet, it has a much lighter flavor than ordinary cabbage and is juicier and more tender. Its pale green leaves have crinkled edges and prominent veins growing from wide stalks or ribs.

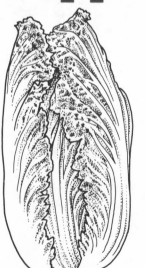

A member of the important crucifer family, nappa has been a staple food in a number of East Asian countries for centuries. California is the biggest producer in the United States, but nappa is also grown in Florida and New Jersey.

There are two varieties: one longer and more slender, with leaves curled outward, the other shorter and stockier, with leaves curled inward. Both varieties are equally good. There is also a Chinese lettuce called chahai that looks like nappa but is much longer. Some stores may offer the Chinese lettuce as nappa, and although it's a different vegetable, the taste is very similar and it's a reasonable substitute.

Season Year round, but October to December is the peak. May is the lowest point in the season.

Choose nappa that has a fresh color and appears firm, not limp.

Never wash nappa until you're ready to use it. Wrap the head loosely in a plastic bag and store in the refrigerator. It will keep a week or two, but for use raw in salads, it is best eaten within a day or two of purchase.

Wash the leaves just before using. Cut a small slice from the base, then remove and wash as many leaves as you need. Drain and use cooked or raw. Shredded raw nappa is good added to salad or made into coleslaw. Nappa can be substituted for cabbage in almost any recipe; unlike cabbage, it doesn't give off a strong odor when it's cooked. It is an excellent vegetable side dish chopped and steamed for about five minutes in one or two inches of water, then served with a little butter and salt.

To make a simple Oriental soup, chop nappa and lightly sauté it with diced onion, minced garlic, and finely chopped cilantro (fresh coriander) and add it to beef or chicken broth. Nappa is good sliced and stirred into any clear soup toward the end of the cooking time.

In the Far East, nappa is marinated for a spicy salad. Called *kimchi*, it is an Asian version of sauerkraut that accompanies many meals. To prepare, chop the nappa coarsely, sprinkle with a moderate quantity of salt, and let stand a few hours at room temperature, turning occasionally until the nappa becomes limp. Squeeze out as much liquid as you can and add a handful of chopped scallions, two or three cloves of crushed garlic, a knob of fresh grated ginger, a dash of chile-flavored rice vinegar, soy sauce, and a little sugar. Toss well, taste and adjust the seasonings, and allow to marinate about twenty-four hours at room temperature. Then refrigerate until ready to use. Sprinkle each serving with a few drops of toasted sesame oil (this is the dark gold seasoning oil sold in small five-or six-ounce bottles).

Nectarine

All summer fruits have their own life: the time for great nectarines is late summer, but they are available from June on. The best way to select a great nectarine is with your nose. When I have a basket or two of ripe nectarines out in the store, you can smell their wonderful fragrance the minute you walk in. A good ripe peach has a sweet fragrance, but you can smell a ripe nectarine a mile away.

Nectarine

Until about 1940 nectarines were a small, drab green fruit with very little red cheek. They were fragile and had a short shelf life, so they weren't popular. Then in 1942 the LeGrade variety appeared, named after the town in California where it was developed. More than a hundred different varieties have been developed in the decades since, and now the industry believes nectarines will surpass peaches as the most popular stone fruit. They're certainly my favorite.

A lot of people think of the nectarine as a fuzzless peach—and it is related to peaches, almonds, and plums—but the nectarine is a different fruit. Like its relatives, it came out of ancient China, but no one knows for sure what its origins are. The flesh is meatier and juicier than that of most peaches; the fruit is also more fragile because it's not protected by a fuzzy skin. For that reason most growers won't ship a really ripe nectarine, and in most instances you'll need to let nectarines ripen at home for a couple of days before eating.

Season Nectarines from Florida and Georgia begin to appear on the market in May, but they tend to be green and hard. In June and July, unless they're local, they're good but not great. It's in August and the first half of September that California nectarines are really superb. If nectarines grow locally and you can get tree-ripened ones at your local farm stand during the summer, by all means buy them.

Imports from Chile and other Southern Hemisphere countries show up in January and February, but those that are shipped by boat are not very good. A few tree-ripened ones are shipped by air, and although they're good, they're very expensive.

Packers are now developing a new technique for shipping that may change that picture soon. It's called controlled atmosphere. The nectarines are put in sealed containers, then the air is pumped out and replaced with air that has a high nitrogen content. This effectively puts the fruit to sleep and prevents the damage caused by chilling. If the technique is perfected—and I hope it is—we may see the unthinkable happen: stone fruits like nectarines, peaches, and plums that are ripe, sweet, and juicy in the middle of winter—just when many of us are longing to get our hands on some fresh fruit.

Selecting Look for unbruised, colorful fruit, although you may have to accept a bruise or two on really ripe nectarines. Avoid fruit that looks green or has a wrinkled or leathery-looking

Nectarine

skin. Choose medium to large nectarines: a gigantic one will be mealy, and a very small one was probably picked too green.

Ripening and Storing

Often your best bet will be to buy nectarines that are still firm, take them home, and let them ripen out on the counter a day or two, until they have a little give and develop a wonderful fragrance. You can refrigerate a nectarine when it's fully ripe, but only for a day or two. Longer refrigeration will rob the fruit of its juice and flavor.

Preparing

Nectarines are great eaten out of hand, but there are other good things to do with them. Try a nectarine antipasto: chill sliced fresh nectarines with sliced green onions, sliced fresh mushrooms, snipped fresh dill, salt, pepper, and an oil and vinegar dressing. Serve in lettuce cups. For breakfast, stir together crisp rice cereal or cornflakes, honey, and flaked coconut. Spoon into ripe nectarine halves placed in a shallow pan, and heat in a slow oven until the nectarines are warm and the coconut is lightly toasted. For a quick nectarine relish, chop equal quantities of fresh nectarines and firm tomatoes, add a generous measure of chopped scallions, and stir in chopped fresh mint or basil. Add salt and use as a relish for hamburgers or fish. Try nectarines in a chicken sandwich: shred the chicken and add alfalfa sprouts and thinly sliced fresh nectarines moistened with well-seasoned mayonnaise or a tart French dressing. Stuff into pita pockets.

Nectarine Surprise   2 servings

2 medium-sized nectarines, peeled and pitted

1 banana, peeled

4 to 5 strawberries, washed and hulled

½ cup orange juice

½ cup pineapple juice

1 teaspoon honey

4 or 5 ice cubes

Cut the fruit into chunks and place in a blender. Add the remaining ingredients. Blend at low speed for about 30 seconds, then at high speed for about 15 seconds.

201   Nectarine

Okra

A beautiful ornamental plant related to the hibiscus and Jamaican sorrel, okra is an ancient vegetable, cultivated for some seven thousand years, that originated in Asia or Africa. It was once called *ngombo,* which became the Creole *gumbo*—a word first used to denote stews thickened with okra and later Creole stews in general. Okra has an unusual texture and a mild, agreeable flavor. It has always been important to Latin American, African, Mediterranean, Middle Eastern, and Asian cooking—as well as to the cooking of the American South. It has just begun to be appreciated by the rest of North America.

Okra is a small, bright green, grooved pod with a small pointed cap. The skin is smooth in some varieties, fuzzy in others, and the pod is filled with soft, edible seeds. Okra must be picked and eaten when the pods are immature; when they're fully developed they are too coarse and fibrous.

Season   Available all year, with the peak season in June through October.

Selecting   Choose pods that look fresh and tender but not limp. Smaller pods, from two to four inches long, are more tender and flavorful than larger pods.

Okra is best used within a day or two of purchase. Keep the pods in a paper bag or **Storing** cover them with a paper towel, place the bundle in a plastic bag, and store in the refrigerator.

If you don't like the slippery texture of cooked okra, cook it as southern cooks do— **Preparing** sautéed or stewed in dishes that include tomato, which seems to be a natural partner for okra. When okra is combined properly in a sauté or ratatouille, its gummy texture dissipates. Okra is especially good added to seafood stews and combines well with vegetables like eggplant, peppers, and sweet corn. It is enhanced by flavorings such as lemon, vinegar, cilantro, and thyme. Creole cooks use okra as both a vegetable and a thickener in shrimp, chicken, or sausage gumbos—highly seasoned stews that usually contain tomatoes and onions and are served with rice. Many Southerners who don't like the texture of stewed okra love okra sliced, dredged in cornmeal, and fried. Surprisingly, pickled okra is firm and crunchy and quite zesty if pickled with some hot peppers.

If necessary, rub the fuzz off the pods with a paper towel or soft vegetable brush, then wash and drain. If you're cooking them whole, remove some of the stem without cutting or breaking the pod. If the okra is longer than two or three inches, remove the upper part of the cap. For soups and certain other dishes, cut off the cap altogether, then slice the okra into rounds and either cook as directed or add during the last ten or twelve minutes of cooking time. Slicing releases some of the sticky juices, which act as a thickener.

Okra can be steamed or simmered just until tender—about ten minutes. It's also good and a bit less sticky cooked in a microwave. Serve it cold with a vinaigrette or hot with lemon, seasonings, and butter or in a tomato-based sauce. Okra freezes well, but blanch it first.

For a simple "gumbo," cut about six slices of bacon into two-inch lengths and fry until crisp but not too brown. Pour off the excess fat, leaving enough to generously cover the bottom of the pan. Slice three or four green onions, including some of the green tops, and sauté them in the fat until the whites just start to turn golden. Add about half a pound of whole cleaned okra, three or four fresh ripe tomatoes cut into wedges, and a few grinds of black pepper. Simmer, covered, for about twenty minutes, stirring frequently, then season with salt and additional pepper as needed. The sauté is done when the okra is tender and the flavors are well combined.

Okra is excellent in a variety of Indian dishes. For a simple curry, stir-fry whole okra with finely chopped onions, curry powder, garlic, ginger, a pinch of chile powder, salt, and finely chopped cilantro. After sautéing a few minutes, add a little tomato paste and enough water to keep everything moist. Cover and cook until tender—ten to twenty minutes, depending on the size of the pods.

Note that when cooked in iron, copper, or aluminum pots, okra will discolor, but it won't affect the taste.

Okra Ratatouille   4 servings

2 to 3 tablespoons olive oil

1 large onion, diced

1 clove garlic

½ pound okra, washed and patted dry

½ red bell pepper, sliced

½ yellow bell pepper, sliced

4 to 6 plum tomatoes, sliced

1 bay leaf

1 teaspoon chopped fresh thyme

2 tablespoons sherry or white wine

pinch chile powder (optional)

pinch sugar

salt and freshly ground pepper to taste

In a large skillet, heat the olive oil over moderate heat and sauté the onion and garlic for 2 to 3 minutes, until the onion is transparent. Add the okra whole to the pan with all the other ingredients. Cover and simmer until the okra is tender, about 20 to 25 minutes, taking care not to overcook it. You may have to add small amounts of water to keep it moist. Served as a side dish along with rice, okra ratatouille is excellent with shrimp, fish, lamb, or chicken.

Okra

Onion

Onions have been an essential cooking vegetable and a household staple for thousands of years. Known to man since prehistoric times, they are alliums—members of the lily family—and their true origins are unclear, although they are believed to be natives of Asia.

Varieties

There are a hundred different varieties, each slightly different in taste, and each has a season. The following are the ones you'll find at most markets. (*See also* Scallion, listed separately.)

Spanish onions are large, round, and yellow, with a dark gold skin. Semisweet and reasonably mild, Spanish onions are very good raw on hamburgers. They're excellent in cooking to flavor more delicate-tasting foods, as their flavor isn't overpowering. In the Northeast they're best in the fall, around harvest time. In June, July, and August, Spanish onions from Texas are available, and in May there are imports from Chile, Argentina, and Mexico. Look for big, hard, dry-skinned onions with a deep golden skin for the best flavor.

Bermuda onions are oval, very white onions with a green or grayish striping from the root to the stem end. Bermudas picked early are usually sweet and can be eaten raw in salads and on sandwiches; like all sweet onions, the early ones are always the sweetest. Early fall is the peak of the crop. Later in the winter and spring, most Bermudas have been in storage and they're likely to be hot. All onions contain sulfur compounds, but because Bermudas have a particularly high sulfur content, they get moldy when they're old, so it's especially important to choose a hard, very white onion. Make sure the stem end is not soft; if it is, the onion may be black at the center.

Red onions are almost always sweet unless they're old. They can be elongated, round, or flattened in shape. California reds, which arrive on the market in September, are usually the flat variety and are among the best of all the red onions. That's because of weather conditions; when the onions are harvested, they're wet, so they are left on top of the ground after pulling to dry. In a warm, sunny, dry climate, the outer skins dry out quickly, and less moisture is lost from the heart in the process. Young, fresh red onions are hard and a deep purple-red, with a dry, shiny skin. Never buy red onions that look like they've been peeled down—they have been in storage too long.

Red onions are also imported from Italy. They are more often long or oval in shape and are frequently sold with the uncut stems braided together. They keep very well hung up in a cool, dry place. The best time to buy the Italian imports is in June, when they first arrive on the market.

Varieties grown and bought locally in various regions of the country may differ, but for most red onions I find that the smaller ones are nearly always the sweetest.

Vidalia onions, grown in Vidalia, Georgia, have become one of the top-selling onions. Vidalias are the sweetest onion of all—that is, if they're true Vidalias, grown in the area from Vidalia seed, and if you get them early in the season. The sweetest Vidalias are harvested in the spring. The season used to last only two or three months, but because of the popularity of the variety, producers are starting to hold Vidalias in storage. Now you can find them on the market in November, but they're not going to be as sweet as they are in the spring and early summer.

There are two other good sweet onions available in some markets—the *Maui*, grown in Hawaii, and the *Walla Walla*, from Washington State. These usually command premium prices.

Yellow globe onions are the most commonly available. They are round, small to medium in size, and very hard, with bright yellow skins. They usually have a stronger flavor than other varieties and are very popular for cooking because they hold their shape and flavor well. If you want an intense onion flavor, use the yellow globe. Yellow globe onions also tend to stay in good condition in storage longer than other varieties—one reason they're abundant almost all year.

Season

Spanish onions: summer and fall, with imports in May

Bermuda onions: fall, beginning as early as August and ending in December

Red onions: from California, beginning in September. Braided Italian red onions are best bought in June.

Vidalias: midspring through summer

Yellow globe onions: year round

Onion   206

For all varieties, look for onions with bright, dry, shiny skins. They should be *hard,* with **Selecting** no soft spots, no sprouting, or signs of mold. Check the stem end to make sure it's firm; if it's soft, the onion may be black at the center.

Store loose in a bin or in a paper bag in a cool, dark, dry place—a dry basement or **Storing** root cellar is best. Some people store onions in the refrigerator, but I think it's too damp and don't recommend it.

You're less likely to cry when peeling and chopping onions if you keep your mouth **Preparing** closed the whole time—breathe through your nose, and no talking until you're finished! If you have a food processor, use it to chop large quantities of onions—and back off a little when you lift the lid of the work bowl.

To remove the odor of onions from your hands (from towels and clothing too), use a little lemon juice mixed with baking soda.

Vidalia Onion Strombolli   4 to 6 servings

dough for 6- to 8-inch pizza
½ pound mozzarella cheese, shredded
¼ pound pepperoni, sliced (optional)
1 small Vidalia onion, diced

Preheat the oven to 375°F.

On a lightly floured board, roll out the dough to form a 6- to 8-inch circle about ⅛ inch thick. Sprinkle half of the mozzarella over the dough, then top with the sliced pepperoni, diced onion, and remaining mozzarella. Roll up the dough to form a log-like loaf. Pinch the seams and ends to seal and place on a greased baking sheet.

Bake for 20 to 25 minutes, or until golden. Slice and serve hot.

Virginia's Stuffed Onions   4 servings

●●●

4 large onions

1 pound lean ground beef

½ cup cooked rice

2 cloves garlic, chopped

2 tablespoons chopped fresh curly parsley

salt and freshly ground black pepper to taste

1 ripe tomato, diced

vegetable oil

½ cup beef stock

Place the whole onions in a large saucepan and add enough water to cover. Bring to a boil over medium heat, lower the heat, and simmer for 15 minutes. Remove the pan from the stove, drain the onions in a colander, and set aside to cool.

In the meantime, prepare the filling by mixing together the beef, rice, garlic, parsley, salt, pepper, and tomato.

When the onions are cool enough to handle, peel them and cut off their tops. Scoop out the centers, leaving enough layers to form a stuffable shell. Spoon the filling into the onions.

In a large skillet, add enough oil to cover the bottom. Place the stuffed onions in the skillet and cook for 5 minutes over medium heat. Lower the heat to simmer and add the beef stock. Cover and simmer for approximately 40 minutes.

Orange

A lot of people understand that fresh oranges are best in the winter, but not many people understand that different varieties have particular seasons. You'll have better luck coming home with good oranges if you learn which varieties are in season when—and keep a simple guideline in mind when you're selecting them at the market. Oranges and *all* citrus fruit should be *heavy in the hand for its size*. This is a simple test and it's your most reliable guide for citrus fruit.

Varieties

The two most familiar varieties are navel and Valencia oranges, which are very good, but if you limit yourself to them, you're missing out on some real treats.

Navel California navel oranges are considered by many to be the best oranges in the world for eating out of hand. They have a meaty flesh, their thick rinds are easy to peel, the segments separate easily, and they have no seeds. All navel oranges have a navel at the blossom end—an opening with a convoluted interior that looks, well, like a navel. Some have a very small navel; others have a larger one. If you're in doubt, inspect several in the bin. A quick poll will identify the variety.

California navel oranges usually arrive around the second week of November and go through late spring. They're not that great at the extreme ends of the season. The earliest ones have less orange color and less sweetness. In February, March, and April, the peak months, California navels get very sweet. Late in the season they are likely to be dry, puffy, and expensive. Avoid them as summer comes on; look for summer fruits instead.

It's not always safe to assume that a Florida orange is a Valencia juice orange and a California orange is a navel. Florida also grows navel oranges, which are on the market between late fall and the end of January. The Florida navel doesn't have as much color as the California variety. They come in all sizes—from tennis-ball to softball size. The rind will be bronze to light orange, with a richer orange color later in the season. Florida navels are, of course, seedless, but they have a higher juice content and a thinner rind that's not as easy to peel as the California navel's. Despite their relatively pale color, they're good oranges and very sweet. Here again, check the blossom end. If it's stamped *Florida* but has a navel, it's a navel orange.

Valencia Valencia oranges are primarily used for their juice. The two varieties most often on the market are the Pineapple and the Hamlin. Both have seeds, thinner rinds than navel oranges, and more juice than pulp. Valencias are slightly elongated—more oblong than round—but the telltale difference between a Valencia and a navel orange is that a Valencia is closed at the blossom end. Navel oranges always have the navel; oranges without the navel will have seeds.

Florida grows the biggest crop of Valencia or juice oranges. The peak season for Florida Valencias is November through the end of June. Early juice oranges in November usually have a tinge of green on the rind. That doesn't mean they're not sweet or juicy—they just haven't had time enough to develop a deep orange tint.

California also grows some Valencias, just as Florida grows some navel oranges. California Valencias have a thicker rind and a higher color both on the rind and in the flesh, but like the Florida Valencias, they have seeds. They have great color, but they're not as sweet and they yield only about half as much juice as a Florida juice orange. I like to mix the two for juicing: California Valencias for their color, and Floridas for their sweetness and yield. California Valencias come in earlier than the Florida fruit, and they have a fairly short season—from June through September. When you see Valencias during these months, they're likely to be from California.

Blood Orange Although they are abundant and familiar in Israel and the Mediterranean, blood oranges are not frequently seen in American markets. In the United States they are grown primarily in California and are shipped in small quantities between December and May. They're easy to spot: they have a red-orange rind, flesh that's flushed with red, and red juice. The flavor ranges from tart to sweet and is generally on the tart side compared to more familiar varieties. Europeans are especially fond of them in salads. My mother used to make an excellent salad with blood orange sections, olive oil, and ground black pepper.

The Mandarin Family Oranges in the mandarin family include: tangerines, tangelos, Mineolas (red tangelos), Murcotts, Temples, clementines, and mandarins—the grandmother of them all. They are basically peeling oranges that began as small, bitter fruits and have been developed by horticulturalists into sweet, easily peeled and eaten oranges.

Orange

Tangerines were named after Tangier; the Italians imported, planted, and made this Moroccan fruit popular in the Western world. Tangerines are flattish, deep orange in color, and have a thinner rind at the stem end, where the peeling begins. They peel easily, but you should take a bit of extra time to remove the white webbing under the rind. Tangerines are available from late November until March, although you'll see them around earlier and later. Steer clear of them in October, when they're usually bitter.

Look for a shiny, tight-skinned, medium-sized tangerine. Very small ones are usually sour and bitter; very large ones puffy and dry. Robinson tangerines have some puffiness or space between the rind and the flesh, but in most varieties you want to avoid excess puffiness. The key again is that a tangerine should be *heavy in the hand for its size*. Late-season tangerines—those that have been in storage—can be decent if you follow the rules for selecting them. Avoid fruit that's too puffy or has a soft, protruding stem end—an indication that the fruit may be starting to ferment.

Of all the mandarins, tangerines are the most nutritious, with a full range of vitamins, especially vitamin A, and vital minerals.

The *tangelo* is the largest orange in the mandarin group. Grown primarily in Florida, it is a cross between the tangerine and the pomelo, which is the ancestor of the grapefruit. Tangelos have a high juice content and a tart to semisweet flavor. Some are round and some are flattened in shape, and they usually have a knobby stem end. The first tangelos of the fall season tend to have a bronze rind and a flattish shape. As the season progresses, the rind color becomes deeper orange. The segments are light orange in color and contain seeds. During October and November tangelos are more like a grapefruit than a tangerine, but they *are* very juicy. I like those that appear during the peak of the season—December and January, a short span of six to eight weeks.

Avoid tangelos with puffy rinds. Look for a hard, shiny, thick-skinned tangelo that feels heavy in the hand for its size.

Mineola oranges are actually red tangelos. They are a little larger than other tangelos, and the rind is a lot more colorful. They're easy to spot at the market because they have a large, knobby stem end. Mineolas are a terrific eating orange—very sweet, easy to peel, and seedless. Most growers will say it's not a juice orange, but it makes wonderful juice, and in Florida it's what farmers use to make juice. Mineolas are on the market from December to March, with the peak usually in January.

There is a variety of red tangelo called the Honeybell that doesn't seem to make it past the Florida state line—maybe because Floridians eat them all themselves. A Honeybell orange is one of the best things I've ever put in my mouth. When I go to Del Ray to visit my father, one of the first things I do is go out to Blood's orchards and buy Honeybells. If you ever have the opportunity to buy them, load up.

California also grows a Mineola variety. It has a highly colored tangerine rind, a refreshingly tart flavor, and no seeds. Smaller than Florida varieties, it has a thick rind and looks a bit like a highly colored navel orange, except it's a bit longer in shape. You can always tell it from a navel by the characteristic knobby protrusion on the stem end, which can be broken off for easy peeling and sectioning. It's an excellent orange.

Murcotts have gained a lot of popularity in the last few years. They're usually marked "honey tangerines" in the stores. As much as I love Honeybells, Murcotts are my favorite of all the oranges. They're even sweeter than Honeybells, with a slightly different taste. Murcotts are tangerine-shaped, but the rind is much tighter than the skin of a tangerine and has bronze speckles. They are a lot firmer and more difficult to peel than a regular tangerine—and loaded with seeds. Regardless of the difficulties they present, they're worth it. Murcotts are great eating and make excellent juice, which is such a deep orange-gold it's almost the color of a Halloween pumpkin. A pitcher of juice is so sweet it's almost too sweet and needs to be cut with the juice of some regular Valencias. Grown only in Florida, Murcotts are in season from January through March.

The *Temple* orange is an old variety that has remained popular. It's a cross between a tangerine and a sweet orange. Shaped like a tangerine but larger, Temples are flattish and have a rough rind that's a bronze-orange color. They have a high juice content but are easy to peel and segment. They also have a lot of seeds. The sweetness key to many oranges—Honeybells being an exception—seems to be the number of seeds. The more seeds, the sweeter the orange.

Clementines are the tiniest of the mandarins. Imported from Spain, Morocco, and other parts of North Africa, clementines are a cross between a sweet orange and a Chinese mandarin. They are small, very sweet, and usually seedless. Most people think of clementines as small tangerines, but they're a different variety entirely, with a distinctive taste. The clementine is an excellent eating orange. Its small size and lack of seeds make it particularly popular with kids. Clementines have been available in Europe for many years, but the market for them in the United States was made only a few years ago, when a devastating freeze in Florida made domestic oranges scarce and expensive. A lot of oranges, including clementines, were imported from Europe, and clementines started to catch on. Over the past few years they've become increasingly popular, and as the demand has gone up, so has the price.

The *mandarin* orange originated in the Far East and has been around since 2000 B.C. If you've never seen a fresh mandarin, you're in for a surprise—the rind is a brilliant emerald green, and the flesh a beautiful deep orange. In the United States mandarins are grown in Florida and California, but they're not often available fresh because canners buy them up. The flavor of a fresh mandarin is much better than that of the canned, however. The flesh is semisweet, with no netting and no seeds. A lot of people pass them by at our store because they think they're just green oranges—that is, until I cut into some and let them have a taste. Then they come back for more. When mandarins are available, you'll find them in produce markets in the late fall. They can be available for two or three months, but later in the season there is heavy competition from the canners. Don't pass up fresh mandarins if you see them.

Ortaniques *Or* for orange, *tan* for tangerine, and *ique* for unique—and this fruit *is* unique.

This orange is one of a kind in more ways than one. Honestly, I've never tasted anything else like it; it's one of the best oranges I've ever eaten. And it grows in only one place—the hills of Jamaica.

Ortaniques don't have that California navel orange look that Americans are so attracted to, but they are incredibly sweet and full of juice. You can section them, you can squeeze or slice them—any way you cut them, they will be delicious. Look for shiny, tight-skinned fruit, as you would with other oranges. Ortaniques are slightly flattened and look a bit like a big tangerine with a bumpy but tight-fitting skin.

Not long ago I flew to the Caribbean to visit Comfort Hall Farm, the largest ortanique farm in Jamaica—for that matter, in the world. It's also the only farm that exports fruit to our markets. The owner, John Sharp, is one of the nicest guys I've ever met. His family has been in Jamaica since the seventeenth century. He took me to the place where one of his forebears, a buccaneer, was hanged. Sharp has a real investment in Jamaica and clearly loves the place. The countryside surrounding his farm, outside Mandeville, is beautiful; the farm itself even more so, with groves of lovely trees numbering in the thousands, many of them growing up the sides of mountains.

The ortanique is a natural mutant, a cross between a Valencia orange and a tangerine. According to Jamaican folklore, it developed with the help of a pair of lovebirds—one living in an orange tree, the other in a tangerine tree. Although attempts have been made to grow ortaniques in Florida and California, none have produced the kind of fruit that grows in the Jamaican hills. Who knows what it is there—the soil, the wind, the rain—but that's the only place this wonderful variety flourishes.

Ortaniques are still new to the United States. Like clementines, they gained a foothold here during the big freezes of the 1980s. Comfort Hall Farm made its first shipment to the United States early in 1987, and as of this writing it's the only source of imports. Although ortaniques have a short season—from February through April—and are a bit more expensive than ordinary oranges, they're worth it.

Selecting Oranges

Whatever the variety, look for oranges that are shiny and *heavy in the hand*. It's a primary rule for a number of fruits, but it's especially important for oranges. Check the scent—the orange should smell good. Except for Robinson tangerines, the rind should never feel puffy—that is, it shouldn't feel like there's any space between it and the flesh. There should be no spotting, no signs of shriveling, no white patches on the rind, and no fermented smell.

Storing Oranges

Tangerines are the most perishable of the oranges. They will keep a day or two at room temperature and up to a week in the crisper drawer of the refrigerator. Other oranges can be kept out at room temperature for three or four days with little problem. Refrigerate them in a plastic bag or in the crisper drawer, and they'll keep well for one to two weeks.

Orange Squares

Makes approximately 24 squares

2 cups flour

2 teaspoons baking powder

½ teaspoon salt

½ teaspoon ground nutmeg

¾ cup unsalted butter, softened

½ cup sugar

1 egg

1 teaspoon vanilla extract

⅓ cup freshly squeezed orange juice

2 teaspoons grated orange zest

½ cup unsweetened flaked coconut (optional)

1 cup mashed cooked carrots

GLAZE

¼ cup freshly squeezed orange juice

1 teaspoon grated orange zest

1½ cups sifted confectioners' sugar (add a few more teaspoons for a thicker glaze if desired)

Preheat the oven to 350°F.

In a small bowl, sift together the flour, baking powder, salt, and nutmeg; set aside.

In a large bowl, cream the butter and sugar until light and fluffy. Beat in the egg and vanilla. Alternately add the flour mixture and orange juice and zest in three parts, beating well after each addition. Stir in the coconut and carrots and mix well.

Pour into a greased 8-by-11-inch baking pan and bake for 35 minutes.

Meanwhile, prepare the glaze. Using a wire whisk, combine the glaze ingredients in a bowl. Spread on the orange squares after cooling and cut into squares.

Orange

Orange-Banana Muffins   Makes 6 muffins

¾ cup whole wheat flour

¾ cup rolled oats

½ cup unbleached flour

1 tablespoon baking powder

½ cup packed brown sugar

½ teaspoon salt

3 tablespoons wheat germ

1 teaspoon ground cinammon

½ cup milk

½ cup freshly squeezed orange juice

1 large egg, lightly beaten

1 cup mashed bananas (about 2 bananas)

2 tablespoons grated orange zest

¼ cup (4 tablespoons) unsalted butter, melted

Preheat the oven to 400°F. Grease six 3-inch muffin cups.

In a large bowl, combine the dry (first 8) ingredients. In a small bowl, combine the liquid ingredients, mixing well. Add the liquids to the dry ingredients all at once and stir until just moistened. Spoon the mixture into the muffin cups, filling each two-thirds full.

Bake for approximately 25 minutes, or until golden and a toothpick inserted in the center of a muffin comes out clean.

Comfort Hall Poached Salmon, Ortanique, and Hollandaise   4 servings

- 2 cups fresh ortanique juice
- 1 cup dry white wine
- 1 bay leaf
- 1-inch strip ortanique peel
- 2 teaspoons salt
- ¼ teaspoon freshly ground black pepper
- 1 tablespoon chopped onion
- 4 salmon steaks, approximately 1 inch thick
- chopped fresh curly parsley for garnish
- hollandaise sauce (optional)

In a large skillet over medium heat, combine all the ingredients except the salmon, parsley, and hollandaise. Bring to a boil, then reduce the heat to a simmer. Add the salmon steaks to the skillet and simmer for approximately 10 minutes, or until done. Using a slotted spoon, transfer the salmon to a serving platter and sprinkle with parsley.

Serve with hollandaise sauce if desired.

Orange

Comfort Hall Ortanique Cheesecake

8 to 10 servings

8 ounces graham crackers

6 tablespoons unsalted butter, melted

5 large ortaniques, peeled and sectioned

juice of 1 large ortanique

½ teaspoon vanilla extract

3 eggs, beaten

⅔ cup sugar

1 pound small-curd cottage cheese

Preheat the oven to 350°F. Grease a 9-inch pie plate or springform pan.

Crush the graham crackers to form fine crumbs. In a small bowl, combine the crumbs with the melted butter until thoroughly mixed. Press the mixture evenly onto the bottom and sides of the plate or pan. Arrange the ortanique sections evenly over the crust.

In a mixing bowl, combine the ortanique juice, vanilla, and eggs. Beat in the sugar, then the cottage cheese, beating until the mixture is smooth. Pour into the pie shell and bake for 35 minutes, or until firm. If you wish to brown the top, increase the heat to 400°F for the last few minutes of baking time.

Cool and refrigerate overnight before serving.

Orange

Ortanique Butter **Makes 1 pint**

This spread is wonderful on bread or toast, or as an icing for cakes and cookies. Also, spoon it into tart shells and serve them chilled with fresh fruit.

> **2 ortaniques**
> **1½ cups sugar**
> **2 eggs**
> **3 egg yolks**
> **pinch salt**
> **½ cup (1 stick) unsalted butter**

Grate the zest from both ortaniques and place in the bowl of a food processor fitted with the metal blade or in a blender along with ½ cup of the sugar. Pulse or blend for 30 seconds, or until the zest is finely chopped. Set aside.

Squeeze both ortaniques thoroughly and reserve the juice. Using an electric mixer or wire whisk, beat together the eggs, egg yolks, and salt until foamy. Gradually add the remaining sugar, then the zest mixture, and continue beating until very thick, about 2 minutes.

Pour the mixture into a medium-sized saucepan and simmer over moderate heat, whisking constantly. Gradually whisk in the reserved juice. Continue whisking until the mixture is thick, steaming hot, and smooth, and the zest pieces are suspended throughout the mixture, about 12 minutes. Add the butter ½ tablespoon at a time, whisking thoroughly after each addition. When the butter is incorporated, spoon the mixture into a hot, dry, sterile jar and allow to cool. Seal and refrigerate for up to 2 months.

Papaya

Also called papitas or pawpaws, papayas are native to the tropics of Central and South America, where they were discovered by Spanish conquistadors and eventually introduced into Asia. Papayas are grown commercially in Brazil, Costa Rica, Hawaii, and elsewhere.

You'll see three main varieties on the market here: Sunrise, Solo, and Amazon Red. Sunrise and Solo range in color from golden yellow to orange-pink; the Amazon Red is generally an orange-red. Different varieties come in different shapes and sizes and can grow to be quite large; generally only the smaller ones are exported. All varieties have a central cavity filled with black seeds that resemble large caviar.

Season Because they're grown in different parts of the world, papayas are available year round. They're most abundant in the spring and fall.

Selecting Look for firm papayas without bruises or scars. The fruit should at least be starting to turn yellow; papayas that have started to ripen will continue to ripen at home. Totally green papayas will never ripen, although the green fruit can be cooked and served as a vegetable.

Papaya

If the papaya has just started to turn yellow, leave it at room temperature until all the green is gone, which can take from three to five days. Don't refrigerate it before it's ripe. A fully ripe papaya will keep a few days in the refrigerator, but it should be eaten as soon as possible. Freezing is not recommended because of the fragile texture of the flesh.

Papayas can be served plain or sprinkled with a little lime or lemon juice. Slice the fruit lengthwise, scoop out the seeds, and eat the flesh with a spoon. Papayas are easy to peel and can be chopped or pureed for a variety of uses. They are good seeded, sliced, and wrapped with prosciutto as you would wrap slices of melon. The flesh can be coarsely chopped and added to shrimp or chicken salad, sliced into fruit salad, or pureed and mixed with other fruit juices.

The seeds themselves can be dried, ground like pepper, and used as a seasoning and tenderizer for meat or in salad dressings. Like pineapples and kiwis, papayas contain papain, the enzyme used in commercially prepared meat tenderizers. Both the seeds and the flesh will tenderize meats. Don't use papaya in gelatin—it will prevent jelling.

For a tasty, nutritious shake, combine one seeded, peeled papaya, ¾ cup of milk, the juice of a lime, three tablespoons honey, and four ice cubes in the container of a blender. Blend at high speed until smooth. Don't try to store this; the enzymes in papaya will cause the milk to curdle in the space of ten hours.

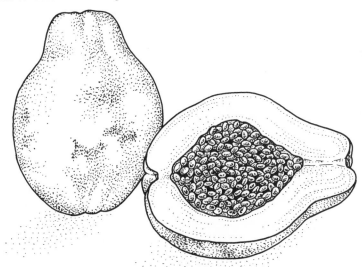

221 Papaya

Papaya Cheese Pie

10 servings

1 cup vanilla wafer crumbs

1 cup flaked unsweetened coconut

⅓ cup unsalted butter, melted

½ teaspoon grated lime zest

½ teaspoon ground nutmeg

2 tablespoons cornstarch

2 tablespoons lime juice

1½ tablespoons anisette

2 cups diced papaya

1 pound cream cheese, softened

1 cup sugar

½ teaspoon salt

3 large eggs, lightly beaten

1 teaspoon vanilla extract

Preheat oven to 350°F.

In a bowl, mix the vanilla wafer crumbs and coconut; add the melted butter and lime zest and blend until well combined. Press the crumbs into the bottom of an 8-by-10-by-1½-inch pan and set aside.

In a large bowl, blend the nutmeg and cornstarch. Add the lime juice and anisette and mix well. Stir in the papaya chunks. Pour the mixture into a 2-quart saucepan and cook over low heat, stirring gently, until the liquid has thickened and the papaya chunks are well coated—about 5 minutes. Cool to room temperature, then spoon into the prepared crust.

In another bowl, work the cream cheese with a fork until it is light and fluffy. Add the sugar, salt, and eggs, and whisk until the mixture is smooth and well blended. Whisk in the vanilla. Pour this mixture on the top of the papaya, making sure that the entire pie is evenly covered.

Papaya

Bake for 1 hour, or until the top is golden brown. Turn off the oven but leave the pie in for another hour. Remove to a cooling rack. Refrigerate before serving.

Parsnip

Parsnips are one of those old-time vegetables a lot of people pass by, but if you've never had them, you've missed something special.

Parsnips are a root vegetable with inedible tops. They are a cousin of the carrot—in fact, they look like carrots, except for their tan color. (There is a new variety out that's more round than long, but I don't think it has half the flavor of the old-fashioned carrot-shaped kind.) Parsnips have a distinctive flavor with a little bite. Raw, they have a slight radish taste, and they retain a bit of a bite even after they're cooked. Like carrots, they also hold their shape well and stay firm even after a fairly long cooking time.

Season

Parsnips are available eleven months of the year, but their flavor increases with cold weather—in fact, parsnips are tastiest if they're picked after a frost or even a hard freeze. In late August and early September they're usually not around.

Selecting

Choose parsnips as you would carrots. They should be firm and crisp, not limp, with no cracks, no root hairs, no signs of wilting or withering. They should have a smooth, light tan color—not brown. Choose medium-sized parsnips for the best flavor.

Storing

Parsnips have a long shelf life. Store them either in a cold room like a root cellar or in the refrigerator.

Preparing

Parsnips can be cooked and served almost any way you'd serve a carrot. Simmer sliced parsnips until tender and serve with a little butter and salt. They're good mashed, and they're wonderful in soups, where they add a little spice. They're also excellent raw; sliced thin into salads, they add crunch and a spicy, peppery flavor.

Peach

Like most fruits, peaches originated in China and arrived in the United States via the Middle East and Europe. Tender, juicy, and aromatic, peaches are thought of as a southern fruit, but California and New Jersey grow huge crops as well. In fact, any temperate area with a long enough growing season will produce peaches, and peaches grown in your area and picked fully ripe are usually your top choice. Of all the places they're grown, though, I think Georgia and the Carolinas still produce the best.

Most of us have no idea how much fuzz peaches have to begin with. Even though they've still got fuzz on them, 90 percent of it has been removed by the time you buy peaches at the market. When I was a kid, New Jersey was about 60 percent farmland. We bought peaches from a man named Francis Johnson, who had a peach farm four or five towns away from us, in Ramsey. I used to go there with my father to pick up peaches for our stand. Although the packing barn was a big red barn, it made me think of a white castle. Peach fuzz covered the whole barn; it was all over the place, completely blanketing the rafters in white, and drifts of fuzz were piled four or five feet high everywhere. That fuzz won't wash off; you have to use a brush or rub it off with a cloth. Now growers use a mechanical brushing system to remove most of the fuzz, and the skins are tender and smooth enough to eat without peeling.

Varieties

There are two basic groups: clingstone and freestone. Clings are so called because the flesh clings to the pit, while a ripe freestone easily breaks away from it. Clings are good for canning and cooking because of their firm texture, but for out-of-hand eating, freestones are by far the juiciest, most tender, and most flavorful peach. Those from Atlantic Coast states are usually juicier than the large, handsome California peaches. This is another case where you don't want to choose fruit with your eyes alone. Cling peaches may look pretty, and California peaches may be big and perfect-looking, but for the best eating, look for smaller freestones and buy local peaches when you can.

Most peaches on the market now have yellow flesh, sometimes shot with red, but in the 1940s and 1950s white peaches were favored—Champion Whites, Georgia Bells, Dixie Belles, and other varieties. Because they were delicate and bruised very easily, commercial growers switched to yellow varieties, which ship a little better. You can still find white peaches on farm stands in some areas, and they're delicious, but the yellow-fleshed peaches have been greatly improved in the last twenty-five or thirty years, so they are sweeter and have a better texture than they did in the past. Many of them were developed by hybridizers in Michigan; you'll find Hale Haven, Red Haven, and Rich Haven peaches at many produce stands, and they're all good. One of my favorites continues to be the Elberta, an older variety with a rich, slightly tart, old-fashioned peach flavor, good for cooking as well as out-of-hand eating.

Season

Peaches are definitely a summer fruit, with the peak of the season beginning in late July and running through early September. In the winter there are imports from Chile, but because ripe peaches are so fragile, they're nearly always picked green and have very little flavor. For the best peaches, wait until they're in season in your area, then get your fill. Peeled, sliced peaches freeze well, so you can put some away to enjoy when good fresh peaches aren't available.

Selecting

When choosing peaches, use your eyes *and* your nose. Choose brightly colored fruit without traces of green, without bruising, and with a plump, smooth skin that shows no sign of wrinkling or withering. A really ripe peach will have a good fragrance.

Storing

Peaches picked hard-ripe but with good color will ripen if you leave them out on the counter, unrefrigerated, for two or three days or put them in a brown paper bag to hasten the process. Don't refrigerate until they're fully ripe, and then don't keep them in the refrigerator for more than a day or two. Like nectarines, peaches lose juice and flavor if they're refrigerated too long.

Preparing

Peaches are great for out-of-hand eating. Leave the skins on for more nutritional value. When you need peeled peaches, you can easily remove the skins by dipping the whole peach into boiling water for ten or fifteen seconds, then immediately plunging it into cold water. You can then peel it like a banana. Peaches are delicious peeled, sliced, and marinated in the refrigerator with some sugar, then served either with plain light cream or over vanilla ice cream. Pies, cobblers, preserves, and ice cream are all traditional peach desserts.

Loel's Peach Kuchen

6 to 8 servings

2 cups flour

1 teaspoon salt

¼ teaspoon baking powder

1 cup sugar

½ cup (1 stick) unsalted butter

6 large peaches, peeled and sliced

1 teaspoon ground cinnamon

1 cup heavy cream

2 egg yolks

Preheat the oven to 400°F.

Sift the flour with the salt, baking powder, and ¼ cup of the sugar. Add the butter and blend until the mixture looks like fine crumbs. Pour into a greased 8-inch square or 9-inch round baking pan, and lightly press the crumbs onto the bottom and sides of the pan.

Arrange peach slices over the pastry and sprinkle with the remaining sugar and the cinnamon. Bake for 15 minutes.

In the meantime, in a small bowl, whisk the heavy cream and egg yolks until well combined. Pour over the peaches and return to the oven for 30 minutes.

Serve warm or cold with whipped cream if desired.

Peaches in Wine

In the old days, Italians would look for late-season peaches which they steeped in wine—usually Chianti and usually homemade. They'd look for these peaches in September, when peaches tended to be drier and would absorb more liquid. Then they'd cut them up, put them in Mason jars, cover them with wine, and let them stand for two or three months. It was a long, drawn-out process, and the peaches were eaten with some ceremony. When my grandfather died and my uncle Joe became the head of the household, he was the one who decided when to bring out the peaches and serve them to guests.

Pea, English or Sweet

The popularity of fresh sweet or English peas largely disappeared after World War II, when homemakers began to choose canned and frozen peas instead of fresh ones—probably about the same time they started choosing packaged white bread over old-fashioned crusty loaves bought at the corner bakery. Convenience may have been only part of the reason. Like sweet corn, green peas start to convert their sugars to starch very soon after they're picked. While pale canned peas are hardly an improvement over a fresh pea too long off the vine, good-quality frozen peas are better than big, starchy fresh ones—and they're generally less expensive. Fresh English peas continue to be a fairly high-ticket item. If you have the space, you might want to consider growing your own—straight off the vine, early green peas are wonderfully sweet, tender, and crisp. Like sweet corn, however, they should be consumed as soon as possible after picking.

Season

A fairly cool-weather crop, English peas are available year round from California and Mexico. Local sweet peas are available in the late spring and early summer—May through early July—with a second, smaller crop appearing in the fall.

Selecting

Look for bright green, lustrous pods with a velvety feel and a green, fresh-looking stem end. Reject pods that are yellowed or limp or tough and dry.

Storing English peas may be refrigerated in the shell, unwashed, for two or three days, but for the sweetest taste consume them the same day you buy them.

Preparing Fresh young sweet peas are delicious added to green salads or eaten as a snack out of hand. Simply break the pods along the seam and pop the peas out of the shells. Rinse briefly in cold water and drain if you wish, although washing is not necessary.

It is extremely easy to overcook English peas. Don't do it! They may be steamed for four to five minutes in a vegetable steamer or simply placed in a pot with about a quarter-inch of simmering water in the bottom, covered, and cooked over moderately low heat just until they're hot—three minutes or so should do it. Toss them two or three times while they're cooking to be sure they cook evenly. The peas should be tender but still crisp when they come to the table. Season with a pinch of salt, butter or cream, snipped parsley or mint, or lemon butter, as desired.

Pea, Field

Most Americans are familiar with black-eyed peas, which we usually see on the market frozen, canned, or dried. There are other delicious peas in the same family that can be bought canned or frozen in northern states; fresh ones are available primarily south of the Mason Dixon line. Depending upon when they are picked, field peas are smaller, more tender, and less starchy than full-sized black-eyed peas, and they have a full, buttery flavor. Like black-eyeds, field peas are actually in the bean family. Also known as lady peas, field peas include varieties called Crowder, Purple Hull, and Cream peas. They are a good source of vegetable protein, especially when combined with rice, as in Hoppin' John, or served with cornbread. Either combination makes what is called a complete protein and is a suitable substitute for meat.

Season Field peas are in season in the summer and early fall.

Selecting The pod color depends on the variety, but look for limber, healthy-looking pods that are neither dried out nor wet. You'll be able to make out the shape and size of the peas inside the pod; generally, the smaller, the more tender, but if the peas are too immature they will be difficult to shell.

Unshelled field peas will keep for several days refrigerated in a paper bag.

Simply shell the peas and rinse. If there are very tiny pods or "snaps" in the bunch, rinse them, snap into bite-sized pieces, and cook with the shelled peas. Two-and-a-half pounds in the pod will yield about a pound and a half of shelled peas, which will serve six people.

To cook field peas southern style, put a piece of salt pork (three ounces or so to a pound and a half of peas) or a small, meaty hambone into a large saucepan, add the peas, cover with water, and bring to a boil. Reduce the heat and simmer, covered, for about an hour, checking the pot from time to time to make sure the peas don't cook dry. Add small quantities of boiling water if necessary to keep the peas covered with liquid. Fifteen to twenty minutes before they're done, taste and add more salt if needed, as well as black pepper and other seasonings if desired. Never drain field peas before serving—the pot liquor is half the point. Many Southerners add a chile pepper to the pot before cooking or serve the peas with a sprinkle of hot pepper sauce; many will recommend you serve them with hot buttered corn bread and dunk the bread into the broth to soak up all its rich flavor. Serve the peas with "sides" of cooked turnip or mustard greens, sliced ripe tomatoes, and raw sweet onions, and you've got soul food.

Pea, Snow

Bright green, crisp, and sweet, snow peas are valued for their edible pods rather than the tiny peas they contain. Although they're most familiar in stir-fries and other Oriental-style dishes, they're excellent as a side dish. They are crisp and refreshing, a snap to prepare, and quick to cook.

Known as the Chinese pea or *mange-tout*, snow peas are a variety of edible pea pods—a kind of pea probably first developed by the Dutch in the sixteenth century. That makes them a real newcomer to the pea family, which has been a staple in the human diet for at least five thousand years. Ideally suited to growing conditions in Asia, snow peas quickly became established in China and other countries in East Asia, where they became a favorite vegetable. Guatemala and other Central American countries are now major suppliers to the United States, along with California. Various regions in Canada also supply area markets.

Pea, Snow

Season Snow peas are available year round, but the peak season is May through September.

Selecting About the same size as regular pea pods, snow peas should be bright green and very flat, with a flexible but crisp texture. The outline of the peas inside should hardly be noticeable. California varieties are a brighter, deeper green than those from Central America, which may be nearly lime green. Avoid snow peas that are fat—they're too mature—or that show excessive moisture or wrinkled pods.

Storing Do not wash snow peas until you're ready to use them. They are highly perishable and should be refrigerated immediately in a plastic bag. They will keep a couple of days refrigerated, but you should use them as soon as possible.

Preparing Wash briefly in cold water and remove the stems. Most snow peas have a fairly tough string down each seam of the pod. These can be removed with the stem if you snap the stem gently and pull toward the opposite end of the pod. If the strings are too tough to eat, they will usually come off with the stem.

Snow peas are delicious lightly steamed or blanched, but don't cook for more than a couple of minutes or you'll destroy their bright color and crispness. As a side dish all they need is a sprinkle of salt or a dab of butter if desired. Snow peas combine well with other Oriental vegetables such as Chinese mushrooms, water chestnuts, and bamboo shoots. Try blanching them and adding to other vegetables for a cold salad, or serve them alone in a vinaigrette. For beautiful hors d'oeuvres, wrap blanched snow peas around shrimp, secure with toothpicks, and serve as is or with a dip. Or split them along one side, blanch, and stuff with a mixture of cream cheese and anchovies.

Stir-fried Chicken and Snow Peas   2 to 4 servings

juice of 1 lemon

2 tablespoons soy sauce

1 tablespoon grated fresh ginger

2 cloves garlic, minced

2 skinned and boned chicken breasts, cut into strips

2 tablespoons peanut oil

1 medium-sized onion, finely diced

5 stalks Chinese celery, cut into short sticks

½ pound snow peas

1 red bell pepper, cut into thin strips

½ root daikon, sliced very thin

½ head bok choy (Chinese cabbage), coarsely chopped

1 cup chicken stock

2 tablespoons water

2 tablespoons cornstarch

salt and freshly ground black pepper to taste

In a medium-sized bowl, combine the lemon juice, soy sauce, ginger, and garlic. Add the chicken and marinate in the mixture for at least 1 hour. Remove the chicken from the marinade, reserving the liquid.

Heat the oil in a wok and sauté the chicken quickly, just until it loses its pink color. Add the onion and celery and stir a minute, then add the snow peas, bell pepper, and daikon and stir a minute or two more. Add the bok choy, chicken stock, and marinade; allow to simmer about 2 minutes. The vegetables should remain crisp. Make a smooth paste of the water and cornstarch and add to the wok, stirring constantly, until the sauce begins to thicken. Remove from heat and season as desired with salt and pepper. Serve with white or brown rice.

Pea, Snow

Pea, Sugar Snap

Although there are several strains of edible-podded peas on the market labeled "sugar snap" peas, Sugar Snap is the proper name of the original hybrid first introduced in 1979—a very new vegetable compared to most we know. The Sugar Snap is a cross between a snow pea and a substandard shelling pea—substandard because it has a thick pod and is hard to shell. The hybrid, developed by botanist Calvin Lamborn, is a very sweet, crisp pea that's completely edible except for the strings. Sugar Snap peas have become very popular in the few years since they were introduced, and for good reason. They are tender, crunchy, and sweet as can be.

Season Sugar Snap peas are available year round.

Selecting Look for bright green, lustrous pods with fresh-looking, green stem ends. Avoid any that are yellowed, limp, coarse, or too dry.

Storing Refrigerate as you would snow peas, but use them as quickly as possible.

Preparing Rinse briefly in cold water and remove the stems. Although Dr. Lamborn has been working on stringless varieties, most Sugar Snaps still have fairly tough strings along one or both sides of the pods. String them as you would snow peas.

Sugar Snaps cook very quickly and should never be overcooked. For the best texture and taste, stir-fry or steam them as you would snow peas.

Pear

Cultivated for nearly four thousand years, pears have been known to man since ancient times. They originated in Asia and spread throughout Europe during the Roman Empire. Until the sixteenth century pears were tough and always eaten cooked, but in the seventeenth and eighteenth centuries, gardeners for European noblemen began to crossbreed varieties, competing with each other to get a pear with a soft, buttery flesh. Most of the pears we know today are derived from those cultivars.

Pear

Pears are grown throughout the United States and Europe and are now being introduced as commercial crops in South Africa, Australia, New Zealand, and Chile. In the United States, Oregon, Washington, and California produce particularly excellent pears.

This is one fruit you do *not* want tree-ripened. Pears have a characteristically gritty texture caused by cells in the flesh called stone cells. Although more and more of these have been bred out, all varieties still contain them. Picking pears before the fruit has matured and holding them under controlled conditions prevents the formation of too many stone cells.

Pears are delicate even when they're hard and green, so they're always picked by hand. Most markets don't sell really ripe pears because they bruise so easily, but it's very easy to ripen them at home.

Varieties

Because pears crossbreed so easily, there are somewhere between four thousand and five thousand cultivated varieties. Eight of those are commonly available to shoppers here.

Anjou Anjou pears are almost always oval, with a very short neck. Immature Anjous are pale green and turn to yellowish green as they ripen. They have a very juicy, spicy flesh that's a bit firmer than the Bartlett. Anjous are available from October through May.

Bartlett and Red Bartlett A bell-shaped pear known as Williams in Europe, the Bartlett is probably the most familiar pear to Americans. It has long been prized for canning. Regular Bartletts turn from green to yellow, with a pink blush. The Red Bartlett is a hardier variety that has a bright crimson skin. An unripe Red Bartlett is actually a darker red than a ripe one: as it ripens, it turns from a darker to a lighter, brighter red. The flesh of both is white. I don't think you can taste much difference between the two. Both have a buttery texture and a mild, sweet flavor. Bartletts are available from August through December.

Bosc Although similar in appearance to the European Conference pear, the Bosc is much juicier and less granular in texture. It is relatively long and slender; of all the pears, it probably has the longest neck. An unripe Bosc has a brown skin that changes to a golden russet, becoming lighter and brighter in color as it ripens. A ripe Bosc can get almost golden yellow, but it will still retain shades of russet. The Bosc has a yellow flesh that's buttery, sweet, and juicy. It has a very long season—August through May.

Clapp The Clapp pear is large, oval, and greenish yellow, with a bit of a red blush. It's a decent pear, but of all the pears, it's the hardest and woodiest. Available in the fall.

Comice A very large, round, short-necked pear, the Comice is my personal favorite. Of all the pears, I think it's the sweetest and most fragrant. Comices have a greenish yellow skin, sometimes with a red blush. Originally a French variety, they have been grown in North America for more than one hundred years. Because they scar very easily, they're sometimes hard to sell here. Ethnic groups buy them, but a lot of Americans just don't like the way they look. With a peak season in November and December, they're one of the best things going around the holiday season. As the demand for them grows, producers are starting to grow more of them, but Comices are still not as commonly available as Bartletts and Anjous, so they're still relatively expensive. Comice pears are available from August to March.

Forelle Another good holiday pear, the Forelle is very small—between a Seckel and an ordinary pear in size—and golden yellow in color, with a bright red blush and characteristic red freckles. Not only is it very sweet and juicy—it's beautiful to look at. An unripe Forelle is green with red specks; as it ripens the green turns to golden yellow. With those red freckles, Forelles are a standout. They have a relatively short season— October to February, peaking in October and November. We still have a good supply during Christmas.

Nelis A winter pear that's small to medium in size, the Nelis has brown freckles over a light green skin that turns golden when ripe. It's fairly round, with almost no neck. The flesh is creamy and sweet raw, and it's also very good for cooking and canning. Nelis are available from October to April, with the height of the season in December and January.

 **Pear**

Packham This is a fairly new strain, developed in Australia. It's similar to a Bartlett in color and flavor, but it's got a rougher shape. Available all winter from Chile.

Seckel Bite-sized, the Seckel is the smallest of the pears. Named after the Pennsylvania farmer who discovered it on his property, Seckels have a short neck and a dark green skin with a dark red blush. I think they have an excellent flavor. Available from August through January, Seckels take a lot more time to ripen than other pears and will stay hard for months in the refrigerator.

Selecting

Green pears should be free of blemishes. Ripe pears—especially tender varieties like the Comice—are going to show a few scars. Avoid bruised or too-soft fruit, but don't be afraid to bring home pears that are still green. That's the way you're going to find most of them.

Ripening and Storing

Place unripe pears in a bowl or paper bag, leave them at room temperature, and they'll ripen in a few days to a week, depending on how green they are when you buy them.

Most pears show a subtle change in color as they ripen, and some develop a sweet fragrance. You can test a pear for ripeness by applying *gentle* pressure to the stem end with your thumb—it should yield a bit. You can hold off the ripening process by refrigerating them, and they'll hold for a long time—as long as three to four weeks. A few days before you want to eat them, bring them out to ripen. You can refrigerate a ripe pear too, but at that point it's only going to last a couple of days.

Preparing

There are a lot of ways to eat pears. They're good with prosciutto. You can use them in any recipe that calls for apples. Use several different varieties, all on the green side, to make a terrific pie. My aunt used to make pear pies just like apple pies, mixing in one or two quinces. You can poach pears and serve them with strawberry sauce for a simple, very pretty dessert that tastes great.

During the holidays, line a basket with napkins, pile up Comices or Forelles or a mix, tuck in sprigs of holly and maybe a few ornaments, and you'll have a pretty centerpiece that's also a good way to ripen the fruit.

Christmas Pears with Strawberry Sauce   6 servings

6 Comice pears, peeled but with stem and base left intact
¾ cup water
1 teaspoon lemon juice
½ cup sugar
Strawberry Sauce

Preheat the oven to 350°F.

Stand the pears in a large casserole. Add the water, lemon juice, and sugar. Cover and bake for 45 minutes. Remove from the oven and set aside.

When ready to serve, place the pears on a serving platter, pouring the cooking liquid over them. Top with strawberry sauce.

Strawberry Sauce   6 servings

2 cups fresh (or frozen, thawed) strawberries, washed and hulled
¼ cup water
1 tablespoon lemon juice
3 tablespoons cornstarch
⅓ cup brandy
red food coloring (optional)

Place the strawberries in a medium-sized saucepan, add the water and lemon juice, and bring to a boil over moderate heat. When the strawberries are soft, remove from the heat and allow to cool slightly.

Pour the mixture into a blender or food processor and puree until smooth. Strain through a sieve, then return the mixture to the saucepan. Gradually stir in the cornstarch, brandy, and food coloring. Cook over low heat, stirring constantly, until thickened.

Pear

Pear Praline Pie 6 servings

PECAN PRALINE TOPPING

½ **cup packed brown sugar**

½ **cup chopped pecans**

⅓ **cup flour**

¼ **cup (½ stick) unsalted butter**

FILLING

5 pears, such as Packham, Comice, Bartlett, Bosc, cored and sliced

⅔ **cup sugar**

¼ **cup flour**

½ **teaspoon grated lemon zest**

½ **teaspoon ground ginger**

pinch salt

1 unbaked 9-inch pie shell

Preheat the oven to 350°F.

First prepare the topping by mixing the brown sugar, pecans, and flour in a bowl. Cut in the butter and blend until the mixture resembles very coarse cornmeal.

Prepare the filling by tossing the pears with the sugar, flour, lemon zest, ginger, and salt. Stir until the pears are well coated.

Sprinkle one quarter of the pecan mixture over the pie crust. Top with the pear mixture and sprinkle with the remaining pecan topping.

Bake for 40 minutes. Serve hot or cold, with ice cream or whipped cream if desired.

Pepper

Peppers are native to America and didn't become known in Europe or Asia until the sixteenth century. Related to the tomato, they come in all shapes and sizes and range in flavor from very sweet and mild to so hot they can actually burn the skin. None of them is related to black pepper, which is actually the berry of an Asian shrub, although red cayenne pepper, paprika, and prepared chile powder are all derived from native American peppers.

Varieties

Sweet peppers include the commonly available bell pepper and thin-walled frying peppers. Chile peppers come in an enormous range of sizes, shapes, and degrees of heat—from very mild green chiles to jalapeños to fiery Scotch Bonnets (or habañeros). These and other varieties too numerous to name are used in Mexican and southwestern cooking, as well as in Indian, Chinese, Thai, and other Asian dishes.

Bell Peppers The green bell pepper, which is available year round at supermarkets all over the country, is a shiny, thick-walled sweet pepper shaped something like a bell. It has a sweet, refreshing flavor and a firm, crunchy flesh. California, Florida, and Texas are the biggest producers in the United States, but bell peppers are grown in almost every state.

Green bell peppers are simply immature versions of sweet red peppers. The red version is sweeter and more tender, and it spoils faster than the green pepper. It's also more expensive because growers get a lower yield of reds from each plant. At the end of the season, however, when they are coming on very quickly, ripe red peppers will be less expensive than they are during the rest of the year. Bell peppers that are green with red patches, usually called "suntans," have reached an intermediate stage. Very good and sweet, they're almost always the least expensive peppers on the market.

Cheese peppers, also called bull-nosed peppers, are simply a strain of bell pepper that has an extra-thick wall and a flattened shape. They are a superb all-round pepper that also makes an absolutely wonderful pickle. My mother made the best pickled peppers in the world.

Yellow, orange, white, and even deep purple varieties of sweet peppers—largely imports from Holland—are now showing up in most markets. These colorful varieties tend to be even sweeter and crisper than their green or red brothers, and they command premium prices. Holland has practically made their cultivation a national pastime, and it produces wonderful peppers—exceptionally crisp and sweet, with a very thick wall.

Frying Peppers Also called Italian frying peppers, Italianelles, or cubanels, these long, pale green peppers are sweet and tender and have a thin skin. They are usually either sautéed in olive oil or stuffed and baked with the stems and seeds intact, as the seeds give the peppers their characteristic flavor and sweet taste.

Chile Peppers Generally, the tinier the chile, the hotter the taste, although there are no hard-and-fast rules. Even the same variety can be mild to hot, depending on local growing conditions. Jalapeños are the ones most often found fresh. Small and plump, with a pointed end, jalapeños range from an inch and a half to three inches long and from dark green to bright red. They are moderately hot to very hot. The smaller serranos, which are also dark green to red and shaped like little bullets, tend to be a bit hotter. They are usually added to sauces and cooked dishes, roasted, or pickled. Banana peppers, which are relatively large and yellow and range from mild to moderately hot, and fresh mild green chiles, which are large and pale green, are available in many markets. If you like the distinctive flavor of jalapeños but can't take the heat, try the mild green chiles, which have a similar flavor without the fire. Most other varieties—including the tiny hot peppers used in Asian cuisines—are either sold dry or are limited to specialty stores and ethnic neighborhoods. Handle *all* of them with care.

Season Bell peppers are excellent bought locally at the peak of the season in your area, but good-quality green bell peppers are available year round, and red sweet peppers nearly year round, although they're most abundant in the summer. The peak season in the United States is between July and November. Peppers are most expensive in midwinter and late spring. Those that are shipped any distance are always waxed to prevent loss of moisture and crispness.

Frying peppers are most abundant during your local growing season—the summer and fall months. Frying peppers out of Florida are available for a little longer into the fall, but shipments tend to taper off in the late winter and early spring, until the next crop comes in.

Chile peppers are a little harder to find. California jalapeños are available pretty much year round, but other varieties like long hot peppers and cherry peppers are easiest to find in season in your local growing area, about the same time local bell peppers are in season.

Selecting Whatever the variety, choose firm, crisp, shiny peppers with a good bright color and a green stem. They should be hard, not limp, with no wrinkles or withering or signs of mold. Those that have lost some crispness or are less than perfect can be fried or chopped and added to cooked dishes, but those that are to be stuffed or eaten raw should be top quality.

Storing Refrigerated in the crisper drawer, peppers will keep for up to three or four days, but they will lose their crispness and get limp in fairly short order. Left at room temperature, they'll lose their crunch in a matter of hours. Don't wash until you're ready to use them.

Preparing Bell peppers should be washed, stemmed, and seeded. They can be sliced raw into salads, added to crudité platters, or used to make salsa. They are good stuffed and baked or added to meat loaf.

The stems and seeds should be left *in* frying peppers during cooking because they add a great deal to the flavor. To fry, simply sauté in a little olive oil until very tender, then remove the stems after they're done. A small seedpod will come away with the stem. Frying peppers are excellent stuffed with ricotta cheese and baked, but be careful handling them, as the walls are thin and will break or tear easily. Frying peppers are also a key ingredient in the classic Italian dish of sausage and peppers. A lot of people use bell peppers instead because frying peppers cook down and it takes more of them to get the same quantity cooked. But to my mind, the frying pepper is the only one to use for sausage and peppers. I don't think anything else compares to its sweet taste!

Handle hot chile peppers with extreme care, and wash your hands thoroughly after preparing them. Not only will the residue burn your lips and really burn your eyes if you touch them after handling peppers, but it will also transfer to other fruits and vegetables.

Pepper

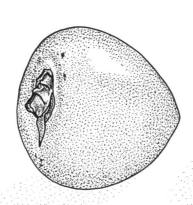
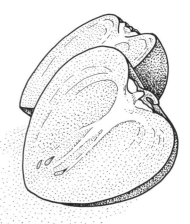

Persimmon

Known as the divine food in Japan because it's so sweet, the persimmon is an orange to orange-red fruit about the size of an apple, with four prominent, large, papery leaves at the crown. It has a very thin, smooth, delicate skin that bruises easily if not handled with care. The persimmon is one of the sweetest of all fruits when it's ripe.

The Japanese have cultivated and improved the persimmon for more than one thousand years. They consider it a national fruit and recommend it for the relief of fatigue and hangovers—probably because it's so nutritious. It is the fruit of the ornamental ebony plant, very rare in a genus that produces almost no other edible fruit. Brought to Europe by Portuguese explorers in the sixteenth century, and later to Brazil and parts of the West Indies, persimmon seeds were introduced to North America by Commodore Perry in 1855.

Aside from China and Japan, major producers include California, Brazil, Chile, Spain, France, Italy, and Israel. Most recently New Zealand and Australia have started to produce and ship persimmons in great quantities.

Varieties

Although there are hundreds of varieties, only two principal types are well known here: Hachiya and Fuyu. The Hachiya which is incredibly sweet when ripe, is full of mouth-puckering tannic acid when it's not. The Fuyu, a newer variety, has had the tannic acid bred out.

241

Hichiya are bright, heart shaped, and orange-red inside and out. They have an exotic taste but can only be eaten fully ripe, when the tannic acid has dissipated—a stage they don't reach until they are very soft. The black seeds in the center are edible, but they can be discarded, along with the skin, which retains tannic acid longer than the flesh and usually isn't eaten unless the fruit is very soft.

Fuyus, sometimes called fujis or marus, look like brilliant orange tomatoes or apples. This new variety is unusual because it can be eaten either soft or while it's still quite firm. Fuyus have a few large brown seeds that should be discarded.

Season Persimmons are available nearly year round. California persimmons are available from September to November, with the bulk harvested in October. Fuyus from Japan and Israel are usually shipped between November and January. Brazilian persimmons are on the market between February and April; those from New Zealand from March to May, and those from Chile from April to May.

Selecting Avoid persimmons with greenish or yellow skins and those that show cracks or splits. The four leaves should still be attached to the stem end.

Storing A Hachiya in good condition will often need to be ripened at home. Leave it out on the counter at room temperature or hasten the process by putting it into a paper bag with a banana or apple. The ethylene gas from the other fruit will help the persimmon ripen. A fully ripe Hachiya will be slightly wrinkled or have a few brown spots. At this very soft stage, almost like a firm jelly, it's at the peak of perfection and should be eaten immediately.

Refrigerate or eat Fuyus while they're still fairly firm—about like a ripe pear.

Once persimmons are ripe, refrigerate them as soon as possible.

Preparing Persimmons can be blanched to remove the skin easily. Just dip in boiling water for a few seconds, then plunge in cold water. Or simply wash before eating. Pluck or cut out the top leaves. A ripe Hachiya can be halved or quartered and the flesh scooped out with a spoon. A Fuyu can be eaten out of hand, like an apple, and the firm flesh makes it a good addition to fruit salad.

A soft, ripe persimmon can be wrapped whole in plastic or foil and eaten partly

Persimmon

frozen like a sorbet. The flesh can also be pureed with a little lemon juice and used as a topping for ice cream or as a filling for layer cakes and crepes.

Because they are readily available during the early winter, persimmons are a good addition to holiday fare and make a wonderfully colorful decoration when arranged and allowed to ripen in a fruit bowl or Christmas basket.

Broiled Persimmons   2 to 4 servings

2 ripe persimmons, halved lengthwise and pitted

4 tablespoons brown sugar

2 tablespoons unsalted butter

Preheat the broiler.

Place the persimmons in a small, greased baking pan. Sprinkle each half with a tablespoon of brown sugar and dot with ½ tablespoon of butter. Broil for 2 minutes, or until the brown sugar begins to bubble. Serve hot.

Stuffed Persimmons   4 servings

4 ripe persimmons, halved lengthwise and pitted

4 figs, halved

½ teaspoon ground cinnamon, or more to taste

½ cup sliced almonds

1 tablespoon Frangelica (hazelnut liqueur), or more to taste

Place the persimmons on a large platter. Using a sharp knife, make an X in each half, and place a fig on the X. Sprinkle with cinnamon, sliced almonds, and Frangelica. Serve at room temperature.

Persimmon

Persimmon and Yogurt Salad   4 servings

12 to 16 Bibb or leaf lettuce leaves, preferably a soft-leafed lettuce

2 to 3 ripe Fuyu or Hachiya persimmons

2 kiwis

1 banana

1 starfruit

½ teaspoon ground cinnamon

pinch ground nutmeg

DRESSING

1½ cups plain yogurt, or ½ cup cream, if desired

1 tablespoon orange liqueur

½ tablespoon vanilla extract

1 to 2 teaspoons sugar

Arrange the lettuce leaves on four salad plates. Slice and arrange the fruit over the lettuce and sprinkle with cinnamon and nutmeg. Blend the dressing ingredients and drizzle over the fruit.

Pineapple

Once known as the fruit of kings, for many years pineapples were available only to natives of the tropics and to wealthy Europeans. Despite the fact that the pineapple has become a familiar item in U.S. markets, it's still a true exotic. For one thing, it is a member of the bromeliad family, in which edible fruits are rare. A pineapple starts out as a stalk of a hundred or more flowers that shoots up from a plant about three feet tall. Each flower develops a fruit that forms one of the scales on the outside of the pineapple. The more scales or marks on a pineapple, the stronger the tropical taste will

Pineapple

be. A pineapple with fewer and larger scales will have a milder but sweeter flavor and more juice.

It was probably the Guarani Indians who took pineapples on sea voyages as provisions and to prevent scurvy, thus spreading the plants from their native Paraguay throughout South and Central America. Columbus called the fruit *piña* when he found it in 1493—*piña* because he thought it looked like a pinecone—and from that we got the name.

The hybrid we know today first appeared around 1700, when the Dutch improved the fruit by crossbreeding. They sold cuttings of the plant to the English, who raised them as hothouse plants. It wasn't until the nineteenth century that canned pineapple began to come out of Hawaii. If you wanted a fresh Hawaiian pineapple, you had to go there to get one. Picked ripe, as the Hawaiian variety has to be, a fresh pineapple simply could not survive the long journey by ship. It was only when air transport became available that fresh Hawaiian pineapple began to arrive in mainland markets.

Varieties

There are two main varieties of pineapples: Red Spanish and Cayenne. The *Red Spanish* is the most commonly available. It is a deep orange color, with white to yellow meat and a crown of hard, spiky leaves on top. A recently developed "thornless" variety has a softer, smoother leaf crown that makes the pineapple easier to handle. Red Spanish pineapples are grown in Honduras, Costa Rica, Puerto Rico, Mexico, and elsewhere in Central America.

The *Cayenne* pineapple is the Hawaiian variety. The scales on a ripe Cayenne tend to be a lighter yellow, the leaves have a smoother edge, and the pineapple itself is much larger and more elongated than the Red Spanish. The flesh is deep yellow.

There are three other less-common varieties. One, called Sugarloaf, is a heavy, round variety with a pointed top that's cultivated in Mexico and Venezuela. Sugarloaf is another big pineapple that can reach ten pounds. Finally, the sweetest pineapples I have ever eaten come from Africa's Ivory Coast. They show up here only rarely—I've had them only two or three times in all the years I've been in the business. If you ever come across them—most likely in June, July, or August—buy some.

Of the pineapples readily available here, to my taste the Cayenne is by far the best, although it can be two or three times as expensive as the Red Spanish. It is sweeter and juicier than the Red Spanish, which is picked greener because it's shipped

245 Pineapple

by boat instead of by air. If you're in the islands where they're grown, by all means buy and eat Red Spanish pineapples—they'll have been picked ripe and they'll be excellent. If you see a Red Spanish in the States that looks and smells good, it's going to be pretty good too. For consistent quality and sweetness, however, Cayennes are your best bet. The tag "Jet Fresh" tells you the pineapple is a Hawaiian Cayenne picked ripe and flown in. The Dole and Del Monte labels also indicate a Cayenne pineapple, although they may not be Hawaiian. Cayennes are now being cultivated in Honduras and Costa Rica by both companies. They're a little more expensive than the Red Spanish, but cheaper than those from Hawaii.

Season For Hawaiian pineapples, the peak season generally comes in April and May, but they're available year round. Caribbean pineapples have two seasons: December through February and August through September.

Selecting Many people think that if you can easily pull a leaf out of the crown, the pineapple is ripe, but this test doesn't tell you anything useful. Like tomatoes, pineapples are considered mature when they develop a little color break. If a pineapple at the market looks green, take a look at the base. If it has begun to turn a little orange or red there, you'll be able to ripen it at home. If there is no break, the pineapple was picked too green. It will have a woody texture and will never be very sweet.

The pineapple should be very firm, never soft or spongy, with no bruises or soft spots. If you find a good-looking pineapple at your market and you're going to use it right away, ask your produce manager to cut it in half to make sure it's not discolored inside. Reject it if it is.

Finally, use your nose. If the pineapple has a good aroma, it's ripe. If you can't smell much of anything, it needs to be ripened. If it has a fermented smell, don't buy it!

Ripening and Storing To ripen a pineapple, stand it upside down on the counter. That's right, stand it on the leaf end. This makes the sugar flow toward the top and keeps the pineapple from fermenting at the bottom. Let it ripen for a few days. When it develops a golden color and smells good, it's ripe.

Peeled pineapple should be wrapped in plastic and refrigerated. If it's not wrapped well, a pineapple will absorb other food odors in your refrigerator.

Pineapple

A lot of supermarkets have a machine that will cut and core your pineapple for you, but it wastes up to 35 percent of the fruit. Pineapples are not that difficult to cut. Just twist off the leaves, lay the pineapple on its side, and slice it like a loaf of bread. Then peel and core each slice. I just cut off the peel and eat the slices with my fingers— around the core, like an apple. That's my favorite recipe for ripe pineapple! If you want to serve the pineapple chilled, I suggest that you chill it whole, then slice and peel after it's cold.

Pineapple Caramel Skillet Cake   12 to 14 servings

4 cups fresh pineapple, cut into cubes

1½ cups sugar

5 ounces unsalted butter

8 ounces pecan halves

2 cups yellow cake batter

Preheat the oven to 350°F.

Divide the pineapple cubes equally into two 10-inch nonstick, ovenproof skillets. Sprinkle half the sugar over the pineapple in each pan. Cook over medium heat about 10 minutes. Drain, reserving the liquid, and setting the pineapple aside. Return the liquid to the skillets, add half the butter to each, and cook over medium heat until the liquid has thickened. Cool.

Arrange half of the drained pineapple over the liquid in the bottom of each skillet. Around the sloping sides of each pan, make a border of pecan halves, top sides down, ends pointing toward the edge of the pan. Divide the cake batter between the skillets. Bake for 35 minutes. Cool 5 minutes and invert on serving platters.

Plantain

In the Southern Hemisphere, a good part of the dinner is this cooking banana, which is served not for dessert but as a main dish. In the tropics and subtropics, it's treated like a staple—fried, baked, boiled, grilled, or combined with other fruits and vegetables.

Imported from Central America, the plantain is often ignored here because people judge it as if it were a banana and decide it's either too green, too black, or too large. Don't let its looks deceive you. Unless a plantain is rock hard, moldy, or practically liquid, chances are it is good. For each stage of ripeness, the plantain has a different taste and different cooking requirements.

When the peel is green to yellow, plantains are bland and starchy and can be cooked like potatoes. As the peel changes from yellow to black, the plantain gradually changes its character from vegetable to fruit, developing greater sweetness and a banana aroma but holding its firm shape, even after cooking. Unlike a banana, a black plantain is merely ripe. Take the greener ones home and let them ripen. At room temperature, they'll ripen slowly to the stage you want.

Season Like bananas, plantains are imported year round.

Selecting You can usually find plantains at all stages of ripeness. Because they're firmer, a ripe plantain is less likely to be bruised than a banana, but you don't want it mushy. A black plantain should still feel firm. Avoid plantains that are cracked or moldy.

Storing Plantains last a long time at room temperature, gradually ripening and changing color. When a plantain is black, it should still feel as firm as a firm banana. If it's still very hard, throw it out. Even when it's ripe, a plantain keeps well. It can be refrigerated if you wish, and unlike a banana it can also be frozen. To freeze, peel the plantain first and wrap tightly in plastic.

Preparing The greener the plantain, the harder it is to peel. A black plantain will peel like a banana; other stages are unpredictable. For greener plantains, cut off both ends, then score the skin lengthwise in several places to make peeling easier.

Plantain

Experience will teach you what degree of ripeness is best for your purposes, but generally, a green or greenish plantain will be very hard and starchy, with little banana flavor and no sweetness. They require a fairly long cooking time and, like potatoes, can be boiled or mashed. They are excellent sliced thin and fried like potato chips, or cut into chunks, boiled, and added to salty or spicy soups and stews.

Yellow-ripe plantains can be prepared in the same ways, but they will have a lovely creamy texture and a light banana scent when they're cooked. They are much more tender than green plantains but much firmer than bananas. You can rinse them, cut into fairly thick cross sections, boil until tender, then peel the chunks and serve them as a side dish. If you plan to add them to soups, stews, or vegetable mixtures, peel them first.

Half-ripe plantains are also excellent grilled. Cuban cooks peel the plantains, cut them on the diagonal, and grill them slowly over a low fire with a little oil or melted butter. Turn and brush them with additional oil or butter until they are tender and creamy inside.

Black-ripe plantains are superb cooked any way you'd cook a ripe banana. They're delicious sautéed and will cook for a longer time than bananas without falling apart, permitting full development of their flavor and aroma. They'll also absorb the flavors of whatever seasonings you use.

Plum

Wild plums have been treasured by the Chinese for two thousand years. In the United States the biggest crop of commercially grown plums comes from hybrids grown in California out of Asian stocks, which were introduced in the 1870s by Luther Burbank. Burbank brought trees back from Japan, planted them on his farm in Santa Rosa, and through crossbreeding produced many modern varieties still popular today. Plums come in a wide variety of sizes and colors—red, yellow, purple, green, blue, and black. Like most produce, they have a season, and that season is summer.

In addition to California, plums are also cultivated in fruit-growing areas of New England and the Midwest, and there are indigenous varieties that grow from the Mississippi River west to the Rocky Mountains and from Canada to the Gulf States. There are also various lovely regional varieties that abound in different parts of the country,

such as the beach plum of the Atlantic Coast, whose astringent fruits are primarily used in jellies and preserves, but these aren't commercially cultivated.

California produces about 90 percent of the commercial crop—more than two hundred different varieties that ripen at different times—from early to late summer, with a few in season into the fall. The following dozen, in order of their appearance, account for the lion's share of the crop.

Early-Season Plums In mid-May, *Red Beauts* are the first on the market, with *Black Beauts* following around Memorial Day. The Red Beaut has a bright red skin and mild-flavored yellow flesh and ranges in size from six to nine plums per pound. The Black Beaut has a thick, tart skin and very juicy flesh that turns reddish as the fruit matures. It closely resembles the Red Beaut, except that the skin is red to purplish black and the fruit runs a bit larger—from four to six plums per pound. Red Beauts stay on the market through early June; Black Beauts until the end of June.

Burbank's classic *Santa Rosa* comes next, generally on the market from the first week of June through the Fourth of July weekend. I like this variety a lot. The plums have a purplish crimson skin with the light freckling that's characteristic of all Rosa-type plums. The flesh is tart and red at the pit, radiating into sweet yellow flesh near the skin. The combination gives them their classic sweet-tart plum flavor. Santa Rosas range in size from five to eight plums per pound.

Another good plum, the *Black Amber,* arrives in early June and continues through mid-July. It has a smooth, black skin with amber flesh and a small pit. It is flattish in shape and large in diameter. The size ranges from four to six plums per pound.

Midseason Plums The *Queen Rosa* is a lightly freckled, purplish red plum with juicy, mild, light amber flesh. When cooked or raw it has a tangy flavor, but leaving the skin on adds some sweetness to the cooked fruit. It's available from mid-June to mid-July and ranges in size from three to six plums per pound.

The *El Dorado* is also available from mid-June to mid-July. It ranges in color from bright red to reddish black with a purple tint. The amber flesh is mellow throughout, and although it's juicy, it retains its firmness in cooking and has a good shelf life. Size ranges from five to eight plums per pound.

Of all the plums, I think the *LaRoda* is the best. It's available from late June through

Plum

the end of July. It has a freckled dark red to purple skin that occasionally shows a little yellow background. The skin is thin and tender, and the flesh is golden, sweet, and juicy. It's great eaten out of hand and very tangy when cooked unpeeled. The size ranges from four to seven plums per pound.

The *Simka,* also known as the "New Yorker" variety, is another good one. It's a larger, heart-shaped plum with a red to reddish purple skin, light freckling, and a firm golden flesh with sweet flavor. It's available throughout the month of July. Size ranges from three to six plums per pound.

Late-Season Plums

The *Friar* begins the later-season plums, available beginning in July and going through Labor Day. It's about the most popular of all the plums. A mature Friar has a deep black skin and a small pit. The light amber flesh is juicy and sweet, with a contrasting tart flavor in the skin. It ranges in size from three big plums to seven plums per pound, and it keeps well.

In my business the *Kelsey* is one of the most valuable plums because its bright green skin is a beautiful contrast to the red and purple varieties on display. As it ripens, the skin turns from green to yellow splashed with red. The sweet, greenish yellow flesh is one of the *least* tart among the plums. The Kelsey is available from the Fourth of July well into August. Size ranges from three to six plums per pound.

The *Casselman,* which starts arriving in late July, has good holding qualities that make it available throughout September. It has a bright red to crimson exterior and light freckling. The firm, golden flesh has a tangy, sweet flavor when ripe. Most Casselmans weigh in at six plums per pound.

The *Angeleno* finishes the plum season. It is a heart-shaped plum with a full dark red to purple-blue skin. The light amber flesh is sweet when fully ripe. Harvest begins the third week in August, but because of their excellent keeping qualities, Angelenos can be shipped through Thanksgiving. They generally run from four to six and a half plums per pound.

Season

Plums are generally available during the summer months; see varieties (above) for specific shipping periods.

Selecting

Choose plums that are firm and plump. A ripe one is tart-sweet and juicy and will give to a gentle squeeze.

Storing Plums are easily ripened at home; just leave them at room temperature in a paper bag with the top loosely closed. (Plums prefer paper to plastic.) This concentrates the naturally occurring ethylene gas that helps the fruit ripen. Check the plums daily and remove when the flesh gives to gentle pressure. Either eat ripe plums immediately or store in the refrigerator, where they'll keep for several days.

Betty's Plum Torte   4 to 6 servings

½ cup (1 stick) unsalted butter

1 teaspoon vanilla extract

½ cup sugar

3 egg yolks

½ cup cornstarch

1 cup flour

1¼ teaspoons baking powder

5 plums, pitted and sliced

2 teaspoons ground cinnamon

3 tablespoons sugar

Preheat the oven to 350°F.

In a large bowl, beat the butter, vanilla, sugar, and egg yolks. Add the cornstarch, flour, and baking powder, beating until the batter is well mixed and has a doughlike consistency.

Place the mixture in a greased 8-inch square or 9-inch round baking pan, pressing the dough onto the bottom and sides of the pan. Top with the plums and sprinkle with cinnamon and sugar.

Bake for 1 hour.

Savory Microwaved Plum Sauce   Makes 2 cups

about 6 plums, cut up

4 teaspoons soy sauce

2 teaspoons cornstarch

2 teaspoons sugar

1 teaspoon grated fresh ginger

1 clove garlic, minced

Puree the plums in a food processor or blender (you should have 2 cups). Combine with the remaining ingredients in a 1-quart glass container and microwave on full power, uncovered, for about 8 minutes, stirring every 3 minutes. The sauce is done when it's thick and clear.

No-Sugar Plum Jam   Makes about 4 cups

about 24 pitted, chopped plums (to equal 9 cups)

2 packets (1¾ ounces each) powdered pectin

¼ cup powdered sugar substitute (usually 40 individual packets)

Place the chopped plums in a heavy 3-quart saucepan. Stir in the pectin. Cook 15 minutes, stirring constantly, until the jam reaches the desired thickness. Remove from the heat and stir in the sweetener.

Ladle into clean, hot jars, leaving ¼ inch headspace. Seal and allow the jam to cool to room temperature, then store for up to 3 weeks in the refrigerator or freeze for as long as a year. If you're using a sugar substitute that doesn't break down in cooking, you may process the jars for 15 minutes in a boiling water bath, then cool and store at room temperature. Refrigerate after opening.

Plum

Plum Kabobs with Plum Sauce

Skewer quartered, pitted plums with pineapple chunks, fresh or canned apricot halves, and drained whole water chestnuts, alternating the fruits. Grill or broil briefly, just until hot, and serve with Savory Plum Sauce. The kabobs are a good accompaniment to grilled chicken, pork, or shrimp.

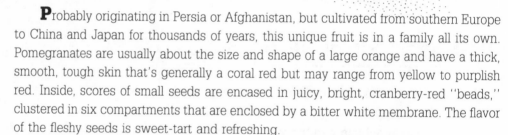

Pomegranate

Probably originating in Persia or Afghanistan, but cultivated from southern Europe to China and Japan for thousands of years, this unique fruit is in a family all its own. Pomegranates are usually about the size and shape of a large orange and have a thick, smooth, tough skin that's generally a coral red but may range from yellow to purplish red. Inside, scores of small seeds are encased in juicy, bright, cranberry-red "beads," clustered in six compartments that are enclosed by a bitter white membrane. The flavor of the fleshy seeds is sweet-tart and refreshing.

The name pomegranate derives from the Latin, meaning "apple of numerous seeds"—and are they numerous! Pomegranates take a fair amount of patience to eat, but they're worth the effort. When I first started working on "People Are Talking," I asked Betty to seed a stack of pomegranates for me. The folks around the station loved it, but it took her six hours to get enough seeds for two bowls full! That's a loving wife for you.

The pomegranate was a symbol of fertility to the Greeks. It is frequently mentioned in the Old Testament, and the pomegranate form was used by the Hebrews as an architectural motif. The remains of pomegranates have even been discovered in ancient Egyptian tombs. In ancient times pomegranate juice was used as a medicine and as a dye. In fact, it's still used to produce the beautiful scarlet color found in many Persian rugs. After the pomegranate was brought to Spain by the Moors, it spread throughout Europe. It was introduced to the Carribean and California by Spanish missionaries about two hundred years ago.

There are a few different varieties, but they show only slight variations in size, skin color, and sweetness.

Season

Pomegranates are available from September to December, with the peak in October.

Selecting

For a juicy, sweet pomegranate, choose unblemished fruit that's heavy for its size. The larger the fruit, the better developed and sweeter the flesh inside—but it should always feel heavy in the hand. That means it has a lot of juice.

Storing

Keep at room temperature for six to seven days or refrigerate. Under refrigeration a pomegranate will last three months or longer if it's in good condition. The thick skin protects the juicy flesh inside. Years ago, in fact, nomads took pomegranates with them into the desert as a source of water because they kept for a long time without drying out.

Both the seeds and juice can be frozen.

Preparing

To remove the edible seeds, either score the skin and peel it back or cut the fruit into quarters. Gently separate the seeds from the white membrane with your fingers. Remove the membrane completely; it's bitter and will make your mouth pucker. And be careful not to get the juice on your clothes because it stains. However you eat it, a pomegranate requires some time and patience.

I often take a shortcut. I roll the fruit back and forth on the counter, much as I do lemons or limes, or thoroughly massage the whole fruit in my hands to gently crush the pulp and release the juice—always taking care not to break the skin. Then I take a small bite out of the skin and suck the juice out.

Pomegranate fruit can be eaten plain or with a sprinkle of sugar or salt. Some people eat the seeds inside the pink flesh; some spit them out. The fleshy seeds make a beautiful ruby garnish when sprinkled over fruit salad, ice cream, or crepes, as well as over various cooked dishes from omelettes to grilled fish.

Pomegranate

Pomegranate juice is delicious on its own, mixed with other juices, or made into sorbet. To prepare the juice, put the fleshy seeds into an extractor or blender, process, then strain and refrigerate or freeze. Try freezing pomegranate juice in an ice cube tray to use later or to put into cold beverages—it makes an exotic drink.

Grenadine Syrup

Pomegranate syrup—grenadine—is excellent as a sauce for baked apples or poached pears and is an ingredient in some cocktails. To prepare, simply mash the fruit lightly with a fork, adding one part sugar to two parts of fruit. Let the mixture stand for a day, then boil, strain out the pits, bottle, and refrigerate.

Sherried Pomegranate Gelatin 4 servings

2 packets unflavored gelatin

3 cups white grape juice

½ cup medium-dry sherry

1 cup seedless red grape halves

3 tablespoons fresh pomegranate seeds

In a small saucepan, sprinkle the gelatin over 1 cup of the grape juice. Let stand for 3 to 4 minutes, until the gelatin softens, then stir over low heat until the gelatin completely dissolves.

Pour the mixture into a medium-sized bowl. Add the remaining grape juice and the sherry. Place the bowl in a larger bowl filled with ice and water, and stir occasionally until the mixture is almost set—about 30 minutes (it should be thick and lumpy).

Using a rubber spatula, gently fold in the grapes and pomegranate seeds, distributing the fruit evenly. Pour into a glass serving dish and chill for several hours.

Pomegranate

Potato

First cultivated in Peru centuries ago, ordinary white or "Irish" potatoes are still grown there—in varieties that include white, blue, red, and even striped and polka-dotted versions. Although we see only a few common ones in most supermarkets, there are more than two hundred varieties of potatoes now being cultivated. A small number of unusual varieties and hybrids can be found in farm markets and specialty produce stores.

A member of the nightshade family, along with the tomato and eggplant, the potato is native to South America. Brought to Europe by Spanish explorers, it was a bit slow to be accepted because many people believed it was poisonous. By the end of the sixteenth century, however, potatoes were regularly taking a place on the table in German households, and now this highly nutritious vegetable is a staple in almost every country in the Western world.

Potatoes store very well, but they don't keep forever. The year-round supply found in the stores is possible because crops from different states are harvested at different times. On the East Coast, for example, potato crops from Florida are the first to arrive on the market. As the season progresses, the potato harvest moves up the coast until the season ends with potatoes from Maine, Nova Scotia, and Prince Edward Island.

"New" potatoes aren't a specific variety; there are many varieties that are good when they're harvested early and shipped directly to market. Although "old" potatoes—potatoes left a long time in the ground—aren't as attractive, they keep a lot better than the new crops and are good winter staples.

White and Russet Potatoes

California new potatoes are light-skinned new potatoes that begin to arrive in May or June. They cook faster and are sweeter than russets or Idaho potatoes, and the tender skin is quite edible. They are fine baked, but because of their thin skin, it's a good idea to wrap them in foil, piercing both the foil and the skin with a fork to release steam.

California russets begin to arrive in August and September. They're often mistaken for Idaho potatoes, but they have a skin that's a bit more leathery. They are excellent baked or made into french fries, and fresh ones are out around the time when the only Idaho potatoes you'll find have been in storage for nearly a year.

The famous *Idaho* potato is harvested in the early fall, but it stores well and is available nine or ten months of the year. Idaho has the right soil and weather conditions to grow a great potato, and it is the variety Americans choose first for baking. The skin is thick and leathery, and the flesh has a relatively low moisture content. Graded by size, Idahos range from 60 to 140 potatoes per 50-pound box.

New York State potatoes start coming in at the beginning of September; that's when they are light, bright, and thin-skinned. By late October the same potato has a thick, dirty-looking skin and will be a good keeper.

Maine potatoes come onto the market next. As Idaho is to baking potatoes, Maine is to mashing potatoes, with soil and weather conditions that produce excellent crops. Growers begin to harvest them from mid- to late fall and continue shipping through the winter and on into May. Early Maine potatoes have a clean skin; as the season progresses, the skin gets dirtier and darker. These "old" potatoes store well, although they tend to sprout. The same holds for potatoes from *Nova Scotia* and *Prince Edward Island,* where the red clay soil produces a potato that has a reddish skin. These winter potatoes have a dirty-looking skin, but they're high in quality.

Redskin and New Potatoes

Although most people think of small red potatoes as "new" potatoes, the terms aren't always synonymous. California potatoes dug early in the season have thin, tender, white skins. Other new potatoes are grown in Florida, North and South Carolina, Virginia, and in states in the Midwest and Northwest.

New red potatoes are harvested at the same time as the whites. They are usually a little sweeter than the whites, with a smooth skin that's a bit thicker (but edible) and flakier than the skins of regular white potatoes. They are best boiled skins on, and can be eaten that way or peeled after cooking.

New red-skin potatoes range from the size of a golf ball to the size of a baseball. They are graded as *A* or *B.* Size B—the smaller of the two—usually costs more per pound than the larger ones.

Florida red potatoes are first shipped in April. They have a very short season, so grab them while they're available. They're at their best when fresh.

Red Bliss potatoes, which are grown in California, Minnesota, and the Dakotas, have a slightly different taste and texture than the Florida reds. The skin is flakier, and the flesh is whiter, harder, and contains less moisture. Red Bliss potatoes are available

Potato

most of the year. The spring and summer varieties go directly to the market and always have a sweeter, milder flavor. Just like white potatoes, the later fall crop of red potatoes is put into storage for shipment during the winter.

Special Varieties

Peewees are very small, thumb-sized potatoes that have become popular for boiling. They were once thought of as culls and left in the field. Less starchy than full-sized potatoes, they now command three to four times their price.

Purple potatoes were originally developed by agricultural schools to be used in the field to mark the boundaries where different varieties had been sown. The purple variety is purple all the way through—and the color does not blanch out with cooking. Although it commands premium prices, it is becoming a popular specialty item. It is a little sweeter than most, and a little starchier. Purple potatoes are novel and colorful mashed or added to other vegetable mixtures.

Yukon Gold, another new hybrid, has a golden color and a buttery flavor. Yellower, sweeter, and heartier than regular potatoes, Yukons whip up beautifully and have a rich look and taste without the addition of butter. You'll have to go to a farm stand or special produce market to find them, and they're likely to be a dollar a pound, but you should definitely try them.

Selecting

Look for potatoes that show no sprouts from the eyes and no wrinkling on the skin, especially if you're buying Maine potatoes. There should be no cuts or dark spots, and the potato should feel heavy in the hand for its size. Avoid potatoes with a greenish tint to the skin—these have been exposed to the light for too long and have a bitter taste. Potatoes prefer the dark, and available light even at the supermarket or at home will make them develop a green tint after a few days. New white potatoes from California are especially susceptible to greening.

Storing

New potatoes should be stored in the refrigerator if you plan to keep them more than a few days. Old potatoes should be kept in a dark, dry place that's not too warm.

Preparing

Thin-skinned potatoes or new potatoes can be eaten skins and all; simply scrub them before cooking. Old or stored potatoes need to be scrubbed very well or peeled.

Potato eyes that have started to sprout can easily be removed if you first push the sprout in with your thumb, then pluck it out.

Potato

Betty's Creamy Potato Soup   4 servings

8 medium-sized potatoes, peeled and cut into chunks

½ cup (1 stick) unsalted butter

1 small onion, diced

2 cups heavy cream

2 cups half & half

2 chicken bouillon cubes

1 cup milk

½ teaspoon salt

1 teaspoon freshly ground black pepper

In a large saucepan of water, boil the potatoes until fork-tender. Drain and set aside.

In a stockpot, melt the butter over low heat, add the onion, and gently sauté until soft and translucent (do not brown). Add the potatoes, cream, half & half, bouillon cubes, milk, salt, and pepper. Simmer over low heat until thickened and thoroughly heated, about 30 minutes. If you'd like a thicker soup, add a little cornstarch or flour.

Potato

Betty's Red Potato Salad

12 to 14 servings

4 pounds red potatoes, cubed but not peeled

1 small onion, diced

6 stalks celery, diced

2 hard-boiled eggs, peeled and sliced

1 cup mayonnaise, or more or less to taste

3 tablespoons chopped fresh parsley

salt and freshly ground black pepper to taste

1 tablespoon oil to taste

1 tablespoon vinegar to taste

In a large saucepan of water, boil the potatoes until fork-tender. Drain and refrigerate in a large bowl until cool.

When potatoes are cool, add the onion, celery, and eggs. Gently mix in the mayonnaise, parsley, salt, pepper, oil, and vinegar. Taste and correct the seasonings.

Potato

Potato, Sweet

Ninety percent of what you see in the stores marked "yams" is actually a variety of sweet potato. The true yam is a tuber that can get as large as 100 pounds and grows primarily in the tropical zones of Africa. The potato with the sweet orange-red flesh that grows in the American South was dubbed a yam by African slaves, and the name stuck.

American sweet potatoes are members of the morning glory family. The rich orange-fleshed variety is harvested beginning in August; the fresh ones that show up on the market then have not been cured. The bulk of the crop is held in a heated, humidity-controlled environment for about a week. This "cures" the potato and converts much of its starch to dextrins and sugar. A cured sweet potato is actually much sweeter than an uncured one and is what usually shows up on the Thanksgiving table.

There are two other varieties of sweet potato that are much less frequently seen these days than the one that masquerades as a yam. The *red sweet potato* has a yellow flesh that's a bit sweeter than the *white sweet potato*, which has a white, more fibrous flesh. The red sweet potato has a dark, reddish skin and is in season about the same time as the yam type—starting in September. It keeps better than the *white sweet potato*, which has a very short season—usually the last couple of weeks in August.

Season Avoid buying sweet potatoes in June and July; by then most of them have been stored for nearly a year. Uncured sweet potatoes start showing up on the market in late August; cured sweet potatoes arrive around the end of October. By Thanksgiving almost all that are on the market have been cured. The less common white and red sweet potatoes have a much shorter season at the end of the summer.

Selecting Look for bright-colored, unbruised skin with no soft spots. Look at the ends of the potatoes, which should be firm. Most sweet potatoes have some fibrous roots on them; these are not a problem.

Store sweet potatoes in a dark, dry place. Cured sweet potatoes will hold longer than **Storing**
uncured ones. Don't refrigerate any of them raw, or the flesh will blacken when it's
cooked. A cooked sweet potato, on the other hand, can be refrigerated for as long as
a week.

Catherine's Sweet Potato Pie   6 to 8 servings

8 medium-sized sweet potatoes, peeled and cut into chunks

½ cup sugar

6 eggs

½ cup (1 stick) unsalted butter, melted

1 8-ounce can sweetened condensed milk

¼ cup flour

1 teaspoon vanilla extract

1 teaspoon lemon extract

2 unbaked 9-inch pie shells

Preheat the oven to 450°F.

In a large saucepan of water, boil the sweet potatoes until fork-tender. Drain
and place in a large bowl. Using a fork or ricer, mash the potatoes. Add the sugar,
eggs, butter, milk, and flour, and blend well. Add the vanilla and lemon extract and
beat with a wooden spoon until light and fluffy.

Fill the pie shells with the potato mixture and bake for 15 to 20 minutes, or
until the tops are light brown. Serve warm or cold, with whipped cream or ice cream
if desired.

Potato, Sweet

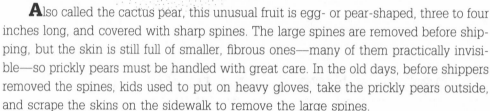

Prickly Pear

Also called the cactus pear, this unusual fruit is egg- or pear-shaped, three to four inches long, and covered with sharp spines. The large spines are removed before shipping, but the skin is still full of smaller, fibrous ones—many of them practically invisible—so prickly pears must be handled with great care. In the old days, before shippers removed the spines, kids used to put on heavy gloves, take the prickly pears outside, and scrape the skins on the sidewalk to remove the large spines.

Depending on the variety and ripeness, prickly pears may have green, yellow, orange, pink, or crimson skins. The thirst-quenching flesh, which ranges in color from green to yellow to red, tastes something like watermelon, but without the sweetness. You may have passed up these exotic-looking fruits at the market, but the prickly pear is an unusually refreshing, juicy fruit that can be prepared in a number of ways. It's well worth trying.

Historically, the prickly pear has been an important source of water to inhabitants of arid and semiarid regions all over the world. Native Americans in the Southwest have long used its juice to help bring down fevers. The cactus grows well without irrigation or pesticides, and it grows everywhere—in Mediterranean countries, Asia, the United States, and Central and South America. Mexico, however, remains the largest producer, consumer, and exporter of the edible prickly pear.

We get two main varieties on the market: Italian imports and those that are grown in California and Mexico. The Italian varieties tend to be greenish yellow to yellow, sometimes with a red blush, and have a yellow flesh. Those from Mexico and California have red flesh and a red skin that's often nearly maroon. Prickly pears from different parts of the world come in a range of colors, but I don't think there's a noticeable difference in the flavor or texture of any variety.

Season Cactus pears from Argentina and Brazil are available year round. Imports from Mexico come in between June and October. Late August to December is the peak season for prickly pears from California and Arizona. These are marketed under the Andy-Boy label and are the top of the line in freshness and ripeness. Prickly pears from the Mediterranean are available in late autumn, and those from Chile from February to April.

Selecting

Always choose a firm, unblemished fruit. Moldy spots are usually an indication of flesh that's too soft and unappetizing. Very firm prickly pears can be ripened at home.

Ripening and Storing

To truly appreciate prickly pears, eat them fully ripe. If the flesh is very firm, let the prickly pear ripen at room temperature until it has a good, relatively uniform color, and just a little give. At that point it's very perishable and should be refrigerated right away.

Preparing

The hundreds of tiny, fibrous, nearly invisible spines in the skin of a prickly pear are very hard to get out of *your* skin once they become embedded in your fingers. Hold the prickly pear by the ends or, better yet, wear protective gloves. To peel, cut a slice off the top and the bottom, then make a skin-deep slash (about one-eighth of an inch) lengthwise down the fruit. Using a couple of forks to start, peel back the skin from the cut; it will come off easily. Then slice the flesh like a loaf of bread. It contains small edible seeds that are excellent for the digestion when eaten in moderation, although many people find them a bit hard and discard them. Discard any fruits that are dry inside.

Ripe prickly pears taste best slightly chilled. They're usually eaten thinly sliced with a squeeze of lemon or lime to enhance the flavor. They're a delicious garnish for chicken or shrimp salad, and they make very good marmalade or sorbet (strain out the seeds for these dishes). Prickly pears make a healthful breakfast when cut into small chunks, mixed with plain yogurt, and sweetened with a little honey.

Prickly pears also make a terrific drink. Peel three or four prickly pears, cut into chunks, and put in a blender with half a cup of orange juice, a squeeze of lemon, and a little honey. Puree the mix until it's smooth, then strain out the seeds and chill or pour over crushed ice. It's delicious as is and also makes a good cocktail mix for tequila or vodka.

Prickly Pear

Cactus Pear Muffins   Makes 12 muffins

2 to 3 cactus pears, peeled, mashed, and drained (about ¾ cup)

½ cup raisins

¼ cup sugar

2 cups flour

2 teaspoons baking powder

½ teaspoon salt

1 egg, beaten

1 cup milk

¼ cup butter, melted

Preheat the oven to 375°F.

In a bowl, combine the cactus pears, raisins, and sugar and set aside.

In another bowl, sift the flour with the baking powder and salt. Add the egg, milk, and butter and stir to just moisten (the batter should be lumpy). Fold in the cactus pear mixture.

Spoon into greased muffin cups, filling each two-thirds full. Bake for 20 minutes, or until a toothpick inserted in the center of a muffin comes out clean. Cool on a wire rack.

Prickly Pear

Pumpkin

Although they're grown in other parts of the world, only in the United States do we use pumpkins to celebrate and symbolize Halloween. Many people never buy pumpkins except to make jack-o'-lanterns, which is too bad because pumpkins supply more beta carotene per serving than any other fruit or vegetable.

Varieties

Some people use *jack-o'-lantern pumpkins* for cooking, but they were developed specifically to be oversized and thin-walled, with a huge seed pocket and a relatively small proportion of flesh.

The smaller *sugar pumpkins,* or pie pumpkins, will give you more meat for cooking purposes and often a better flavor and texture. Sugar pumpkins make an especially delicious pumpkin soup. Buy an extra one, clean out the cavity, and use it as a striking tureen.

If you can find it, I suggest using a variety called the *cheese pumpkin* for pies. It is a medium-sized to large pumpkin with a very flattened shape, a light tan shell, and orange flesh. Found most readily at farm stands and in New England, cheese pumpkins make delicious pies. Regular pumpkins—sugar and especially jack-o'-lantern—sometimes make a stringy filling.

Season

October through December.

Selecting

Whatever kind of pumpkin you're buying, select one with no bruises or soft spots. It may be greenish in color, but left whole in a cool place—not refrigerated—it will ripen and turn orange. Never handle a pumpkin by the stem because it breaks off easily.

Decorating Jack-o'-lanterns

There's a way to decorate pumpkins that's different and colorful. Instead of cutting and hollowing out a pumpkin for your jack-o'-lantern, try leaving it intact and creating a face with fresh vegetables. Depending on what you use, you can give the pumpkins a wide range of personalities. My mother decorated pumpkins this way because it preserved the pumpkin, which she could use in cooking after Halloween was over. She'd use a carrot or parsnip to make a long, witchy nose. She'd make lips out of red peppers, use radishes for the eyes and add string bean eyelashes. She'd slice potatoes to make ears, and make "hair" out of fennel tops. The result was unusual and very striking. My wife, who is quite artistic, picked up a lot of kitchen techniques from my mother, and she has decorated pumpkins for my show that were really something to see.

Peter's Pumpkin Soup 6 to 8 servings

2 small pumpkins

salt and white pepper to season

2 sprigs fresh thyme

2 tablespoons butter

1 carrot, finely diced

1 medium-sized onion, finely diced

2 tablespoons flour

6 cups chicken stock

6 tablespoons heavy cream

ground nutmeg or grated Parmesan cheese

Preheat the oven to 400°F.

Cut the pumpkins in half, scoop out the seeds, and rub the insides with salt and pepper. Put a thyme sprig into each half, invert onto a baking sheet or roasting pan, and bake until tender, about 45 minutes to an hour. Remove from the oven and set aside to cool.

When the pumpkins are cool, scoop out the flesh first and puree in a food processor fitted with the metal blade.

In a stockpot, melt the butter over medium heat. Add the carrot and onion and sauté gently until soft. Add the flour and cook for 2 to 3 minutes. Add the chicken stock and pumpkin puree and bring to a boil. Reduce the heat and simmer, stirring often, for 20 minutes. Add the cream and salt and pepper to taste.

Before serving, garnish with ground nutmeg or Parmesan cheese.

Pumpkin

Quince

A member of the rose family, the quince is related to apples, pears, plums, and many other fruits. It has an ancient history, and some people believe it may have been the fruit named in Genesis as the fruit of the tree of knowledge. Although quinces were a favorite in Grandma's day, they have fallen out of general use, and ordinarily you'll find them only at farm or specialty markets.

Quinces are completely inedible raw; cooked, they're a different story. The yellowish white flesh is firm, dry, and sour when it's raw but turns bright pink when it's cooked, and with a bit of sweetening, it makes wonderful desserts and preserves. Quinces have a smooth green to yellow skin and are either round or pear-shaped. Most are about the size of an apple, with a similar core but more pits. One variety—the *pineapple quince*—is about three times the size of the others. All of them have a lovely fruity fragrance when they're ripe, and a single quince will fill an entire room with its scent.

Quinces originated in western Asia. Long a symbol of love and happiness, they were known as golden apples to the Greeks and Romans, and as a part of the wedding ritual they were dedicated to Aphrodite and Venus. In Portugal, quince is called *mar-*

melo—the origin of the word *marmalade,* which was originally made with quinces. In France they have been used for hundreds of years to make *cotignac,* a kind of sweet cognac or brandy. Because of its high pectin content, the quince was important commercially before the arrival of artificially extracted pectins. In fact, it jells so well that hairdressers once used it to keep elaborate hairdos in place.

Quince trees, once common in gardens throughout New England, now grow in all parts of the world, including the Mediterranean area, Latin America, and the United States.

Season The main season for quinces both here and in Europe starts in September or October and ends in December or January. Quinces from South America are available in April and May.

Selecting Choose large fruit with at least some yellow showing on the skin; as on tomatoes, this color "break" indicates the fruit was picked at a mature stage. As the quince ripens, the skin turns from green to yellow and is easily bruised, often giving the skin a blotchy appearance. Bruising is usually unavoidable; if it's not extreme it won't affect the quality of the fruit.

Storing Leave green quinces at room temperature for three to five days to ripen. Wrap ripe quinces individually in paper towels for protection, then refrigerate. They'll keep as long as several weeks if they're not too badly bruised.

Preparing Wash, peel, and core the fruits before cooking. (You will need a sharp knife.) Because the cut flesh quickly discolors, keep peeled pieces in cold water with some lemon juice if you're preparing a lot of them. Unless you're making marmalade or using a recipe that calls for cooking with sugar, sweeten the quinces after they've been cooked. The cooked flesh will turn dark pink.

Quinces don't fall apart like apples or pears when they're cooked, so they're very good in dishes that have to cook a long time. They make wonderful old-fashioned marmalade and jelly, but there are a dozen other ways to cook them. A quince added to an apple pie will improve the flavor and aroma tremendously. Quinces can be made into a sauce like applesauce that's excellent with roast lamb, pork, or poultry. Prepare

Quince

it as you would applesauce, adding sugar or other sweetening as desired. My mother added a little ginger and it was delicious.

Try baking or stewing halves or slices with raisins, honey, and vanilla; serve with cream for an excellent dessert.

Quince syrup is great on pancakes, ice cream, or fruit salad. Leave a quince out or hang it up, and it will scent a room or closet with a sweet, fruity fragrance.

Quince Compote   4 servings

4 quinces

½ cup water

¼ to ½ cup sugar

1 teaspoon grated fresh ginger

1 cinnamon stick

Wash, peel, and core the quinces to remove all the seeds, then cut the flesh into cubes. In a medium-sized saucepan, combine the water, quinces, sugar, and ginger. Bring to a boil, then reduce heat and simmer 15 to 20 minutes, or until tender. After cooking, add the cinnamon stick and refrigerate until cool.

This simple, delicious compote has a texture and flavor that's almost like chutney.

Radicchio

Radicchio is the Italian name for chicory. *Not* a red cabbage, radicchio is actually the only member of the chicory family that turns red. Young radicchio actually starts out with bright green leaves that turn bright red when the weather gets cool. The radicchio we eat originated in the province of Veneto, where it once grew wild. Italians have cultivated it since the sixteenth century, and much of what we have on the market continues to be imported from Italy.

The best-known variety here has a dark, ruby-colored leaf with round, smooth, shiny, white-ribbed leaves. It's shaped something like a very small head of lettuce, but its leaves are fairly loose—almost like the petals of a flower. There are other, less common varieties that may show flecks of pink, red, or green, but they all have a similar taste. Radicchio has a sharp, slightly bitter flavor akin to that of endive or green chicory, and it adds great zest and color to the salad bowl.

Ten years ago radicchio sold for about six dollars a pound, but as it became more popular it began to be cultivated more widely, and the price has come down. It's still relatively expensive, but a little will go a long way added to other salad greens.

Season

Available year round in California, New Jersey, and Mexico. Italian radicchio is harvested from November through mid-February.

Selecting

Look for compact, firm heads with no brown on the tips of the leaves or at the base. If there's anything to discard, you don't want to buy the head in the first place.

Storing

Radicchio will stay crisp for up to a week if it's enclosed in a plastic bag and refrigerated. Pull off and wash leaves as needed.

Preparing

A zesty and colorful addition to other greens for tossed salads, radicchio is also a colorful garnish and makes an attractive bed for seafood or chicken salad. Italians make salad with radicchio alone, which they dress with olive oil, white wine vinegar, salt, and pepper. Radicchio is also excellent cooked briefly and added to pasta or omelettes—or even breaded and fried, as my mom used to do.

Radish

The fastest-growing of all vegetables, radishes are a favorite in home gardens because they usually are the first thing to come up in the spring. Good radishes are crunchy, spicy, juicy, and low in calories. They're a bright and inexpensive addition to salads and raw vegetable platters. The round red varieties are the most common, but there are also *icicle* radishes—so called because they're long, thin, and white—and a round white radish that to me seems hotter than the red variety.

Radishes are underground roots or bulbs with leafy green tops. The leaves have a spicy flavor something like arugula, although their texture is a bit cottony for my taste. Because the leaves turn yellow quickly, radishes are often sold with the tops removed. Once the tops are cut off, radishes dry out quickly, so these are always packaged in plastic.

Season

Local radishes are in season early in the spring, but radishes from Florida and Texas—the biggest producers—are available all year.

Radish

Whenever they're available, buy bunch radishes with the tops still on. They may cost a little more than cello-pack radishes, but I think they're 100 percent better. The color is often brighter, they have a fresher, spicier flavor, the texture is more tender—not as likely to be woody—and they'll stay fresh and crisp longer.

The earliest radishes are always hotter than those that have stayed in the ground a bit longer, so if you like them mild, wait a few days after the new crop begins before purchasing.

Storing Refrigerate radishes with the tops still on in the crisper drawer or in a plastic bag.

Preparing Twist off the tops, rinse well, and cut a thin slice off each end. Radishes can be prepared a bit ahead of time, covered with water or chopped ice, and refrigerated until you're ready to use them. Enjoy them as is, slice them into salads, or make decorative radish "roses" by making one or two rows of deep slashes all around the circumference. Then put the bulbs in ice water and refrigerate until the "petals" swell and curl out into a flower shape.

Rhubarb

Because we tend to eat rhubarb sweetened and in desserts, we may tend to think of it as a fruit, but it is a vegetable that looks something like very big red celery. That's where the similarity to celery ends. Rhubarb is never eaten raw but is cooked and sweetened to make a delicious sweet-tart pie filling or alternative to applesauce.

There are basically two different types. One is field-grown rhubarb, which has broad, deep pink to red stalks, sometimes streaked with green. The other type is hothouse-grown rhubarb, which is a lighter, softer pink and has much smaller stalks. It is usually more tender and nearly always stringless, but it's expensive and is available mainly in fancy produce stores.

Season Early spring through early summer.

Selecting Look for firm, crisp stalks with no spots or dark patches. The leaves are poisonous and must not be eaten, so rhubarb is usually sold with them already cut off. If the leaves are attached, they should be stiff and vivid green. Avoid rhubarb that has wilted leaves or flabby stalks. On field-grown rhubarb the youngest stems—those on which the leaves aren't fully grown—are more tender and more delicately flavored than the larger stalks.

Storing

Remove any leaves and store rhubarb in the refrigerator *unwashed* in a plastic bag for as long as a week.

Preparing

Rhubarb is sold ripe and, if the leaves have been removed, ready to wash and cook. Again, the leaves contain toxic quantities of oxalic acid, so all leaves *must* be removed and discarded before cooking. If the stalks are especially big, tough, or stringy, you can peel them as you would celery.

Rhubarb is good steamed, stewed, or baked with sugar. For the simplest preparation, wash the stalks, cut into one-half to one-inch pieces, add a little sugar and just enough water to cover, and cook, uncovered, until tender—around ten minutes, depending on the tenderness of the stalk. Start with about half a cup of sugar per pound of rhubarb, tasting and adjusting for sweetness near the end of the cooking time.

Sometimes mixed with apples, rhubarb is a great companion to strawberries. Add the berries near the end of the cooking time and spoon the mixture over ice cream or use it for shortcake. Better yet, make the traditional strawberry-rhubarb pie, which is one of my personal favorites.

Rutabaga (Yellow Turnip)

Each year Americans consume greater quantities of almost every sort of fresh vegetable except rutabagas. This neglected vegetable deserves better. Rutabagas can be cooked like potatoes, and if they're prepared right, they have a creamy, potatolike texture and a distinctive taste. They've been a must on my family's Thanksgiving table for years, thanks to my Irish mother. Sure, the rutabaga is homely, but this inexpensive vegetable has a long shelf life, can be cooked in a number of ways, is very nutritious, and is generally a terrific, hearty winter vegetable.

Large and squat, a rutabaga looks a lot like a big darkened white turnip with the top and tail cut off. The skin is purple at the top, yellowish below, and the whole root

Rutabaga

is heavily waxed to prevent it from losing moisture and shriveling. Rutabagas are grown in cooler climates everywhere, but for the U.S. market, Canada grows the best.

Season   Rutabagas are in season from October through early summer.

Selecting   Choose roots that are heavy in the hand for their size, more rounded than pointed, and hard as a rock—with no soft spots. The tops should be purple and bright looking, and the wax should have a good shine on it. You can tell right away if a rutabaga is old: the wax will look dull, and the rutabaga will feel light.

Storing   If you can, store rutabagas in a cool, dark place like a root cellar. Even at normal room temperature, however, rutabagas in good condition will keep for a couple of months.

Preparing   Prepare rutabagas as you would potatoes, or as if they were acorn squash, with a little sweetening (they aren't stringy like acorn squash). We mash them just like potatoes: peel, cube, boil, and mash, then add butter, salt and pepper. Or combine with potatoes before mashing for a milder flavor. I love mashed rutabagas straight: they've got a distinctive taste and they really stick to your ribs. They're excellent as a side dish with turkey, roast chicken, pork roast, pork chops, or ham.

Rutabaga

Scallion (Green Onion)

Also called green or spring onions, scallions are in the lily family like onions but are not a true onion or even a true bulb. In the old days, when no one did much more than nibble the white ends, scallions were very strong—even hot—in flavor, but the taste has improved over the years and scallions are now milder and sweeter. People have also discovered the virtues of the fresh green tops, which can be chopped and added to salads, stir-fries, omelettes, fried rice, and other dishes.

Season

Scallions are usually sweetest during the early summer months, although they're available year round, with shipments from California (the largest producer) supplemented by substantial crops from Ohio, New Jersey, and Texas.

Selecting

Look for a pure white bulb end and straight, emerald green tops. Tops that are curved or starting to curl usually indicate the scallions are old and tough. Yellowed or discolored scallions have definitely been around too long.

Storing

Refrigerate as is if you have a good crisper drawer or wrap in plastic and refrigerate.

| **Shallot and Pearl Onion** | Dry shallots and pearl onions are both members of the lily family, along with more than three hundred other varieties of onions and onionlike vegetables that include leeks, scallions, and garlic. |

Some believe the word *shallot* derived from a Middle Eastern city named Ashkelon or Ascalon. The ancient Greeks grew shallots and traded them to other countries, and the Romans prized them both as a food and as an aphrodisiac. The shallot is a small bulb roughly the size of a small head of garlic that sometimes separates into two or three cloves when you remove the outer skin. Shallots are graded into small, medium, and jumbo sizes. The most widely cultivated is the pink shallot, which has a pinkish papery skin and an oblong shape. There is also a copper yellow shallot, which has a yellowish skin and a more elongated shape. Top-quality shallots are grown in the Brittany region of France and in other European countries; Canada and the United States also produce crops.

Pearl onions may have originated in the Middle East or in southern Europe, where they've long been popular. In the early part of this century, immigrants introduced pearl onions to California, which now grows them in large quantities. Mild, marble-sized pearl onions come in three colors—silvery white, red, and golden yellow.

Season Thanks to cold storage, both shallots and pearl onions are available year round. Like other onions, they have a more delicate flavor in the spring, a stronger flavor in the fall.

Selecting Both shallots and pearl onions should be firm, with a dry, papery skin. Avoid any that show sprouts—green shoots—or dark spots.

Storing Keep shallots and pearl onions in a cool, dry, dark place, and they will stay in excellent condition for about a month. If you don't have a cellar or cool closet, refrigerate them and use within two weeks. Once they are peeled or cut, wrap them in plastic and refrigerate, or place in a jar, cover with olive oil, and refrigerate. Be sure to use the aromatic oil in salad dressings afterward.

Preparing *Shallots:* Cut both ends off each shallot, slit the peel lengthwise, and the papery skin will come off easily. Keep the outer skins for soup stock—they add great color and flavor. Tie them up in cheesecloth or put them in a tea ball, and discard before serving.

Scallion (Green Onion)

The shallots themselves add a subtle flavor and aroma to casseroles, pasta dishes, soups, and stews. Use whole, slivered, or minced. Mince shallots finely and add to a vinaigrette to dress tossed salad or avocado. Mince and add to diced leftover boiled potatoes before frying to give a whole new flavor to hash browns. Shallots are excellent in sauces and are essential to such traditional French ones as *beurre blanc, sauce merchand de vin,* and *sauce à la bordelaise.* They are also delicious roasted whole with very small turnips or chunks of potatoes or a combination of both, and seasoned with rosemary, thyme, salt, pepper, and a little olive oil.

For a hearty, healthy soup, sauté eight to ten shallots with two cloves of garlic in a little olive oil. Add one or two grated carrots, a cup of orange or brown lentils, two-and-a-half cups water, and one whole chile pepper. Bring to a boil, then simmer until the lentils are cooked through. Discard the chile, add finely chopped cilantro and a squeeze of lemon, and season to taste.

Pearl onions: The easiest way to peel pearl onions is to blanch them in boiling water for one minute, then plunge into cold water. Cut a thin slice off the root end, hold the onion by the top, and squeeze—it will pop right out.

Pearl onions are good whole or sliced into salads. They're excellent added to sauces or combined with other vegetables such as English peas or fresh string beans. They make a zesty pickle and are tasty and attractive added to skewers of beef, chicken, fish, and other vegetables for outdoor grilling.

Creamed or glazed pearl onions are traditional on many families' Thanksgiving tables. Just remember that most onions have a stronger flavor in the fall than they do in the spring. To make sure they're sweet, blanch the pearl onions for two minutes, drain, peel, and finish cooking in fresh water.

Snow Pea. *See* Pea, Snow.

Spinach

Spinach was introduced to Europe by the Moors more than a thousand years ago. Over the years it has been grown in Italy as a Lenten food—planted in the fall and harvested in February, in time for Lent, when meat cannot be consumed. Spinach has become more popular as consumers have discovered the sweet flavor of properly pre-

Spinach

pared fresh spinach. It's used for every part of a meal: raw in salads, as a hot vegetable, to make creamed soups, in soufflés and casseroles, and stuffed into ravioli.

Although there are many varieties, the two distinguishable types of spinach on the market are those with dark green, very crinkly leaves, and those that have smaller, lighter green leaves that are nearly flat. Although some people think flat-leaf spinach is sweeter and more tender, I still like the crinkly-leafed kind, which has a lot more flavor and definitely more crunch. Texas is the number-one producer; California, Colorado, New Jersey, and Ohio also have major crops.

Flat-leafed spinach is usually sold in bunches. It is popular in California, which produces the biggest crop. Because it is tender and easy to clean, its popularity is spreading beyond the West Coast.

Crinkly-leafed spinach is sold bunched, loose, or partially washed and packaged in ten- and twelve-ounce cello packs. Most restaurants I deal with like it bagged because it's handy and much cleaner than other fresh spinach. It's fine if it's fresh; its disadvantage is that some merchants keep cello-pack spinach around too long. By the time you take it home, it may be four or five days old and starting to rot, so inspect the cello pack carefully before buying. *See also* Greens.

Season Spinach is available twelve months of the year but is most plentiful in the spring and fall. It breaks down very easily in hot weather, so it's usually best in the cooler months.

Selecting Whatever variety you choose, look for bright-colored stems and leaves. The leaves should be unbroken, crisp, and show no dark edges or signs of slime or wilting.

Storing and Preparing Spinach can be washed, towel dried, and stored in a plastic bag in the refrigerator for two or three days, but it's fairly fragile and should be eaten as soon as possible.

Spinach can be very sandy, so it needs to be washed carefully. First remove the purple stem ends and break away the toughest part of the ribs. Soak the leaves in very cold water for about twenty minutes; most of the sand will sink to the bottom of the container or the sink. Then carefully wash the leaves one or two at a time under cold running water. After washing, place them in a colander and run them under the tap again, gently tossing the leaves to give them one final rinse. You can also use a salad

Spinach

spinner and spin gently after each rinse until no sand remains in the bottom of the outer bowl. Pat dry.

Eva's Strawberry and
Spinach Salad with Lemon Dressing   4 to 6 servings

10 ounces fresh spinach, washed, stemmed, and coarsely torn

1 pound fresh strawberries, washed, hulled, and sliced

LEMON DRESSING

¼ cup sugar

juice of 1 large lemon

1 egg yolk

6 tablespoons vegetable oil

Place the spinach in a salad bowl and arrange the berries artfully on top. Refrigerate until well chilled.

Meanwhile, prepare the dressing. In a medium-sized bowl, combine the sugar and lemon juice, and whisk until sugar is mostly dissolved. Add the egg yolk and whisk until the sugar is completely dissolved. Add the oil 1 tablespoon at a time, whisking after each addition. The dressing should be thick and creamy. Cover and refrigerate until you are ready to serve.

When you are ready to serve, toss the salad gently with the lemon dressing.

Spinach

Baked Spinach-Stuffed Tomatoes 6 servings

6 medium tomatoes

3 tablespoons butter

¼ pound mushrooms, wiped and sliced

½ pound fresh spinach, washed and chopped

1 cup bread crumbs

4 eggs

salt and freshly ground black pepper to taste

Preheat the oven to 350°F.

Cut the tops off the tomatoes and scoop out the pulp, leaving a ¼-inch-thick shell. Turn the tomatoes upside down to drain.

In a medium-sized skillet, melt the butter over moderate heat. Add the mushrooms and sauté for 2 minutes. Stir in the spinach and cook for 2 minutes. Remove from the heat and stir in the bread crumbs, eggs, salt, and pepper.

Place the tomatoes in a lightly greased 9-by-13-inch baking pan and sprinkle them lightly with salt. Fill the tomatoes with the spinach mixture and bake for approximately 25 minutes, or until tops are golden.

Spinach

Sprouts

Sprouts are the tender young shoots of seeds that germinate very quickly. Mung and soybean sprouts have been a staple vegetable in China and East Asia for many centuries, probably because they are so fast-growing and easy to produce; they are now popular in the West as well. What other fresh vegetable can be grown in the middle of winter, without a greenhouse? Only a few of the many kinds are available commercially here, but the list is varied. It includes the familiar mung bean and the slightly strong-tasting soybean sprouts, which are often cooked; tiny alfalfa sprouts, peppery-tasting radish sprouts, mustard cress, and garden cress, which are usually eaten raw.

Season

Year round.

Selecting

Choose sprouts that are fresh and crisp and show no signs of discoloration.

Storing

Refrigerate in a plastic bag and use within a day or two of purchase.

Preparing

Simply wash, drain, and pat dry with a paper towel. If the sprouts seem to be limp, revive them by soaking in ice cold water for a few minutes.

All sprouts taste good raw. They are crisp and refreshing in salads and make an attractive edible garnish. Alfalfa sprouts, radish sprouts, and sprouting cress are tasty in most sandwiches—especially pita pocket sandwiches. Not all sprouts are good cooked, but mung and soybean sprouts are excellent in stir-fries.

Squash

Squash was a food staple in the Americas for some eight thousand years before the first European explorers arrived here. Like melons and cucumbers, squashes are edible gourds that are indigenous to North, Central, and South America. The name comes from the Algonquin word *askútasquash,* which means "eaten raw" and probably derives from the kind of summer squash encountered by early European settlers. The Native Americans taught them how to store and use winter squashes as a staple and

Squash

demonstrated the curative and hygienic properties of squash seeds. Following the practice of the natives, the settlers ate whatever was available in the wild—fish, fowl, venison—which often carried parasites, and cured themselves by eating squash.

Varieties The squashes commonly found in the United States are divided into summer and winter varieties. Summer varieties are immature squashes, usually small in size, with a soft skin, white flesh, high water content, and crunchy texture. Summer squashes are 100 percent edible, seeds and all, and very perishable. Winter varieties are fully mature squashes that are usually larger in size, with a hard outer shell and a long shelf life. They are always eaten cooked. Most have an orange flesh that is sweeter and nuttier in flavor than the more delicate summer squashes and contain large quantities of beta carotene. The larger, harder seeds of winter squashes are usually discarded, but they can be salted, roasted, and eaten like nuts.

Summer Squash Yellow squash and long, slender, dark green zucchini are probably the two most familiar summer squashes, but there are other good varieties. These include the *chayote*, which is pear-shaped, with white, pale, or dark green skin; the *cocozelle*, which is shaped like a zucchini and striped green and yellow; and the tiny scalloped *pattypan*, which has white, yellow, or green stripes and looks like a little flying saucer.

Winter Squash Winter squashes all have a hard skin. There are many varieties and a hundred ways to cook them.

Acorn squash, so named because it's shaped a bit like a large acorn, is one of the smaller winter squashes. It has a dark green skin and orange flesh.

Banana squash is cylindrical in shape, with an ivory to pink shell and ivory to pink flesh.

Buttercup squash is turban-shaped, with a green or orange skin and yellow flesh.

Butternut is fairly large and pear-shaped, with a smooth, cream-colored skin and orange flesh.

Delicata, which I think is one of the best-tasting squashes, is long and slender—something like a cucumber. It has a green and beige striped skin and yellow flesh.

Golden acorn looks just like acorn squash, except the skin is bright orange and the flesh is sweeter than that of the green acorn squash.

Squash

Golden nugget is closely related to the acorn variety. A very deep orange color inside and out, it is mostly available in small, single-serving sizes. It can be opened like a small pumpkin, which it looks exactly like, scooped out, basted with butter, and baked whole.

Hubbard squash may be the least attractive-looking of the lot, but it's terrific. Very large in size, with a hard, thick, bumpy, gray-green or orange shell, it has a very sweet orange flesh. An uncut one can be stored in a cool, dry place for months without losing its flavor and sweetness. An average Hubbard squash can weigh twenty pounds, so most produce stands will sell cut halves or quarters. Cut Hubbards should be wrapped and refrigerated, and they'll keep about a week. Hubbard squash can be baked, mashed, added to soups, or mixed with other vegetables in a casserole. It makes an excellent pie; although it has the same flavor as a pie pumpkin, it's sweeter and requires less sugar. It also has a thicker, firmer texture than fresh pumpkin, so that it sets up better. An especially nutritious variety, Hubbard squash has a high vitamin content and delivers enormous quantities of beta carotene.

Pumpkins are another variety of winter squash, with an orange or tan shell and orange flesh. It provides more beta carotene per serving than any other fruit or vegetable. (*See* Pumpkin.)

Spaghetti squash has a round or oval yellow shell. The yellow- to cream-colored flesh inside comes out in strands, giving the squash its name.

Sweet dumpling squash is another one of my favorites. It has a green skin streaked with white and yellow-orange flesh.

Turban squash has bumpy orange to red skin with green stripes. The flesh is usually orange.

Season

Summer squashes, especially zucchini, are generally available year round, but the peak season is between April and September.

Winter squashes are also available year round, but some varieties are hard to find in the summer. The peak season is September through March.

Selecting

All squashes should have a solid, heavy feel. A squash that feels light for its size may be soft and dehydrated inside. Summer squashes should have a firm but tender, sleek, unblemished skin. A shiny skin on yellow squash and zucchini is a good indication that

it was picked young and tasty. Choose small to medium-sized squashes, rather than large ones, for the best flavor and texture.

Winter squashes vary widely in size, but most of them are quite large. For that reason they're often sold in halves or quarters. The hard shell of a winter squash should be undamaged, but the skin, unlike that of summer squashes, should be *dull,* which indicates the squash was picked when fully mature. Make sure the stem is still attached; a missing stem means the squash has been in storage too long.

Storing *Summer squash:* Store refrigerated in an *un*sealed plastic bag and use within three or four days. Handle summer squash carefully because the tender skin is easily nicked.

Winter squash: Never refrigerate unless it's been cut; then wrap in plastic and store only a day or two before using. The smaller the winter squash, the shorter the shelf life; acorn squash, for example, should be used within two or three weeks of purchase. Some of the larger varieties of winter squash will stay sweet and good-tasting as long as six or seven months if kept in a dry, cool (*not* cold) place, out of direct sunlight.

Preparing Summer Squash Summer squashes have a high water content—never overcook or they will turn to mush. Overcooking is probably why so many kids hate squash! There are exceptions, but zucchini, chayote, crookneck, and cocozelle never need peeling. If the squash *looks* nice and tender, leave the peel on. Simply wash it and discard a thin slice from each end.

Summer squashes are terrific brushed with a little oil and cooked on the grill, and they can be steamed, sautéed, stir-fried, or baked in casseroles. Use very little water if you're going to boil a squash. Cut it into horizontal slices about a quarter of an inch thick, put in just enough water to cover the bottom of the pan, add salt, pepper, and butter if desired, cover, and cook no more than three to five minutes. Turn the squash a few times to cook evenly and test frequently for doneness—it's done when it's easily pierced with a fork but retains some crunch.

To grill, slice the squash lengthwise, marinate or brush with an oil-based salad dressing or with olive oil, herbs, and perhaps some garlic, then grill over hot coals, turning occasionally so it doesn't burn.

Young, tender summer squashes, especially zucchini, are good raw in salads or

with dips. They are delicious lightly steamed, stir-fried in a little oil, or fried tempura-style in batter. There are many Mediterranean recipes that call for squash—it's good in a ratatouille or baked with Parmesan cheese. Zucchini can also be used in zucchini bread—a sweet bread, almost like cake, that makes a good dessert—and muffins.

Pattypan squash is good stuffed and baked. Cut off the stem end and carefully scoop out the seeds and some of the flesh. Stuff with a combination of bread crumbs, minced, sautéed onions, herbs, and grated cheese, *or* with sweet corn, diced sautéed red sweet peppers, and minced scallions. Bake in a moderate oven about twenty minutes, or until tender.

Preparing Winter Squash

Cutting a winter squash can present an interesting challenge. When I did a show on winter squash, I invited Matt Lauer, an NBC reporter, to demonstrate—then gave him a pair of goggles and heavy gloves and pulled a chain saw from under the counter. It was a joke but not too far off the mark. We have a customer at the store whose husband cuts the winter squash with a band saw! The problem is that the shell is very hard, the squash tends to roll, and the blade of a knife tends to slip off the smooth skin.

A kitchen saw or even a small saw from the workshop will make short work of it, but another reasonably simple way to cut into a winter squash is to look for the area on the squash that has indentations or ribs. Lay the squash so it's as steady as you can get it, insert the point of a sturdy knife in a crease, give the handle a couple of taps with a hammer to start the cut, then proceed as if you were cutting a watermelon. (Need I say that you have to be *extremely* careful when you do this?) Remove the seeds before cooking.

Smaller winter squash are best baked. Cut in half, brush with butter, sprinkle with brown sugar, and bake for about thirty minutes, or until tender. Acorn squash are typically baked. Golden acorn, golden nugget, delicata, and sweet dumpling squashes are particularly delicious prepared this way; because they're so sweet, they'll need less sugar than green-skinned acorns.

Very large squashes can be peeled, cut in chunks, and boiled for ten to twenty minutes, or until tender. The chunks can then be pureed or mashed and prepared as you would mashed potatoes; butternut squash is at its best prepared this way. Winter squash is delicious added to soups and stews or sliced, battered, and fried; precook it in water until the flesh is tender-crisp before frying.

Spaghetti squash is best baked whole in a moderately hot oven for one to one and a half hours, depending on the size of the squash. Pierce the squash in two or three places before baking to release steam. After it's done, cut in half and use a fork to remove the flesh, which looks and handles like spaghetti. You can toss it with a marinara sauce or top it with butter or cheese. A lot of people like to eat spaghetti squash cold with a vinaigrette.

At home Betty makes a cold zucchini salad that's very simple, quick, and delicious. Slice the zucchini and sauté briefly in olive oil with a bit of garlic. Remove from the heat and, while the zucchini is still hot, splash a top-quality vinegar over it. It can be a good wine vinegar or a balsamic or herbed vinegar, depending on your preference. Add some salt and pepper and serve either warm, at room temperature, or chilled.

Because of its versatility, zucchini is a good staple to keep around the house. The other night we got home late, and neither of us wanted to bother with a big meal, so Betty sliced and sautéed zucchini and potato, added beaten eggs to the pan when the vegetables were almost done, and made a terrific fritatta.

Marinated Zucchini   4 to 6 servings

¼ cup olive oil

4 large zucchini, sliced ⅛ inch thick

½ cup vinegar

1 teaspoon fresh or dried mint leaves

3 cloves garlic, chopped

½ teaspoon salt

½ teaspoon freshly ground black pepper

In a large skillet, heat the oil over moderate heat. Add the zucchini and sauté on both sides until golden brown. Set aside.

In a medium-sized casserole, layer the sautéed zucchini with the vinegar, mint, garlic, salt, and pepper. Stir and cover the casserole. Let the zucchini marinate at room temperature for 1 hour. You may serve at room temperature or you may heat it before serving.

Squash

Zucchini Bread

8 to 10 servings

3 cups flour

2 cups sugar

1 teaspoon salt

1 teaspoon ground cinnamon

½ teaspoon baking powder

1 teaspoon baking soda

3 eggs

1 cup corn or vegetable oil

2 teaspoons vanilla extract

½ cup chopped walnuts

2 cups grated zucchini

Preheat the oven to 350°F. Generously grease two 9-by-5-inch loaf pans. In a large bowl, mix the first 6 ingredients. Add the eggs, oil, vanilla, walnuts, and grated zucchini. Beat together until well blended. Pour the mixture equally into both loaf pans and bake for 1 hour.

The zucchini bread may be served warm with your meal or as a dessert.

Zucchini and Chicken 4 servings

··

1 tablespoon olive oil

1 3- to 4-pound frying chicken, cut into pieces

2 large onions, sliced

2 large tomatoes, chopped

1 green bell pepper, sliced

4 small zucchini, sliced

1 tablespoon garlic powder

1 teaspoon dried oregano

pinch salt and freshly ground black pepper

In large skillet, heat the oil and add the chicken pieces. Sauté the chicken until browned, then remove and set aside. In the same skillet, cook the onions until soft, then add the tomatoes, bell pepper, and zucchini. Cover and simmer until all the vegetables are soft.

Return the chicken to the skillet and add the garlic powder, oregano, salt, and pepper. Cover and simmer for 45 minutes. (You may add potatoes to this dish if you like.)

Squash

Patsy's Linguine and Zucchini 2 to 4 servings

¼ cup olive oil

4 medium-sized zucchini, sliced into rounds

4 cloves garlic, sliced

4 fresh basil leaves

4 fresh sprigs Italian parsley

1 teaspoon salt

½ teaspoon freshly ground black pepper

1 pound linguine

In a large skillet, heat half of the olive oil over moderate heat. Add the zucchini and sauté until golden brown, about 5 to 7 minutes. Remove from the heat and transfer the zucchini to paper towels to drain.

Pour the remaining oil into the skillet, add the garlic, and sauté until golden. Remove the skillet from the heat, and when it has cooled slightly, add the basil, parsley, zucchini, ¼ cup water, salt, and pepper.

In the meantime, bring 3 quarts of water to a boil and cook the linguine until al dente. Drain and toss with the zucchini.

Squash

Swiss Chard

Swiss chard, sometimes simply called chard or leaf beet, is a hard beet prized for its succulent stalk and leaves rather than its roots. It has large flat or crinkled green leaves growing from a thick, greenish white central stalk or rib. There is also a red-stemmed variety that almost looks like rhubarb, and other varieties that have a dark red leaf. Both the leaves and the stems are eaten, which leads some cooks to call Swiss chard two vegetables in one. The cooked leaf is similar to spinach; the stalks can be cooked separately like asparagus.

Despite its name, Swiss chard has no special association with Switzerland. A member of the chenopod family, along with beets and spinach, it originated in the Mediterranean region and is thought to be the ancestor of the beet root. It was well documented by the ancient Greeks and Romans, who used it as an herbal remedy. Swiss chard is much more popular in Europe than it is here, and is grown in every European country, as well as in parts of Asia, Africa, and South America and to a lesser extent in North America. *See also* Greens.

Season Swiss chard is available from April to December and is most plentiful between June and October.

Selecting The leaves and stalks should be crisp and fresh-looking. Avoid wilted or brown leaves.

Storing Keep refrigerated in a perforated plastic storage bag for no more than three or four days. Swiss chard always has a better flavor when it's fresh.

Preparing To prepare, discard a thin slice at the base of the stalk and wash thoroughly in a sink full of cold water. Avoid cooking Swiss chard in aluminum or iron pans, which will discolor it. Many cooks separate the stalks from the leaves if the stalks are more than half an inch wide. The leaves are either cooked separately or added to the pot when the stalks are almost done.

If they're very young and fresh, the leaves can be eaten raw in salads. To cook, steam or sauté rather than boiling them—they'll have more flavor. Treat them as you would spinach, but cook them a bit longer. Swiss chard is a good substitute for bok choy in stir-fried dishes, is very good creamed, and makes a delicious soup. The leaves are excellent chopped and added to a variety of other soups—including chicken, minestrone, vegetable, and lentil—during the last few minutes of cooking time.

The stalks are great steamed whole or cut on the diagonal and steamed or braised for just a few minutes. They should be slightly crisp when done. Serve as you would asparagus, either hot or cold. They're good with a variety of sauces, including vinaigrettes and even hollandaise.

Try using a seasoned Swiss chard and ricotta cheese filling to stuff pastas like ravioli or tortellini. For a great fish dish, put a bed of steamed leaves in a baking dish or in individual ovenproof shells, place cooked stalks over them, then spread a mixture of crab meat and Mornay sauce over the top. Sprinkle with Parmesan cheese and bread crumbs and heat in a 325°F oven until the sauce is browned on top.

Swiss chard leaves are excellent stuffed. Cut them away from the stalks, then wilt them by barely steaming or blanching. Hold the stalks for another use or cook and mince them and add to the filling. Make a filling of ground meat and rice or wild rice sautéed with onions, garlic, seasonings, and herbs. Put a spoonful on each leaf, wrap, and place in a shallow baking dish, seam side down. Add tomato sauce, a creamy cheese sauce, or any braising liquid to barely cover the stuffed leaves. Sprinkle with Parmesan cheese and bake in a 325°F oven about forty-five minutes.

In Europe, Swiss chard is served hot or cold after being sautéed in a little olive oil and garlic. It's seasoned with nutmeg, pepper, and salt, and finally given a generous squeeze of lemon juice or a sprinkling of wine vinegar. Sautéed shallots, onions, or anchovies are good added to this dish if you're serving it hot.

For a delicate treat, try Swiss chard pancakes. Cook a bunch of Swiss chard, mince fine, and squeeze out all the water you can. Put it in a bowl with some grated cheese, a few spoonfuls of sour cream, and enough bread crumbs to make the mixture hold together. Add about one tablespoon of mixed vegetable spices or chicken bouillon granules, a little lime juice, salt, and pepper. Mix well and form into small patties. Dip each patty first into a plate of flour, then into a bowl of beaten eggs thinned with a little water, and finally into a plate of bread crumbs, coating both sides each time. Fry in a nonstick pan with just a little oil until golden brown. Serve with sour cream or yogurt. The cooked patties freeze well if you have extras.

Swiss Chard

Malfotte   4 to 6 servings

½ cup (1 stick) butter

1 cup finely chopped onion

4 cups Swiss chard, cooked, drained, and chopped

2 pounds ground beef

1¼ cups grated Parmesan cheese

4 eggs

¾ cup bread crumbs

½ cup flour

4 cups tomato sauce

Preheat the oven to 350°F.

In a skillet, melt the butter, add the onion, and sauté until lightly browned. In a large bowl, mix the sautéed onion, Swiss chard, ground beef, 1 cup grated cheese, eggs, and bread crumbs. Take a small handful of the mixture and form into sausage-like rolls about 3 inches long.

Place some flour in a dish and roll each malfotte in flour until well coated. Bring a large saucepan half full of water to a boil. Place the malfottes into the pan and boil until they float to the top, about 5 to 7 minutes. Remove them with a slotted spoon and drain.

Cover the bottom of a baking pan with tomato sauce and place the malfottes in the pan in a single layer. Cover with sauce and sprinkle with the remaining Parmesan cheese. Bake for approximately 20 to 30 minutes.

Swiss Chard

Tomatillo

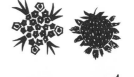

Also called Mexican green tomatoes (*tomates verdes* in Spanish) or sometimes Chinese lantern plants because of the way they look—almost like an Oriental lampshade—tomatillos are in the nightshade family along with tomatoes but are a genus commonly called ground cherries or husk tomatoes. The lime-green fruits are enclosed in a dull green papery husk that's easy to peel off. The fruits are generally one to two inches in diameter. The interior is firm, with the texture of a crisp, hard green tomato, and scattered with very small, edible seeds. Tomatillos have a fresh, lemon-herbal flavor that's tart and acidic raw, more mellow cooked. They are a key ingredient in *salsa verde* and are delicious added to many vegetable dishes.

Tomatillos became popular in the 1970s, when the popularity of southwestern and Mexican cuisines began to spread throughout the country. Although they're easily grown, they're cultivated commercially only in Mexico and southern California—with India the only other grower of note.

Season

Look for tomatillos year round. Their availability is still unpredictable; this is a fruit you need to ask for wherever you shop, in order to create the kind of demand that will give tomatillos wider distribution.

Selecting Choose firm, dry fruit with clean, close-fitting husks that show no blackness or mold. The fruit should be quite firm—tomatillos don't have the "give" of a regular tomato.

Storing If wrapped in paper or kept in a paper-lined basket, tomatillos will keep in the refrigerator for nearly a month without deteriorating. Tomatillos can also be frozen, but they should be cooked first.

Preparing Husk the tomatillos and remove the stems, then wash the fruit carefully until the skin no longer feels sticky. The sticky residue under the husk can make tomatillos taste bitter.

To freeze, place cleaned tomatillos into a pan and barely cover with water. Simmer until tender but not mushy—which can take anywhere from two to fifteen minutes, depending on the size. Cool and then freeze *in the cooking liquid,* and use the liquid, as well as the fruits, in recipes.

Slivered or chopped raw tomatillos add a fresh, tart, lemony taste when mixed with gazpacho or other cold soups or tossed into a green salad. Chop or puree them to make a tart dressing, and use them either raw or cooked for different versions of *salsa verde.*

Cooked tomatillos have a fuller, mellower flavor. Tomatillo salsa—made with raw or barely cooked fruits combined with chile peppers, onions, garlic, cilantro, and seasonings—is delicious on tacos and many other Tex-Mex dishes and is a great sauce for potatoes. Tomatillos can even be made into pies and add a great twist when added to apple pie.

Tomatillos can be roasted instead of parboiled. Begin with tomatillos that are all about the same size, so they will cook in the same amount of time. Leaving the husks on, rinse and place the tomatillos in a preheated 450° to 500°F. oven. Cook until tender—usually ten to fifteen minutes. Watch them carefully to make sure they don't burst during cooking. When tender, remove from the oven, allow the tomatillos to cool, twist off the husks, and gently rinse the fruits.

Tomato

A fruit—oh yes, it's a fruit—but in the United States we treat the tomato like a vegetable. Thomas Jefferson grew tomatoes at Monticello back in 1781, but they didn't really start to become popular here until after the Civil War. Now the tomato is the third most popular vegetable in the United States—after potatoes and lettuce.

Once called the Peruvian apple, the tomato is a member of the nightshade family. It originated in South America, and our name for it comes from the ancient Nahuatl name *tomatl*. The French called it the love apple, and the Italians named it the golden apple because the first tomatoes were small yellow fruits. After the early Spanish explorers sent seeds to Naples, the Italians went crazy for tomatoes, and the rest—all the way down to pasta and pizza sauce—is history.

A really good tomato is sweet, tender, juicy, and except for the yellow varieties, a deep rich red color. When you get one of those hard tomatoes that tastes like cardboard, you've got one of the hybrids that started coming onto the market in the 1950s, when the businessmen and scientists got together and produced a tomato that could be shipped from one coast to the other without bruising. Unfortunately, at the same time they also bred out all the flavor.

A great tomato is worth looking for. And the way you handle it at home is almost as important as what you choose in the first place. The three most important rules to remember about tomatoes are

1. Never refrigerate!
2. Never refrigerate!
3. Never refrigerate!

Refrigerating kills the flavor, the nutrients, the texture. It just kills the tomato—period.

Varieties

There must be a thousand varieties of tomatoes. Some of the more popular are *Burpee Big Boy*, *Early Beefsteak*, *Rutgers* (after the university that produced the seed), *Ramapo*, *Fireball*, and *Jet Star*. Many people think that *Beefsteak* got its name because it's big, but Big Boy is the really big one. The Beefsteak is so named because it doesn't have

Simple Pleasures

We have all kinds of upscale restaurants, and there is a lot of interest in complicated cuisines, but sometimes it's the really simple things that give you the most pleasure. When I was a kid, I had to help my father sell produce out of the back of his truck. At lunchtime he'd stop at some little store and buy a loaf of Italian bread. Then we'd find a place where we could pull off to the side of the road. He'd put down a piece of cardboard for a cutting board, slice the bread, cut up a tomato and an onion, and make tomato sandwiches.

Sometimes when I come home from the store and I'm too bushed to prepare or even eat a full meal, I'll make myself a tomato sandwich. Food brings back memories. You can sit down with the most ordinary things on your mind and eat something good and it will bring back memories—things you haven't thought about in years. Even memories that might not start out being so good seem to improve as time goes by. At the time I hated peddling fruits and vegetables out of that truck with Pop, but now I wish I had the time to pull off to the side of the road the way we did then. We don't have the luxury of slowing down—everything is geared to working and being productive. Produce, produce, produce. Wouldn't I love to be able to take my son and go sit by the side of the road and have a tomato sandwich? With the perfect ripe red tomato and good bread, there's nothin' better.

the hard, greenish-white core most tomatoes have. A ripe Beefsteak will be solid red and edible all the way through, like a good steak that's solid red meat.

Unless you live in a really cold climate, the best tomatoes you can buy will be at your local farm stand, when tomatoes are in season in your area. That's true for most produce, but it's doubly true for tomatoes. About half the tomatoes shipped and sold in the United States come from Florida. They are the ones you find in the store in the winter. They're hard, they're thick, they never turn red, and they have no taste. A few winter tomatoes come out of Mexico and California, as well as from Holland, Belgium, and Israel. There are also more and more hydroponic tomatoes on the market.

Tomato

I may be biased, but I think that in season the Jersey tomato is the best around—maybe because of the soil. The truth is, any local tomato, picked ripe, is going to be good. In the summertime, in season, buy local tomatoes.

In the winter I think Israelis beat out the rest, with hydroponics a close second. Israeli tomatoes are grown in greenhouses, picked ripe, and then shipped by air. For that reason they're very expensive. If you have to have a good tomato in the dead of winter, choose an Israeli one. Hydroponics grown in the U.S. are also excellent.

Mexican tomatoes are a little better than most of the other winter varieties here because they're usually picked by hand and are a little riper when they come off the vine. Most tomatoes in the U.S. are shipped green because ripe tomatoes are just too fragile for machine picking.

California tomatoes, which usually arrive in the late spring, have a thick wall and are very solid inside. A lot of people like them because they're easy to slice, but I don't think they're any better than Florida tomatoes. They look better and ripen more easily, but they're very dry.

Don't get me wrong. There's nothing wrong with a Florida tomato in Florida. Or a California tomato in California. The problem isn't the source—it's that the tomatoes are picked green, gassed with ethylene to make them turn more or less red, then refrigerated and shipped. Even if the tomatoes are picked ripe, they're refrigerated before they're shipped, and that's the final insult!

Plum Tomatoes Most plum tomatoes sold here are an Italian variety called Roma. Plum tomatoes are available year round now, and if your choice in the winter is between a plum tomato and the usual California and Florida varieties, take a plum tomato. They'll have a better flavor. The best time for plum tomatoes, however, is in the late summer and early fall. Local ones are usually available in August and September.

Although plum tomatoes are good raw in salads, they are *great* for sauce. Late plum tomatoes are the best for sauce; they're the ones that have been on the vine the longest, and they're really ripe.

Cherry Tomatoes Like other tomatoes, local cherry tomatoes, picked ripe, are going to be the best. Look for small ones. One local variety, called Tiny Tim, is not much bigger than your fingernail, and it's as sweet as sugar.

In the winter cherry tomatoes from Israel again are your best bet. Picked ripe, they're very small and very sweet. The Israelis have also produced a "baby tomato" that's a little smaller than a golf ball. It has excellent flavor too. Your next best bet is Mexican cherry tomatoes, which again are picked a little later and a little riper. I don't recommend cherry tomatoes from California. They tend to be too watery and mushy.

When choosing cherry tomatoes, look for a good red color—avoid those that look orange. Also check to see if the stems are still on. If the stems are missing, chances are those tomatoes have been sitting around too long.

Yellow Tomatoes Yellow tomatoes are low-acid tomatoes that still retain their unique tomato flavor and texture. The yellow tomato is a deep, bright yellow color—almost school-bus yellow. It is usually medium to large, round, and very smoothly shaped, with a thin skin, thick meat, and solid seed pockets. The juice is very thick. Yellow tomatoes go well in salads and are especially tasty and beautiful in an all-tomato salad or platter that combines both red and yellow varieties. Yellow tomatoes aren't grown in large commercial quantities here, but a few come out of Florida and California, and Holland exports them as well. Holland has developed an excellent acid-free yellow tomato that is very tasty and, like other produce from Holland, consistently high in quality. The California varieties are what they call genitori seeds, which means that the seeds have been passed on from one farmer to the next, one generation to the next, and although some are shipped, most stay in the area. The local crop usually appears in late August and early September, but they may stay in season as late as November.

There is a beautiful yellow tomato that's quite small—about the same size as a cherry tomato but pear-shaped. They have become very popular among those who've been lucky enough to discover them at local farm stands. They're sold in pint cartons, and straight off the farm they're super sweet.

Other Varieties Tomatoes come in scores of different varieties, colors, and markings—striped, purple, even white—but these are found almost exclusively in season, from local sources like farm markets or markets that carry specialty produce. Again, if you want to see a wider variety where you shop, *ask* for what you want and help create a customer demand.

Tomato

Local Tomatoes: Depending on the local climate, from July through September, with the peak in late July and August

Florida Tomatoes: October to July, with the peak from December through May

California Tomatoes: May to December, with the peak from June through October

Imports: Usually year round, with the peak usually from January through April

Tomatoes are considered "vine ripe" by the industry if they have developed a little color "break"—that is, a small yellow or reddish patch of color on the skin or a starburst of yellow at the blossom end. If the tomato has a color break or the starburst, you'll be able to ripen it at home.

Don't ripen tomatoes on the windowsill. Never put them in the sun to ripen. Just put them out on the counter, stem end up, in a relatively cool place—not right next to the stove or the dishwasher. Put on a little Frank Sinatra music if you want them to ripen fast. If you want them to ripen faster—well, you can always put on the Stones. Never, ever refrigerate—not even after the tomato is ripe. If you've got too many ripe tomatoes, make a salad or a raw tomato sauce for pasta. Or make a cooked sauce, freeze it, and you'll have something nice for the winter.

Pop's Tomato Sandwich

1 serving

2 slices Italian semolina bread

1 medium-sized to large ripe tomato, sliced

2 or 3 thin slices sweet onion

olive oil

balsamic vinegar

dried oregano

salt and freshly ground black pepper to taste

For this sandwich, you need the best semolina bread, perfectly ripe tomatoes, and the best olive oil. (We always had olive oil and vinegar in the truck.) If we were near a delicatessen or general store, sometimes my father would buy a little jar of mayonnaise and use that too. If you're using mayonnaise, spread a thin layer on both slices of bread. Then cover one piece with a thick layer of tomato slices, then thinly sliced onions. Sprinkle some hot peppers on top. Dress with olive oil, vinegar, oregano, salt and pepper. Top with the second slice of bread.

Take a bite, and you know it's summer.

On tomato sandwiches now I use mayonnaise, salt, pepper, and onion. I don't make these with oil and vinegar anymore. I don't know why. I think I'll go make a tomato sandwich with oil and vinegar!

Tomato

Jersey Tomato Salad Italiano   4 servings

2 large ripe beefsteak or other slicing tomatoes

¼ cup olive oil

red wine vinegar to taste

¼ cup chopped fresh basil

3 cloves garlic, finely chopped

2 tablespoons finely chopped fresh Italian parsley

1 medium-sized red onion, finely chopped

½ teaspoon salt

½ teaspoon freshly ground black pepper

2 teaspoons dried oregano

Cut the tomatoes into chunks and place in a salad bowl. Add the remaining ingredients and toss well. Toss again right before serving.

Tomato

Fresh Plum Tomato Sauce   8 to 10 servings

5 pounds plum tomatoes

¼ cup olive oil

2 tablespoons chopped fresh garlic

1 teaspoon salt

1 teaspoon freshly ground black pepper

¼ cup sugar

2 tablespoons fresh or dried oregano

2 tablespoons chopped fresh Italian parsley or dried parsley

1 teaspoon fresh or dried basil

Rinse the tomatoes well; cut out the cores and cut the tomatoes in half. Place the tomatoes in a blender and puree until smooth.

In a large saucepan, heat the oil over moderate heat. Add the garlic and brown for 1 minute, then add the tomatoes. Add the remaining ingredients and cover the pan. Simmer for 1 hour, stirring occasionally. Serve over your favorite cooked pasta or freeze for later use.

Tomato   304

More and more tomato lovers are discovering another option to ethylene-gassed tomatoes in the winter. Geneticists have now bred a tomato that can be left on the vine until it's ripe and red but remains firm enough to ship without heavy damage to the fruit. Calgene, the company that produced that MacGregor variety, has begun shipping their tomatoes to a few areas in the United States, and they may be at your market now.

Such genetic "engineering" has caused a lot of controversy, but in fact growers have been fooling around with the genetic structure of plants for centuries by cross-breeding. Cross-breeding in the field was a haphazard way to produce better genes, but by the 1930s growers had bred genetic resistance to twelve different diseases into tomatoes, with huge increases in production and quality. In the most recent development, scientists managed to isolate the gene that makes a tomato become soft. By adding a copy of that gene to the plant DNA, but in reverse, they've produced a tomato that develops vine-ripened flavor and color before the softening process begins. Were animal genes employed? No. The manipulated gene—polygalacturonase or p.g. for short—is derived from tomatoes and introduced at the seed stage. There are no chemicals or other additives pumped into the tomato itself—in fact, genetically manipulated produce may result in fruits and vegetables arriving on the market with *fewer* applications of chemicals and pesticides than are used today.

The new tomato—marketed by Calgene under the name MacGregor—will be clearly labeled so that consumers will know exactly what they're getting. It's a matter of choice for each consumer to make, but I'm enthusiastic and look forward to improvements in other produce. I've tasted the MacGregor and it has excellent flavor. As far as I'm concerned, this new hybrid is a home run for the produce industry.

Tomato

Turnip

The southern cousin of the rutabaga, white turnips are a very big crop in the South, where they're grown as much for their green tops as for the roots. Unlike rutabagas, white turnips are pure white with pink or purple tops, and they can be consumed raw as well as cooked. From late spring to early summer, they are sold with their edible green tops on. The tops can be prepared as you would spinach, although they take a bit longer to cook (see Greens). Southern cooks often cube the turnip roots and braise them with the greens, seasoning it all with salt pork. White turnips can be cooked in a number of ways and can also be cut into sticks for a crudité platter or sliced into a salad.

Season   Year round. During the fall and winter, white turnips are sold without the greens. Late spring and early summer turnips are sold with their edible green tops on.

Selecting   Smaller white turnips have a better flavor and texture than larger ones. Look for firm, fresh-looking roots that are heavy in the hand for their size, with bright pink or purple crowns and no sign of shriveling or rusty color. Turnips sold with the tops cut off should not be showing new sprouts at the top—an indication they are old or improperly stored.

Storing   Turnips will keep for months in a cool, dark place.

Preparing   Rinse and peel, discarding a thin slice from the crowns and root ends.

White turnips are a good side vegetable for poultry or roast pork and are excellent cooked with carrots. Sliced raw into a salad, a turnip will add crunch and a mildly spicy flavor.

Turnips are delicate-tasting peeled, boiled, pureed and seasoned with butter, salt, a pinch of sugar, and a sprinkle of nutmeg or mace. They are also excellent pureed together with carrots or potatoes—vary the seasonings according to the combination of vegetables you use. In French provincial cooking, small, tender turnips are traditionally added to braised duck or goose dishes. Turnips are very tasty in a cream of potato and leek soup. They can enhance the flavor of other soups and stews, but because they have a slightly sharp flavor they should be added last. If you're making extra soup or expect leftovers, add turnips only to the portion you're sure you'll use immediately. The turnip flavor will predominate in soups that are stored and reheated.

Watercress

When I was a kid, there was a stream behind a neighbor's house around the corner. It made a path through their backyard and must have come from a well or spring, although I never knew exactly where it started or ended. The water was ice cold, even in the middle of the summer, and it ran over moss-covered rocks. It was a place we liked to go on a hot day when we were thirsty from running and playing. We could drink the water and not be afraid of it, and pull up a handful or two of wild watercress and chew on the cool, peppery leaves. Unfortunately, this isn't a scene you're likely to discover in your neighborhood anymore, and eating wild cress isn't something I'd recommend either, unless you're sure the water hasn't been polluted by people or animals.

Watercress is a creeping plant with a long stem that branches out into clusters of small, rounded, dark green leaves that have a fresh, peppery taste. It originated in the Mediterranean area and was brought to North America by the early settlers. Watercress was once thought to be a cure for madness; the Greeks thought it improved mental abilities.

Because it's perishable, you'll usually find watercress tied into bunches and displayed upside down in ice or ice water. Properly called nasturtium, watercress is a crucifer that's particularly high in vitamin C. Not only does it make a great salad; it's also delicious made into soup or chopped into cream cheese.

Season   Year round, but most plentiful in the spring and summer.

Selecting   Watercress should be crisp and bright green, with no wilting or yellowing.

Storing   Because watercress is fragile, it's best to buy and use it the same day. If you need to store it, undo the bunch, wash in very cold water, and spin in a salad spinner or pat dry. Enclose in a plastic bag, store in the refrigerator, and it will last a few days.

Preparing   The entire plant, including the roots, is edible, although in the summertime the stems start to get thick and tough.

To use the leaves, wash, discard the base stems, and cut into bite-sized pieces. Watercress is excellent in salads and on sandwiches—try it on a cheese and tomato sandwich. It makes an excellent cream soup that tastes something like leek soup. Mince and add it to sour cream or a soft cheese for dips. It can be added to stir-fries at the last minute, but be careful not to overcook. Watercress is also very attractive as an edible garnish.

For an especially good salad, cut up watercress, a little endive, and a ripe avocado. Add a dressing of olive oil, lemon juice, a touch of Dijon mustard, a little garlic, and salt and freshly ground pepper to taste.

Watercress

Index

·····················

Acorn squash, 284
Alar, 9
Alfalfa sprouts, 283
Allsweets watermelons, 178
Amazon Red papayas, 220
American parsley, 134
Anchovy sauce, cardoon
    tempura with, 64–65
Andy's raw broccoli salad,
    54
Angeleno plums, 251
Anjou pears, 233
Antioxidants, 68
Antipasto, nectarine, 201
Apple(s), 3–9
  Baldwin, 7
  Braeburn, 7, 8–9
  cider, 7
  Cortland, 4
  crisp, Lib's, 11
  crumb pie, Betty's, 10
  Empire, 5
  Gala, 7, 8
  Golden Delicious, 3
  Granny Smith, 7, 9
  Greening, 5

Jonathan, 6
Lady, 5
McIntosh, 3–4
Macoun, 5–6
Northern Spy, 7
Opalescent, 6–7
pie, 8
Red Delicious, 2–3
Rome Beauty, 4
Royal Gala, 7, 8
Winesap, 6
Winter Banana, 7
York, 7
Apple pears, 11–13
Apricot(s), 13–14
  mousse, 14–15
Artichoke(s), 15–17
  Betty's stuffed, 18
Arturo's Caesar salad, 162
Arugula, 19–20
  salad, 20
Asian pears, 11–13
Asparagus, 21–22
  baked crusty-crumb, 23
Avocados, 24–27
  as houseplants, 28

Italian-style, 27
spinach salad with stars,
    101

Baby artichokes, 16
Baby salad mix, 186
Bacon avocados, 25–26
Baldwin apples, 7
Banana(s), 29–30
  crisp, 30
  health benefits of, 31
  nectarine surprise, 201
  -orange muffins, 216
Banana passionfruit, 99
Banana peppers, 239
Banana squash, 284
Bartlett pears, 233
  praline pie, 237
Basil, 128–130
  Gabby's pesto sauce, 131
Beans, 31–32
  and escarole, Mom's, 167
  string, and potato salad,
    Mama Louise's, 33
Beefsteak tomatoes, 297–298

Beet greens, 123
    see also Swiss chard
Beets, 33–34
Belgian endive, 35
    salad, 36
Bell peppers, 238, 240
Bergamot, 109
Bermuda onions, 205, 206
Berries, see specific berries
Beta carotene, sources of:
    apricots, 13
    broccoli, 51
    carrots, 68
    mangoes, 171
Betty's cherry cheesecake, 76
        Betty's creamy potato
        soup, 260
Betty's plum torte, 252
Betty's red potato salad, 261
Betty's stuffed artichokes,
    180
Beverages:
    apple cider, 7
    papaya milk shakes, 221
    pomegranate juice, 256
    prickly pear juice, 265
Bibb lettuce, 164
    salad with greens, reds,
        and whites, 43
Bing sweet cherries, 74
Black Amber plums, 250
Black Beaut plums, 250
Black Beauty grapes, 116
Blackberries, 37–38
Black-eyed peas, 228
Blood oranges, 210
Blueberry(ies), 38–39
    tea cakes, 40
    torte, 39
    watermelon basket, 185
Borage, 109
Bosc pears, 233–234
    praline pie, 237
Boston lettuce, 163
    salad with greens, reds,
        and whites, 43

Boysenberries, 41
Braeburn apples, 7, 8–9
Bread:
    cactus pear muffins, 266
    cranberry, 86
    orange-banana muffins,
        216
    strawberry muffins, 48
    zucchini, 289
Breba figs, 107
Broccoli, 51–52
    à la Dolores, 55
    and kumquat salad, 154
    Patsy's pasta primavera,
        56
    salad, Andy's raw, 54
    soup, cream of, 53
Broccoli rabe, 57–58
    and sausage, Betty's,
        59
Brussels sprouts, 59–60
Bull-nosed peppers, 238
Burpless cucumbers, 87
Bush basil, 129
Bush beans, 31–32
Butter:
    cookies with raspberry
        preserves, 45
    ortanique, 219
Buttercup squash, 284
Butternut squash, 284
Button mushrooms, 187–
    188

Cabbage, 61–62
    Chinese, 198–199
Cactus pear(s), 264–265
    muffins, 266
Caesar salad, Arturo's, 162
Cake(s):
    Betty's cherry cheesecake,
        76
    blueberry tea, 40
    carrot, 67
    cherry dessert, 77

Comfort Hall ortanique
        cheesecake, 218
    pineapple caramel skillet,
        247
    see also Torte
Canary melons, 184
Cannonball watermelons,
    178
Canteloupes, 175, 176
    mango fruit salad, 175
    watermelon basket, 185
Carambola, 100–101
    spinach salad with stars,
        101
Cardoon, 62–64
    tempura with anchovy
        sauce, 64–65
Carrot(s), 65–66
    cake, 67
    and ginger soup, pureed,
        115
    Patsy's pasta primavera,
        56
Casaba melons, 184–185
Casselman plums, 251
Casserole, cauliflower and
        cheese, 71
Catherine's sweet potato
        pie, 263
Cauliflower, 69–70
    and cheese casserole, 71
    salad, 70
Cayenne pineapples, 245–
    246
Celery, 72
Celery cabbage, 198–199
Celery root (celeriac), 73
Chahai, 198–199
Champagne grapes, 116
Champion White peaches,
    224
Chanterelle mushrooms, 189
Chard, 292–293
Charleston Gray
        watermelons, 178
Chayote squash, 284

Cheese:
    and cauliflower casserole, 71
    eggplant and zucchini Parmesan, 93
    fennel Parmesan, 106
    papaya pie, 222–223
Cheesecake:
    Betty's cherry, 76
    Comfort Hall ortanique, 218
Cheese peppers, 238
Cherry(ies), 73–76
    cheesecake, Betty's, 76
    dessert cake, 77
    mango fruit salad, 175
Cherry tomatoes, 299–300
Chicken:
    cranberry, 85–86
    and grapes, Oriental, 119
    and snow peas, stir-fried, 231
    spinach salad with stars, 101
    and zucchini, 290
Chicory, 165–166
    see also Radicchio
Chile peppers, 239, 240
Chinese cabbage, 198–199
Chinese flowering cabbage, 57–58
Chinese gooseberries, 147–148
    chiffon pudding, 149
Chinese lantern plants, 295
Chinese parsley, 132
Chinese wood ear mushrooms, 193
Chive flowers, 109
Chives, 132
Chocolate-covered strawberries, 49
Chow choy, 198–199
Choy sum, 57–58
Christmas melons, 185

Christmas pears with strawberry sauce, 236
Chrysanthemums, 109
Cider, apple, 7
Cilantro, 132–133
Clapp pears, 234
Clementine oranges, 212–213
Clingstone peaches, 224
Coconut, 78–79
    cookie bars, 80
    crisps, 79
Cocozelle squash, 284
Collard greens, 123–124, 125, 126
Comfort Hall Farm, 213, 214
Comice pears, 234
    praline pie, 237
    with strawberry sauce, 236
Concord grapes, 117
Cookie(s):
    bars, coconut, 80
    butter, with raspberry preserves, 45
Coriander, 132–133
Corn, 81–83
    fritters, 83
Corn salad, 169–170
Cortland apples, 4
Cos (romaine) lettuce, 160
    Arturo's Caesar salad, 162
Crabmeat, Ken Otto's stuffed mushrooms with, 196
Cranberry(ies), 84–85
    bread, 86
    chicken, 85–86
Cream cheese icing, 68
Cream of broccoli soup, 53
Creamy potato soup, Betty's, 260
Crenshaw melons, 181–182
Creole gumbo, 202, 203–204
Crimini mushrooms, 189

Crimson Sweet watermelons, 178
Cubanel peppers, 239
Cucumbers, 87
Curly endive, 165–166
Curly parsley, 134
Curuba passionfruit, 99

Daikon, 88–89
Japanese pickles, 89
    see also Radishes
Daisies, 109
Dandelion greens, 124, 125, 126
    mixed green salad with, 127
Delicata squash, 284
Desserts:
    apricot mousse, 14–15
    Betty's apple crumb pie, 10
    Betty's cherry cheesecake, 76
    Betty's plum torte, 252
    blueberry tea cakes, 40
    blueberry torte, 39
    butter cookies with raspberry preserves, 45
    carrot cake, 67
    cherry cake, 77
    chocolate-covered strawberries, 49
    coconut cookie bars, 80
    Comfort Hall ortanique cheesecake, 218
    cream cheese icing, 68
    grape pie, 118
    kiwi chiffon pudding, 149
    kumquat tart, 155
    Lib's apple crisp, 11
    Loel's peach kuchen, 226
    orange squares, 215
    pineapple caramel skillet cake, 247

Desserts (*continued*)
    raspberry filling, 44
    raspberry torte, 44
    strawberry angel pie, 50
Diet, and disease
    prevention, 31
Dill, 133
Dipping sauce, anchovy, 64–
    65
Dixie Belle peaches, 224
Dressing:
    lemon, Eva's strawberry
        and spinach salad
        with, 281
    raspberry vinaigrette,
        43
Duncan grapefruit, 120

Eggplant, 90–93
    gumbroit, 95
    stuffed, 94
    and zucchini Parmesan,
        93
El Dorado plums, 250
Elephant garlic, 112
Empire apples, 5
Endive, 35
    salad, 36
English peas, 227–228
English thyme, 136–137
Enoki mushrooms, 190
Escarole, 165–166
    and beans, Mom's, 167
    salad, Pop's, 166–167
Eva's strawberry and
        spinach salad with
        lemon dressing,
        281
Exotic fruits, 96–101
    carambola (starfruit), 100–
        101
    feijoa, 96–97
    kiwano, 97–98
    passionfruit, 98–99
    see also specific fruits

Feijoa, 96–97
Fennel, 103–104
    Parmesan, 106
    salad niçoise, 105
    and tomato salad, 107
Field peas, 228–229
Field salad, 169–170
Figs, 107–109
    stuffed persimmons, 243
Fish:
    Comfort Hall poached
        salmon, ortanique,
        and hollandaise, 217
    smoked trout with
        horseradish sauce,
        139
Flat-leafed parsley, 134
Florida mangoes, 172, 173
Florida red potatoes, 258
Flowers, edible, 109–110
    salad with, 111
Forelle pears, 234
Freestone peaches, 224
French tarragon, 136
Friar plums, 251
Fritters, corn, 83
Fruits, exotic, 96–101
    carambola (starfruit), 100–
        101
    feijoa, 96–97
    kiwano, 97–98
    passionfruit, 98–99
    see also specific fruits
Frying peppers, 239, 240
Fuerte avocados, 24–25, 26
Fuyu persimmons, 241–242

Gabby's pesto sauce, 131
Gala apples, 7, 8
Galia melons, 182
Garden cress, 283
Garlic, 112–113
    flavored olive oil, 130
Gelatin, sherried
        pomegranate, 256

Genetic engineering, of
        tomatoes, 305
Georgia Bell peaches, 224
Gherkin cucumbers, 87
Ginger, 113–115
    and pureed carrot soup,
        115
Globe artichokes, 16
Golden acorn squash, 284
Golden celery, 72
Golden Delicious apples, 3
Golden Doll watermelons,
    178
Golden needle mushrooms,
    190–191
Golden nugget squash, 285
Gourmet salad, 186
Granny Smith apples, 7, 9
Grape(s), 115–118
    and chicken, Oriental,
        119
    mango fruit salad, 175
    pie, 118
    seeded, 117
    seedless, 115–116
    watermelon basket, 185
Grapefruit, 119–121
    Pete's broiled, 122
    salad, 122–123
Green bell peppers, 238, 240
Greening apples, 5
Green onions, 277–279
Greens, 123–127
    Jimi Quick's mixed, 127
    mixed green salad with
        dandelion, 127
Green tomatoes, Mexican,
    295
Grenadine syrup, 256
Gumbo, creole, 202, 203–204
Gumbroit, 95

Haas avocados, 24–25, 26
Hachiya persimmons, 241–
    242

Haden mangoes, 172
Haitian mangoes, 173
Hen-of-the-woods
        mushrooms, 193
Herbs, 128–137
    basil, 128–130
    chives, 132
    cilantro (fresh coriander),
        132–133
    dill, 133
    flavored olive oil, 130
    Gabby's pesto, 131
    mint, 133–134
    parsley, 134–135
    rosemary, 135
    sage, 135–136
    tarragon, 136
    thyme, 136–137
Hibiscus, 109
Hollandaise, poached
        salmon, and
        ortanique, Comfort
        Hall, 217
Honeydew melons, 180–181
    mango fruit salad, 175
    watermelon basket, 185
Honeysuckle, 109
Horned melons, 97–98
Horseradish, 137–138
    sauce, smoked trout with,
        139
Houseplants, avocado, 28
Hubbard squash, 285

Iceberg lettuce, 158–160
Icebox watermelons, 178
Icicle radishes, 273
Icing, cream cheese, 68
Idaho potatoes, 258
Impatiens, 109
Insect repellant, 9
Iron, beets as source of, 33
Italian frying peppers, 239
Italian parsley, 134
Italian-style avocados, 27

Jack-o'-lanterns, 267–268
Jalapeño peppers, 239,
        240
    flavored olive oil, 130
Jam, no-sugar plum, 253
Jamaican honeysuckle,
        99
Japanese pickles, 89
Jasmine, 109
Jersey tomato salad Italiano,
        303
Jerusalem artichoke(s), 140–
        141
    pickled, 143–144
    salad, 142
Jicama, 144–145
    and mango salad, 146
Jimi Quick's mixed greens,
        127
Jonathan apples, 6
Jubilee watermelons, 178
Juice:
    apple, 7
    pomegranate, 256
    prickly pear, 265

Kadota figs, 107
Kale, 123–124, 125, 126
Keith mangoes, 172
Kelsey plums, 251
Ken Otto's stuffed
        mushrooms with
        crabmeat, 196
Kent mangoes, 172
Kentucky Wonder beans,
        31
Kirby cucumbers, 87
Kiwano, 97–98
Kiwi(s), 147–148
    chiffon pudding, 149
Kohlrabi, 150–151
    Chinese style, 152
Kumquat, 153–154
    and broccoli salad, 154
    tart, 155

Lady apples, 5
Lady peas, 228
Lambert sweet cherries, 74
Lamborn, Calvin, 232
Lamb's lettuce, 169–170
LaRoda plums, 250–251
Lavender, 109
Leaf basil, 129
Leaf beet, 292–293
Leaf lettuce, 164–165
Leeks, 156–157
Lemon, 157–158
    dressing, Eva's strawberry
        and spinach salad
        with, 281
    thyme, 136–137
Lettuce, 158–165
    Bibb, 164
    Boston, 163
    chicory, 165–166
    escarole, 165–166
    iceberg, 158–160
    leaf, 164–165
    mesclun, 186
    Mom's escarole and
        beans, 167
    Pop's escarole salad, 166–
        167
    romaine (cos), 160–162
    salad with greens, reds,
        and whites, 43
Lib's apple crisp, 11
Lime, 167–168
Lime blossoms, 109
Limestone lettuce, 164
Linguine and zucchini,
        Patsy's, 291
Loel's peach kuchen, 226

Mache, 169–170
McIntosh apples, 3–4
Macoun apples, 5–6
Magnolias, 109
Maine potatoes, 258
Malfotte, 294

Mama Louise's potato and string bean salad, 33
Mandarin family oranges, 210–213
Mango, 171–174
  fruit salad, 175
  and jicama salad, 146
Maracuya passionfruit, 99
Marigolds, 109
Marsh seedless grapefruit, 120
Maui onions, 206
Melons, 175–185
  Canary, 184
  canteloupes, 175, 176
  Casaba, 184–185
  Crenshaw, 181–182
  Galia, 182
  honeydew, 180–181
  mango fruit salad, 175
  muskmelons, 175, 176–177
  Persian, 182–183
  Sharlyn, 183–184
  Spanish, 185
  watermelon basket, 185
  watermelons, 177–179
Mesclun, 186–187
Mexican green tomatoes, 295
Mexican mangoes, 172, 173
Mexican turnips, 144–145
  jicama and mango salad, 146
Milk:
  coconut, 78, 79
  shakes, papaya, 221
Mimosa, 109
Mineola oranges, 211, 212
Mint, 133–134
Mission figs, 107
Mom's escarole and beans, 167
Morel mushrooms, 192
Mousse, apricot, 14–15
Muffins:
  cactus pear, 266
  orange-banana, 216
  strawberry, 48

Mung bean sprouts, 283
Murcott oranges, 212
Mushroom(s), 189–194
  chanterelle, 189
  Chinese wood ear, 193
  crimini, 189
  enoki, 190
  hen-of-the-woods, 193
  marinated portobello, 197
  morel, 192
  oyster, 190–191
  Patsy's pasta primavera, 56
  porcini, 192–193
  portobello, 191
  portobello, and pasta, 195
  salad with greens, reds, and whites, 43
  sautéed, 195
  shiitake, 191–192
  stuffed, with crabmeat, Ken Otto's, 196
  truffles, 193–194
  white cap, 187–188
Muskmelons, 175, 176–177
Mustard cress, 283
Mustard flowers, 109
Mustard greens, 125

Nappa cabbage, 198–199
Nasturtiums, 109, 110
Navel oranges, 209
Nectarine(s), 199–201
  surprise, 201
Nelis pears, 234
New potatoes, 257, 258–259
New York State potatoes, 258
Northern Spy apples, 7
No-sugar plum jam, 253
Nova Scotia potatoes, 258

Okra, 202–204
  ratatouille, 204

Olive oil, flavored, 130
Onion(s), 205–207
  green, 277–279
  pearl, 278, 279
  shallots, 278–279
  strombolli, Vidalia, 207
  Virginia's stuffed, 208
Opalescent apples, 6–7
Orange(s), 209–214
  -banana muffins, 216
  blood, 210
  Comfort Hall ortanique cheesecake, 218
  Comfort Hall poached salmon, ortanique, and hollandaise, 217
  Mandarin family, 210–213
  navel, 209
  nectarine surprise, 201
  ortanique butter, 219
  ortaniques, 213–214
  squares, 215
  Valencia, 210
Orange-fleshed honeydew melons, 181
Orchid grapefruit, 120
Oregano flavored olive oil, 130
Oriental chicken and grapes, 119
Oriental pears, 11–13
Ortanique(s), 213–214
  butter, 219
  cheesecake, Comfort Hall, 218
  poached salmon, and hollandaise, Comfort Hall, 217
Oval artichokes, 16
Oyster mushrooms, 190–191

Packham pears, 235
  praline pie, 237
Palmer mangoes, 172
Pancakes, Swiss chard, 293

Pansies, 109
Papaya, 220–221
  cheese pie, 222–223
Parmesan:
  eggplant and zucchini, 93
  fennel, 106
Parsley, 134–135
  Gabby's pesto sauce, 131
Parsnips, 223
Pascal celery, 72
Passionfruit, 98–99
Pasta:
  Patsy's linguine and
    zucchini, 291
  and portobello
    mushrooms, 195
  primavera, Patsy's, 56
  stuffed with Swiss chard,
    293
Patsy's linguine and
  zucchini, 291
Patsy's pasta primavera, 56
Pattypan squash, 284
Pea(s), 227–232
  English or sweet, 227–
    228
  field, 228–229
  snow, 229–230
  snow, and chicken, stir-
    fried, 231
  sugar snap, 232
Peach(es), 224–225
  kuchen, Loel's, 226
  in wine, 227
Pear(s), 232–235
  Anjou, 233
  Bartlett, 233
  Bosc, 233–234
  Christmas, with
    strawberry sauce,
    236
  Clapp, 234
  Comice, 234
  Forelle, 234
  Nelis, 234
  Packham, 235

  praline pie, 237
  Red Bartlett, 233
  Seckel, 235
Pearlette grapes, 115–116
Pearl onions, 278, 279
Pears, apple, 11–13
Peewee potatoes, 259
Peppers, 238–240
Persian melons, 182–183
Persimmon(s), 241–243
  broiled, 243
  stuffed, 243
  and yogurt salad, 244
Pesto sauce, Gabby's, 131
Peter's pumpkin soup, 268
Pete's broiled grapefruit, 122
Pet-sai, 198–199
Petunias, 109
Pickled Jerusalem
  artichokes, 143–144
Pickles, Japanese, 89
Pie:
  apples for, 8
  Betty's apple crumb, 10
  Catherine's sweet potato,
    263
  grape, 118
  papaya cheese, 222
  pear praline, 237
  strawberry, 49
  strawberry angel, 50
Pineapple(s), 244–247
  caramel skillet cake, 247
  nectarine surprise, 201
  watermelon basket, 185
Pineapple guava, 96–97
Pink grapefruit, 120
Plantains, 248–249
Pleurottes, 190–191
Plum(s), 249–252
  early-season, 250
  jam, no-sugar, 253
  kabobs with plum sauce,
    254
  late-season, 251
  midseason, 250–251

  sauce, savory
    microwaved, 253
  torte, Betty's, 252
Plum tomato(es), 299
  sauce, fresh, 304
Pole beans, 31–32
Pomegranates, 254–256
Pomelos, 119
Pony Boy honeydew melons,
  181
Poppies, 109, 110
Pop's escarole salad, 166–
  167
Pop's tomato sandwich, 302
Porcini mushrooms, 192–193
Portobello mushrooms, 191
  marinated, 197
  and pasta, 195
Potassium, sources of:
  bananas, 31
  beets, 33
Potato(es), 257–259
  pie, Catherine's sweet,
    263
  salad, Betty's red, 261
  soup, Betty's creamy, 260
  and string bean salad,
    Mama Louise's, 33
  sweet, 262–263
Praline pear pie, 237
Preserves, raspberry, butter
  cookies with, 45
Prickly pears, 264–265
  cactus pear muffins, 266
Primrose, 109
Prince Edward potatoes,
  258
Pudding, kiwi chiffon, 149
Pumpkin(s), 267–268, 285
  soup, Peter's, 268
Purple potatoes, 259

Queen Rosa plums, 250
Quince, 269–271
  compote, 271

315

Radicchio, 272–273
  and arugula salad, 20
  see also Chicory
Radishes, 273–274
  daikon, 88–89
  Japanese pickles, 89
  salad with greens, reds,
    and whites, 43
Radish sprouts, 283
Rapini, 57–58
Raspberry(ies), 41–42
  filling, 44
  preserves, butter cookies
    with, 45
  salad with greens, reds,
    and whites, 43
  torte, 44
  vinaigrette, 43
Ratatouille, okra, 204
Red Bartlett pears, 233
Red Beaut plums, 250
Red bell peppers, 238, 240
Red Bliss potatoes, 258–259
Red cabbage, 61
Red Delicious apples, 2–3
Red onions, 205–206
Red potato salad, Betty's,
  261
Red seedless grape(s), 116
  and Oriental chicken, 119
  pie, 118
Redskin potatoes, 258–259
Red Spanish pineapple, 245–
  246
Reed avocados, 24–25, 26–
  27
Relish:
  cranberry, 85
  nectarine, 201
Rhubarb, 274–275
Ribier grapes, 116
Romaine (cos) lettuce, 160–
  162
  Arturo's Caesar salad,
    162
Rome Beauty apples, 4

Rosemary, 135
  flavored olive oil, 130
Roses, 109, 110
Royal Anne sweet cherries,
  74
Royal Gala apples, 7, 8
Ruby Red grapefruit, 120
Ruby seedless grapes, 115
Russet potatoes, 257–258
Russian tarragon, 136
Rutabagas, 275–276

Sage, 135–136
Salad:
  Andy's raw broccoli, 54
  Arturo's Caesar, 162
  Betty's red potato, 261
  cauliflower, 70
  with edible flowers, 111
  endive, 36
  Eva's strawberry and
    spinach, with lemon
    dressing, 281
  fennel and tomato, 107
  gourmet, 186
  grapefruit, 122–123
  with greens, reds, and
    whites, 43
  Italiano, Jersey tomato,
    303
  Jerusalem artichoke, 142
  jicama and mango, 146
  kumquat and broccoli, 154
  mango fruit, 175
  mixed green, with
    dandelion, 127
  niçoise, fennel, 105
  persimmon and yogurt,
    244
  Pop's escarole, 166–167
  spinach, with stars, 101
Salmon, poached, ortanique,
  and hollandaise,
  Comfort Hall, 217
Sand pears, 11–13

Sangria watermelons, 178
Santa Rosa plums, 250
Sauce:
  anchovy, cardoon tempura
    with, 64–65
  fresh plum tomato, 304
  Gabby's pesto, 131
  hollandaise, poached
    salmon, and
    ortanique, Comfort
    Hall, 217
  horseradish, smoked trout
    with, 139
  plum, plum kabobs with,
    254
  plum, savory microwaved,
    253
  strawberry, 236
Sausage and broccoli rabe,
  Betty's, 59
Savoy cabbage, 61
Scallions, 277–279
Seckel pears, 235
Seeded grapes, 117
Seedless grape(s), 115–116
  and Oriental chicken, 119
  pie, 118
Serrano peppers, 239
Shaddocks, 119
Shalea pears, 11–13
Shallots, 278–279
Sharlyn melons, 183–184
Sharp, John, 213
Shellfish:
  Ken Otto's stuffed
    mushrooms with
    crabmeat, 196
Sherried pomegranate
  gelatin, 256
Shiitake mushrooms, 191–
  192
Simka plums, 251
Snap beans, 31–32
Snow peas, 229–230
  and chicken, stir-fried, 231
Solo papayas, 220

Soup:
    Betty's creamy potato,
        260
    cream of broccoli, 53
    Peter's pumpkin, 268
    pureed carrot and ginger,
        115
Sour cherries, 75, 76
Soybean sprouts, 283
Spaghetti squash, 285
Spanish melons, 185
Spanish onions, 205, 206
Spinach, 125, 126, 279–281
    salad with stars, 101
    and strawberry salad with
        lemon dressing,
        Eva's, 281
    -stuffed tomatoes, baked,
        282
Sprouts, 283
Squash, 283–288
    eggplant and zucchini
        Parmesan, 93
    gumbroit, 95
    marinated zucchini, 288
    Patsy's linguine and
        zucchini, 291
    summer, 284
    winter, 284–285
    zucchini and chicken,
        290
    zucchini bread, 289
    see also Pumpkin
Starfruit, 100–101
    spinach salad with stars,
        101
Star Ruby grapefruit, 120
Stone cells, 233
Strawberry(ies), 45–47
    angel pie, 50
    chocolate-covered, 49
    muffins, 48
    nectarine surprise, 201
    pie, 49
    sauce, Christmas pears
        with, 236

    and spinach salad with
        lemon dressing,
        Eva's, 281
    watermelon basket, 185
Straw mushrooms, 190–191
String bean(s), 31–32
    gumbroit, 95
    and potato salad, Mama
        Louise's, 33
Strombolli, Vidalia onion,
    207
Sugarbaby watermelons, 178
Sugarloaf pineapples, 245
Sugar pumpkins, 267
Sugar snap peas, 232
Sui choy, 198–199
Summer squash, 284, 285–
    287
    marinated zucchini, 288
    Patsy's linguine and
        zucchini, 291
    zucchini and chicken, 290
    zucchini bread, 289
Sunchokes, 140
    see also Jerusalem
        artichoke(s)
Sunrise papayas, 220
Super select cucumbers, 87
Sweet cherries, 73–75, 76
Sweet dumpling squash, 285
Sweet peas, 227–228
Sweet peppers, 238–239
Sweet potato(es), 262–263
    pie, Catherine's, 263
Sweet William, 109
Swiss chard, 125, 292–293
    malfotte, 294
Sycamore honeydew
    melons, 181
Syrup, grenadine, 256

Tagetes, 109
Tamarillos, 102
Tangelos, 211–212
Tangerines, 211

Tanimoto, George, 147
Tarragon, 136
Tart, kumquat, 155
Taxo passionfruit, 99
Tea cakes, blueberry, 40
Temple oranges, 212
Tempura, cardoon, with
        anchovy sauce, 64–
        65
Thompson grapes, 116
Thyme, 136–137
    flavored olive oil, 130
Tientsin, 198–199
Tokay grapes, 117
Tomatillos, 295–296
Tomato(es), 297–301
    baked spinach-stuffed,
        282
    cherry, 299–300
    and fennel salad, 107
    genetically engineered,
        305
    gumbroit, 95
    Mexican green, 295
    other varieties of, 300
    Patsy's pasta primavera,
        56
    plum, 299
    salad Italiano, Jersey, 303
    sandwich, Pop's, 302
    sauce, fresh plum, 304
    yellow, 300
Tommy Atkins mangoes,
    172
Torte:
    Betty's plum, 252
    blueberry, 39
    raspberry, 44
    see also Cake
Toxic flowers, 109
Tree mushrooms, 190–191
Tropical fruits, 80
    carambola (starfruit), 100–
        101
    feijoa, 96–97
    kiwano, 97–98

Tropical fruits (*continued*)
passionfruit, 98–99
see also specific fruits
Trout, smoked, with
horseradish sauce,
139
Truffles, 193–194
Turban squash, 285
Turnip greens, 125
Turnips, 306

Valencia oranges, 210
Vegetables:
gumbroit, 95
okra ratatouille, 204
Patsy's pasta primavera,
56
selection of, 91
*see also specific
vegetables*
Vidalia onion(s), 206
strombolli, 207
Vinaigrette, raspberry, 43
Violets, 109, 110

Virginia's stuffed onions,
208
Vitamins, as antioxidants,
68

Walla Walla onions, 206
Watercress, 307–308
salad with greens, reds,
and whites, 43
Watermelon(s), 177–179
basket, 185
mango fruit salad, 175
White cap mushrooms, 187–
188
White celery, 72
White grapes, 116
White potatoes, 257–258
Wine, peaches in, 227
Winesap apples, 6
Winter Banana apples, 7
Winter squash, 284–285,
286–287
Witloof chicory, 35
Won bok, 198–199

Yams, *see* Sweet potato
Yellow crookneck squash,
284
Yellow globe onions, 206
Yellow tomatoes, 300
Yellow turnips, 275–276
Yogurt and persimmon
salad, 244
York apples, 7
Yukon Gold potatoes,
259

Zucchini, 284
bread, 289
and chicken, 290
and eggplant Parmesan,
93
gumbroit, 95
and linguine, Patsy's,
291
marinated, 288
Patsy's pasta primavera,
56
Zutano avocados, 25–26